The LEVELLING

The LEVELLING

What's Next After Globalization

MICHAEL O'SULLIVAN

PUBLICAFFAIRS

NEW YORK

PublicAffairs
Hachette Book Group
1290 Avenue of the Americas, New York, NY 10104
www.publicaffairsbooks.com
@Public_Affairs

Printed in the United States of America
First Edition: May 2019

Published by PublicAffairs, an imprint of Perseus Books, LLC, a subsidiary of Hachette Book Group, Inc. The PublicAffairs name and logo is a trademark of the Hachette Book Group.

The Hachette Speakers Bureau provides a wide range of authors for speaking events. To find out more, go to www.hachettespeakersbureau.com or call (866) 376-6591.

The publisher is not responsible for websites (or their content) that are not owned by the publisher.

Library of Congress Cataloging-in-Publication Data
Names: O'Sullivan, Michael, 1957– author.
Title: The levelling: what's next after globalization / Michael O'Sullivan.
Description: First Edition. | New York: PublicAffairs, [2019] |
    Includes bibliographical references and index.
Identifiers: LCCN 2018049629| ISBN 9781541724068 (hardcover) |
    ISBN 9781541724082 (ebook)
Subjects: LCSH: Equality. | Social stratification. | Populism.
Classification: LCC HM821 .O88 2019 | DDC 305—dc23
LC record available at https://lccn.loc.gov/2018049629

ISBNs: 978-1-5417-2406-8 (hardcover); 978-1-5417-2408-2 (ebook)

LSC-C

10 9 8 7 6 5 4 3 2 1

For Myrna

CONTENTS

ONE

THE LEVELLING

Brexit, Trump, Noise, and Disruption

THAT OUR WORLD IS CHANGING AT A TECTONIC LEVEL IS CLOSE TO UNDENI-able, yet we often do not seem able to see beyond headline-grabbing events of recent years—the election of Donald Trump, Brexit, and new governments in Mexico and Italy, to name a few. These events simply represent the smashing of the old order; they are the detonators, the wrecking balls of the system that has grown up since the fall of communism.

The Levelling is about how the center of gravity in our world, societies, and economies is changing, the confusion those changes create, and the ideas that will help bring new structure to what is a disordered world. At the time of writing, the debate in countries as diverse as the United Kingdom, China, the United States, and Brazil is focused on uncertainty and the breakdown in well-established ways of doing things. Many people feel that their countries have strayed off the path to progress, and many more feel that the road ahead is an uncertain one.

My aim is to provide the frameworks and ideas that can help breathe new life into politics, policy making, and economic growth. They are not magic bullets but simply ways of focusing attention on fundamentally important issues, such as what makes a stable society and how to think through important political issues of the twenty-first century, including the role of intangible infrastructure in generating economic growth, the demise of international institutions, the rise to power of central banks, and the legal aspects of genetic engineering. The world we live in today, be the reader in Shanghai or Santiago or Stockholm, is very different from that of any other point in history. Forms of human interaction like social media didn't exist before. In economics, central banks have never before exerted so much influence on the world economy. In markets, the United States used to be the locus and architect of stability across emerging markets, either through the International Monetary Fund (IMF) or the US Treasury Department; now it is the provocateur of volatility. This time, as they say, is different.

There is also a sense that the cycles of the rise and fall of nations are repeating themselves and that, as over the past four hundred years, we are again grappling with basic issues such as the quality of public life, equality, and the workings of democracy. As a result, history can help prod today's debate in the right direction. It also provides ammunition for many scaremongers, and warnings—with some reason—that the world will soon revisit the bleak 1930s are now commonplace.

There is plenty in our history books to both inform and mislead us as to what might happen next to our societies. However, one period I am drawn to is the middle of the seventeenth century and its momentous events. The end of the Thirty Years' War through the Peace of West-phalia gave rise to the concept of nation-states as we know them. It was also a moment when laws and institutions were formed and began to be respected.

In England and, later, the United States and France, the first stir-rings of democracy arose, along with the notion of popular rule. My own country, Ireland, is bounded by these three Atlantic powers, and much of its history has been determined by its relationship with them. I have spent my life moving between Ireland, England, America, France, and

Switzerland and am naturally biased toward this corner of the world and its heritage. One thread that runs through all four Atlantic-facing countries is the idea of the republic. In simple, modern terms, a republic is a state that is run by its people, with equality among them. I would add strong institutions and laws to this mix.

The echo of this idea still courses powerfully through the twenty-first century. In France, the currency of the "republic" is still strong and prominent. In America, the institutions and checks and balances created by the Founding Fathers are still working and relevant. One of those Founding Fathers, Alexander Hamilton, will make a guest appearance later in this book.

The American and French Revolutions represent the explosion into life of democracy and what we understand as the republic, but their seeds were sown a century earlier, in the mid-seventeenth century. A hidden gem in English history—which gives its name to this book—is a good basis for the repair of politics, economics, and finance today. Later in the book, we will discuss this gem in full, and at the risk of perhaps sounding a bit like the writer Dan Brown, I will take you on a tour of old churches, missing manuscripts, and historical intrigues.

To give a quick glimpse, the inspiration for this book came from running alongside the River Thames, frequently passing St. Mary's Church in Putney. Having heard of the Putney Debates, which took place there in 1647, I eventually stopped to explore the church and, by extension, the Putney Debates. The debates have recently been acknowledged as one of the most important moments in English history and as the crucible of modern constitutional democracy. More than a year earlier, King Charles I had lost the English Civil War—a conflict fought over how England would be governed—to forces led by Oliver Cromwell. The debates took place between the officers and the rank and file of Cromwell's New Model Army to discuss the future constitution of England following the imprisonment of Charles.

The largest group involved in those debates, the Levellers, crafted arguments for equality and constitutional democracy, arguments that they framed as the "Agreements of the People." Those agreements resonate today as the first popular, written expressions of constitutional democracy. With democracy now under attack, it is to the Levellers we must turn for inspiration.

As political ruptures occurred across Europe during and after the eurozone crisis and as the 2016 US presidential campaign intensified, the Putney Debates and the Levellers who inspired them kept coming to my mind. One of the first texts on the Levellers I read was *The World Turned Upside Down*, by the historian and former master of Balliol College Christopher Hill. In it Hill tracks the emergence of radical political groups in mid-seventeenth-century England as they played a formative role in the emergence of democracy as we now know it. It is hard not to draw comparisons between the Levellers' demands and the strong desire by many people in many countries today for more satisfying political choices and more balanced economic circumstances.

The Levellers' story and the agreements they crafted deserve to be dusted off and reexamined. Their aims, their sentiments, and the forces that propelled them are relevant to the world in which we live and provide an apt starting point for processing and ordering the many changes percolating through the international political-economic order today. Their achievement was to set out a contract between the people and those who represented and governed them. Today there is little sense that such a contract is in place.

In fact, today the contract people thought they had with politicians, governments, institutions, and potentially each other is disintegrating. If anything, the order of the last thirty years is crumbling. Across politics, economics, finance, and geopolitics, the world has been and is increasingly dogged by a series of strange events, puzzles, and rising tensions. In economics, for instance, we have growth with low productivity, high profit margins but tepid wage growth in the United States, and record indebtedness at the same time as odd, multicentury lows in interest rates in countries like France and Spain. Wealth creation and wealth inequality are both at all-time highs, though many business leaders and politicians don't seem to mind this contradiction. These phenomena are rare historically and have tended to be followed by social, political, and economic crises. Predictably, I can cite the late 1920s as an example.

Additionally, central banks, now more powerful than governments, own enormous pools of assets, which they bought in an effort to keep the side effects of the global financial crisis at bay. As they unwind these holdings, this will make financial markets more jumpy and fragile economies more vulnerable.

In politics, there is Brexit, the election of Donald Trump, and the emergence in Europe of new, mostly right-wing political parties that are starting to disrupt traditional parties and politics. The rise of radical politics is spreading to emerging nations, notably Brazil. Voter volatility, apathy toward established political parties, and distrust in politics have risen to levels not seen since the Second World War. Gravely, democracy as a political choice looks as if it has peaked. More countries are now veering toward rule by strongmen, or to be more polite, toward "managed democracy." Other countries no longer see democracy as an indispensable part of the road map of progress and development.

In geopolitics, the rise and fall of nations is playing out at a seemingly accelerated speed. The election of Emmanuel Macron now gives France a leader with the ideas and energy to lead Europe, at a time when Angela Merkel's domination of European politics draws to a close. Internationally, the United States is no longer seen as a leader, and some places see it as an aggressor. Syria has used chemical weapons, there are calls for Germany to have nuclear weapons,[1] North Korea has fired missiles over Japan as part of its "path to disarmament," and the internet has entered the arsenal of warfare.

If Crisis or War Comes

Smaller countries are not immune to this upheaval and are perhaps emblematic of the new fears and geopolitical threats that nations face today. For example, in May 2018, Swedes were issued a booklet entitled *If Crisis or War Comes*.[2] They have not had such an alarming communication since 1961, when the fear of a nuclear war was very real.[3] The aim of the booklet is to teach Swedes how to respond in the event of total war (cyber and propaganda attacks as well as military conflict), terrorist attacks, and extreme climate change. Sweden, alert to risks from Russia, has increased military spending, introduced conscription, and begun holding full-scale military exercises.

Beyond Europe, one of the world's other megatrends is the Chinese Dream.[4] China's quest is to regain the level of economic and geopolitical power it enjoyed up to three centuries ago and "make China great again." However, it is likely to face a reality check over the next five years as its economy slows, its citizens begin to desire more social and political self-expression, and America's elite seeks to check China's geopolitical progress. There was a time when emerging markets like China would sit quietly while Western nations and institutions told them what to do, but in the post-global-financial-crisis world, the West is no longer in a position to do so.

The sense of topsy turvy is not restricted to economics and international relations. The structure of our everyday lives is more volatile than ever before. The way we use our time and socialize has been utterly changed by social media. Obesity is now a significant health issue for nearly one in three Americans. More broadly, in a number of developed countries, the level of what the United Nations calls human development (e.g., life expectancy and education) is stalling and in some cases reversing. To cap it all, sixteen of the seventeen warmest years on record have occurred since 2000.

Though my intention is not to be pessimistic or to scaremonger, there is plenty of scope to heap more misery on the outlook for the future. What is astonishing is that so many of these trends are ignored. To brush them off ignores some very deep undercurrents—such as lack of political accountability, inequality, rapid social change that fuels a profound dissatisfaction with the political class, the diverging fortunes of large corporate actors and households, and the slowing of globalization*—and barely recognizes the concerns and issues that everyday people now grapple with and express through increasingly contorted political choices.

As at other turning points in history, many policy makers act as if a continuation of the glorious and happy past is the only way forward. A large number of politicians, academics, policy makers, business consultants, and writers still believe that globalization as we have experienced it over the past decade or so will persist in more or less the same fashion, or better.

For instance, recent work from the McKinsey Global Institute points to soaring digital globalization and stable financial globalization, but in my view, finance and technology will soon run into the reality of a more fractured, multipolar world. For example, China increasingly controls its internet space, partitioning it off from the global internet.

Many politicians and commentators still dismiss voter behavior as populism while failing to recognize that ordinary people feel increasingly confused and uncomfortable about the world they live in. Their consensus attitude might be summed up by a quotation attributed to Winston Churchill: "The best argument against democracy is a five-minute conversation with the average voter." Already, the example of the Levellers looks apt—the key social division in their day was that between the elite (the Grandees) and the ordinary people (the Levellers), which chimes with political debate today.

The same complacent mind-set sees financial markets thriving despite many structural economic risks. It also presumes that the liberal democratic order will continue to act as a beacon to emerging nations. It is in the interest of many politicians and commentators to believe that nothing will change.

This book sets out a different view, one of the world entering a new era, a fundamental transition phase. On almost every vector,

---

* We can define globalization as the increasing interdependence and integration of economies, markets, nations, and cultures.

the world is turning away from globalization and toward a multipolar order. This process is undercut by many risks—debt is too high,
humans are less productive, trade and military tensions are rising, to
name a few.

The exciting and challenging element of the new era is that it is one
where new political templates and parties are either in the process of being created or will need to be created, a world in which a new framework
for organic economic growth will need to be discovered, and a world
where many artificial stimulants to growth—such as indebtedness
and central-bank asset purchases—will need to be pared back. In this
emerging multipolar world, many of the international institutions of the
twentieth century will become redundant as new formations of nations
and new institutional arrangements spring up.

In this "levelling," Brexit and Trump are the first catalysts. More
signs will come, and we will be less and less able to ignore them. We are
at a turning point similar to that of the late 1980s, when many people
focused on the fall of communism itself and few saw that a bigger trend,
globalization, was about to take hold. In today's world, what initially
appear as isolated events are beginning to form a pattern breaking down
what we might call the old order.

An Interconnected World

It is important to understand how interlocked and connected the spheres
of economics, politics, finance, and geopolitics shaping the changing
world are today. The economic crises of the past ten years demonstrate
that the world is not siloed and that actors in one area (e.g., politics) do
not have the luxury of isolating themselves from the impact of other
fields (such as finance).

This interlocking and connection happens in many fascinating ways.
Technology is a good example. For instance, it complicates diplomacy
through the rise of cyberwarfare and what could be called diplomacy by

tweet, and it accelerates economic change and changes the way central banks look at inflation (what could be called the Amazon effect of apparently driving retail prices lower). Then, the sheer size of technology companies like Facebook and the pervasiveness of technology in society is one of the new challenges to law and philosophy (biotechnology is another). In financial markets, new data and algorithmic trading are changing the ways in which markets operate.

The Levelling will fully illustrate and synthesize the transition going on in world politics, economics, finance, and international relations. It will also show that as globalization falters and gives way to a more multipolar form of world order, the relative power between countries and regions will level out, and then new constellations will emerge.

At this juncture, some readers might comment, This is all very interesting, but what has it got to do with me? Most people can be forgiven for thinking that terms like "globalization," "quantitative easing," "trade protectionism," and "international diplomacy" have little to do with their everyday lives. In fact the opposite is true. Our mortgages and pensions, the stresses on our working environments, what we are pushed and pulled to view on the internet, the prices and quality of the goods and services we consume—all are driven by these factors. The trouble is that they are presented and discussed in technical and abstract ways, partly, I suspect, to hide their true impact.

This also opens up the possibility for the misuse and abuse of these terms. Though a politician might fail to win many votes with a call for "more globalization," he or she might do better with a demand for "China to give us back our jobs." The distance between the technical aspects of some of the tectonic changes in our world and their impact on our lives is large. Climate change is an example. We feel it happening, but most of us do not understand the complex science behind it. That gap also helps explain why some people apparently tire of experts who don't speak the language of everyday people. Equally, the tenor of public debate and of policy discussions on social media is at times appalling and, for many people, uninspiring and demoralizing. The divide between expert and layman is also a challenge for political leaders, who often struggle to bridge it. What we really need to ask is, Are the forces acting on our societies and economies good or bad? And what can constructively be done about them?

In this sense, the goal of this book is to jump to the next stage in the debate and to set out some ideas and frameworks that will help tease out how public life will evolve in the next fifteen years, what kind of society people in developed and developing countries really want, and how their wishes can be better represented by their elected leaders.

One of the most prominently discussed policy fault lines is inequality, together with a broader sense of a world divided between insiders and outsiders. The extent of income inequality and its social and economic implications are increasingly well understood, but wealth inequality is perhaps a more serious issue. Wealth inequality means that many people are cut off from the positive effects of rising property and asset prices, in a way that makes their social standing and the opportunities they enjoy (or not) permanent. Many other markers of the way we live now are also stretched. For example, sugar, artificial foodstuffs, and drugs have permeated our diets and have changed our behavior and health to such an extent that they have provoked a global crisis of obesity (eight of the twenty countries with the fastest-rising obesity rates are in Africa) and declining health.[5] Furthermore, aging and demographics will have complex effects on growth and investment. Older populations consume less and work less, demonstrably lowering the rate of economic growth and placing a burden on younger generations. "Gray" generations also invest more conservatively.

The World Turned Upside Down

There are other elements of "the world turned upside down." The West appears to be in decline and the rise of liberal democracy is slowing.

The component parts of globalization—the flow of ideas, people, and money—are retreating, and the United States is now erecting barriers to trade with Europe and Asia. At a more sinister level, technology—which was once regarded as an outright positive—is breeding more-sinister threats in cyberspace and in new forms of warfare, such as cluster drones.

Many of the extremes now evident across technology, economics, and politics mark the end of a period in history, or even bookend a period in history. The last thirty years have been kind in terms of growth and progress (advances in technology and human development are just two areas of development). The average level of economic growth has been much higher than the historical norm, poverty has been eradicated in many parts of the emerging world, and there have been no major wars. The next thirty years, however, will not be so kind and easy. There is great complacency about this, and many politicians, consumers, and investors seem to assume or internalize the prosperity of the last thirty years and expect it to be reproduced.

There is plenty more. Imagine if political dislocation, extremism, and volatility become the norm. If racism becomes more overt and more accepted. If productivity plunges because of triple crises in obesity, poor education, and drug dependency. If wealth inequality grows and if, for many, unfunded pensions turn retirement into purgatory. If protectionism rises, not only in the realm of trade but also in the sense that the flow of ideas and internet access between countries becomes more bounded. If, in the emerging countries, governments become more authoritarian as growth slows, more dismissive of the West, and more dangerously innovative in the areas of internet censorship, military adventurism, and genetic engineering. This kind of nasty end to globalization has happened before, in 1913. It was followed by world war, depression, financial crashes, and political extremism. Although the probability of disasters of this magnitude is still low, very few consumers, investors, or politicians are attuned to the long-term implications of the changes facing the world.

Four Challenges Ahead

I would like to strike a different, more constructive note. There are at least four problems that need solutions if we are to avoid the darker scenarios that threaten the world we live in. Each represents a way of levelling out the many imbalances that face our world, and they provide new ideas that form the basis for future political-economic structures.

The first problem relates to political discontent, expressed initially through Brexit and then in the US presidential election of 2016. It is now cropping up in Europe in the form, for example, of the rise of the right-wing party Alternative für Deutschland (AfD) in Germany (not to forget the rise of Aufstehen on the left); the Catalan independence movement; high political turnover in Australia (where the style of politics is especially brutal and which has now had six prime ministers in ten years); battles against corruption in African countries, including Kenya and South Africa; and the general rise in aspirations toward more political openness in emerging markets.

There is a broader crisis of democracy in that voter turnout is dropping, voters are more fickle, and elections seem to be less predictable. The rise of social media as a political tool and the accompanying voter polarization are among the underlying currents here, as is the reality that lower economic growth and the aftermath of the global financial crisis have had a delayed, disruptive impact on politics. Much of this is now well documented. What is less obvious is how positive, grassroots-based solutions can be found to overcome discontent and produce a better form of politics.

This is where the Levellers come in. They were a key part of the Putney Debates, held in order to discuss what a new, modern British constitution might look like. Remarkably, ordinary men (and notably in some cases, women) were allowed the chance to express their views on what a new, less unequal political system might look like, which makes the debates one of the most important episodes in the history and development of democracy.

The Agreement of the People

The Levellers will strike a chord with many people who are disenchanted with politics and world affairs. For one thing, they were ordinary people, soldiers and tradespeople, men and, remarkably for the period, women. They were angry at a world where Parliament had lost touch with the people, where the law was applied differently to the rich ("Grandees") and the poor, and where there was little sense of fairness in social and economic affairs. Unlike in much of the political debate on social media today, the aim of the Levellers was a tangible, constructive solution to a political problem. Their methods would also be recognized today. They canvassed opinions across society and used pamphleteering in the same way we use social media today.

Their great contribution was the Agreements of the People. The agreements (three of them evolving from 1647 to 1649) set out the remedies proposed by the Levellers to the problem of what we might call political-democratic recession.[6] The agreements are recognized as the first popular attempt to craft democratic constitutions. The agreements called for elected officials to be more responsive and responsible to those who elected them, the simplification of the law in plain English, an end to onerous indebtedness procedures, suffrage for most males, religious freedom, and political and electoral reform. They demanded an end to corruption in politics and within the judiciary.

The Levellers wanted a political system that fostered responsibility to the people on the part of their leaders, a system where these leaders or representatives were accountable, and a political-legal environment where there was no uneven distribution of outcomes. Imagine then, if, using the Levellers as an example, an "Agreement of the People, Twenty-First Century" were to be struck across countries through social media. Imagine the way it could frame the responsibilities of political leaders. Imagine the ways it could make for a more positive, focused political debate that will be led by new parties and new political blood. Imagine the way it could help structure principles that could guide how societies and governments approach indebtedness, trade, diplomacy, and economic development.

Running Out of Steam

The second challenge is economic growth. Since the turn of the twenty-first century, economic growth worldwide has been running out of steam; only stimulants in the form of very high levels of debt and aggressive central-bank action have kept it going. This does not stop politicians, however, from promising a return to prosperity or, in more glorious terms, pledging to make their country great again. The Trump administration is a case in point, demanding, as the basis for its economic model, large tax cuts for corporations and high earners rather than reskilling and education for workers threatened by the rise of technology.

My strong view is that countries (and companies too) should focus on stable, organic growth—growth that comes from factors such as the skill base of the labor market, innovation and technology, intangible infrastructure, and the system of laws and institutions that form the backbone of a nation. A truly great country is a resilient one that does not need to bully its neighbors in order for its economy to grow. Neither does organic growth come from accounting tricks, the ramping up of large levels of debt, or spurious tax breaks that cause economic imbalances. The next recession will lay this bare in a very bleak way.

In truth, what governments need but often avoid is a framework for rediscovering long-term growth. This requires careful, long-term policy making that often doesn't lend itself conveniently to rhetoric. This is a question not of probing economic theory or of coming up with new mathematical models but of setting out a coherent framework for growth and of providing politicians and those who vote for them with an understandable and tangible policy checklist. Success for a country comes not necessarily as a result of its military might or the size of its gross domestic product (GDP) but rather from its capacity to stimulate human development, to withstand economic shocks, and to have a stable society. One of the central ingredients in such an approach is a country's "intangible infrastructure," that is, "the set of factors that develop human capability and permit the easy and efficient growth of business activity."[7]

These factors can be essentially political, legal, or socioeconomic in nature. Political factors include the degree of political stability or the strength of a country's institutional framework. The rule of law, tax policies, and the protection of intellectual and physical property rights are important legal factors. Examples of socioeconomic factors include research-and-development capabilities, business processes or employee training, and education. Stating that governments should focus more on education and should prosecute it in a clever and progressive manner is, to the ears of cynics, rehearsing the obvious. However, the reality is not so easy. Many countries get education wrong. Greece is an example. Many, if not all, of my Greek friends have had the privilege of a third-level education outside Greece, usually at universities in the south of England: the City University of London, the University of Essex, Oxford University, and the London School of Economics. There is an apparent aversion among Greeks to their own educational system. An extreme case in point: the two individuals who dueled over Greece's future in the heat of the eurozone crisis—George Papandreou, leader of the Panhellenic Socialist Movement (PASOK), and Antonis Samaras, leader of New Democracy—were roommates together at Amherst College. The cause and the effect is a poor education system, which is, correspondingly, held in very low esteem among Greeks. The consequence is that many young Greeks, once educated abroad, stay abroad. They are not invested in their country. Other examples abound: Italy, for example, has no major university in the top two hundred universities in the world,[8] whereas Germany has ten in the top one hundred.

Conversely, one of the successes of some American cities (such as Pittsburgh) is that they have succeeded in keeping the graduates of good local universities (such as Carnegie Mellon University and the University of Pittsburgh). With Greece now finally emerging from the eurozone crisis, I can think of few better investments than an overhaul of the Greek secondary and tertiary educational system (with a very large helping hand from the European Union) so that promising Greek students feel they can have as good an education at home as abroad.

Education is just one vital ingredient in the system of factors that produces organic economic growth. Yet before we can set off on an unencumbered path to steadier, organic growth, as I hope *The Levelling* will make clear, the obstacles and detritus of previous crises first need to be removed. I have two obstacles and two provocative solutions in mind. I conceive of them as "a Westphalia Treaty for Finance," and they make up the third idea in this book.

The two obstacles are debt and central banks. It seems the world has learned little from the 2009 global financial crisis or, indeed, the long history of financial crises going back to the tulip mania, the South Sea Bubble, and the Mississippi scheme. Debt levels (global debt to GDP) today are higher than at the beginning of the financial crisis. China, emerging-market governments, corporate America, and select European countries (that is, France) have taken on most new debt. Most of this debt is not productive, in that it doesn't fuel growth; rather, it has been taken on to patch up economic holes, fuel financial engineering, and buy time rather than to fund new investments. In China, for instance, the impact on the GDP of a dollar (or renminbi) spent on investment (mostly infrastructure) has fallen steadily in the last five years. If interest rates rise, as they are beginning to as of this writing, the burden of this debt will weigh down economic activity and fuel future crises.

One cause of so much debt accumulation since the 2009 crisis is the monetary policy of "quantitative easing" (QE), that is, the buying of bonds and other securities by central banks, something that would have been unthinkable to earlier generations of central bankers. Quantitative easing is the financial equivalent of morphine, helping take pain away. Medicinal morphine is not supplied to patients on a continuous basis, and it is not known to cure cancer, heart disease, or other ailments. Central bankers, however, appear to have a different view of the uses of financial morphine.

A Westphalia for Finance

Since 2009 central banks have aggressively pursued quantitative easing (and "zero" interest rates) in the hope of lowering borrowing costs and pushing up investment by companies and households. This has helped forestall financial crises but has done little else. It has not cured underlying economic problems and at the same time has fostered an addiction to low interest rates and accommodative central banks. Even the start of QE decommissioning by the US Federal Reserve is proving difficult for markets to digest.

My proposal for provoking change is a framework to level debt and risk taking through a global conference leading to a treaty on debt and risk. The assumption, unfortunately, is that the only way governments would agree to this is if they were in the midst of a nasty market crisis and were facing a deep recession.

This kind of conference, though not unprecedented in history (think of the 1924 and 1953 debt conferences that allowed Germany debt relief), would be highly unusual and would be both a sign and an acknowledgment of how bloated debt levels have become. Such a conference would be part of the laying down of the initial rules of the game for a multipolar world. Like the system put in place by the historic Peace of Westphalia (1648), it could be one where nation-states bear greater responsibility, in this case for their financial health. The overriding aim would be to encourage risk bearing rather than risk sharing of debt, in much the same way that Westphalia encouraged individual states and statelets to bear political and identity risk.

This world treaty on financial risk could be crafted along the lines of existing large-scale environmental or nuclear weapons deals. Under this agreement, the world's major central banks would agree—or rather, their political masters would agree for them—to use extraordinary measures like quantitative easing only in truly exceptional preset conditions of great market and economic stress. The effects would be that markets would properly price economic and political risks, politicians would therefore act to address those risks and fault lines, and, when extraordinary monetary policy needed to be launched, it would be more effective.

By prohibiting quantitative easing or such extraordinary uses of the monetary toolbox (central banker speak for the many options they have invented to express their power), such a treaty would attune political leaders to the fact that the monetary comfort blanket could not be deployed against every threat and that governments would thus have to adopt a more proactive approach to avoiding and curing economic crises.

Multipolar World

The final idea in *The Levelling* relates to geopolitics. Many people remain attached to a world that has been globalized by the United States. The debate over America's place in the world under President Trump is testament to this. The same is also true of debates in the United Kingdom and Europe. As these debates are raging, my own experience is that US and British citizens are still in denial about the way their countries' international influence is slipping. Europeans do not yet recognize the urgency with which their community needs to better align and organize itself. Similarly, the almost exclusively Western commentariat does not countenance the possibility that globalization as we know it is over and is giving way to a multipolar world dominated by three to four specific regions that increasingly do things in a distinctive way.

Geopolitics will be dominated by three significant players: China-centric Asia, the Americas, and Europe. India may constitute a fourth pole, but its time has not yet arrived. These will be the players in the Great Game of the twenty-first century. (Peter Hopkirk's book *The Great Game: On Secret Service in High Asia*, on the strategic battle between Britain and Russia in the nineteenth century, is a must-read as background.) For example, China's One Belt, One Road infrastructure and trade project is a definitive Great Game–like maneuver. Each of these blocs, poles, or great powers will take a distinct approach to economics, society, the military, and the internet, to name a few areas. As regards the internet, for instance, the United States owns the companies that have built it, Europe will regulate it, and China has already erected a cordon sanitaire around its internet space.

If the world comes to be dominated by three great intercontinental powers, several things may happen. Countries that fall between the cracks of these great power blocs, such as the United Kingdom, Japan, Russia, and Australia, will be forced to redefine their place in the world. Countries that lack the economic power to match the military might of the big three, such as Russia, may have to rethink their national development models. Countries with vast economic potential, such as India, may have to remake other facets of their power base, such as India's military. And new coalitions may form.

One potential new coalition could be made up of the small developed countries of the world (e.g., Switzerland, Sweden, Ireland, Singapore, and New Zealand), which in many cases represent the canaries in the coal mine of globalization and which increasingly suffer similar policy challenges and seek to compare notes with each other. In general, these countries represent enlightened democracies that in many cases demonstrate best practice in policy making. As all this happens, some regions may be increasingly left behind. More importantly, many of the institutions set up in the twentieth century—the World Bank, IMF, World Trade Organization (WTO), and North Atlantic Treaty Organization (NATO)—may become defunct. In many cases they may be replaced by great-power diplomacy.

The relevance of geopolitical change to the notion of levelling is twofold. First, it will involve a decades-long process of changing power distribution, or levelling out of power and wealth between countries. Second, it will provoke a swell of nationalism, regionalism, and friction and, in turn, a great swirling competition of ideas. Consider China and India. India is behind China militarily and economically but arguably ahead of it in terms of its democracy.

What Would Hamilton Say?

Finally, one of the fascinating trends of the next decade or so will be watching how regions and countries change and evolve and how this drives political change within them. In the spirit of the Levellers, it is to be hoped that this happens in a progressive, constructive way. One figure in history who, in terms of intellectual outlook, is relevant to the idea of this levelling is Alexander Hamilton. I single him out because, like the Levellers, he was interested in both democracy and the idea of the classical republic (i.e., its institutions and laws) and was keenly aware that they served different purposes. Hamilton was an architect and implementer of intangible infrastructure to such an extent and level of excellence that few historical figures can match him.

So I use "Hamilton" as shorthand for the establishment of institutions, laws, and skill sets needed for countries—or here, regions—to be able to enjoy durable economic growth, high human development, and a stable public life. In the last part of the book, I use Hamilton to tell the story of what needs to be done in institution building and diplomacy so that the "levelling" may become reality.

The levelling will happen in many ways: The levelling of political accountability and responsibility between political leaders and "the people" (Grandees versus Levellers, insiders versus outsiders, elites versus masses). The levelling of institutional power—away from central banks and defunct twentieth-century institutions such as the WTO and IMF and toward new treaties (on risk and monetary policy) and new institutions (e.g., a truly effective and powerful climate body and an institution or agreement that oversees cybersecurity). The levelling out of wealth—between rich and poor countries and between the very rich and "the rest," preferably with "the rest" enjoying both better organic growth and a greater share of this growth. Then the levelling out of power between nations and regions is what the concept of the multipolar world is about, and within it, different regions will have different reserves of power.

There is so much change and challenge ahead. It is important that we, and notably the media, move beyond the symptoms of a changing world and focus on the tectonic shifts happening under our feet. My objective with *The Levelling* is to try to set the world we live in in some context and to draw out reference points that people may find useful in addressing the many changes that face us. I propose new ideas—from new political parties to new rules for the way finance functions—that are essential in moving on from the sense of disorder today.

TWO

THE TIDE GOES OUT

*Running Out of Breath Economically,
Losing Patience Politically*

I SPEND QUITE A BIT OF TIME IN FRANCE, AND ON A RECENT TRIP OUT OF Paris to Versailles I unexpectedly came across a stand selling evangelical books, which carried the following sign: "The World Is Out of Control." Two thoughts came to mind. One is that doomsaying is always a good advertising strategy, and various religious organizations have been guilty of using this ploy through the ages. That the stand was in Versailles underlined this history, since the town has seen quite a few "out of control" periods. Versailles is an echo from history that serves to remind us that absolute power, and absolute inequality, can have violent and unpredictable consequences.

My second thought was to ask whether the world is really "out of control." In absolute terms, world GDP and wealth are at all-time highs, unemployment is at a decade low in many large countries, technological advances are spellbinding, and there has been a sharp fall in poverty at a global level in the past twenty years. So it seems that things are really not so bad.

However, if we scratch beneath the surface, it all looks very different.[1] The world economy has so strained and contorted itself to arrive at a postcrisis recovery that debt levels and intervention by central banks are at record highs. Though growth through 2018 has been positive despite trade tensions, forecasts from bodies like the IMF and the US Federal Reserve show that trend growth—long-run average rate of growth—in the next five to ten years will be considerably lower than the average of the past thirty years. It seems that households already sense this, and the stock and bond markets have become more nervous. More importantly, the sources of growth we have come to rely on are reversing. Productivity, the world's ability to generate growth, is pallid, and most notably, globalization and open trade are under attack and retreating. President Trump's trade dispute or trade crusade has begun to cleave apart the world order and to decouple trade flows between large economies. One memorable image of 2018 comes from the June G7 meeting, where Trump is surrounded by disapproving counterparts. Beyond the G7, America's role in the world is also being reconsidered. Historically the United States has resolved emerging-market crises, but in the summer and fall of 2018, trade tariffs deployed against China and Turkey risked causing one. The long-term effect of such trade disputes will, I believe, make investment by other countries into the United States less rather than more likely.

In another echo of Versailles, a deepening fault line is the distribution of the spoils of economic growth and wealth within and between countries. At one end of the spectrum, the share of the economy that companies have—corporate profits relative to GDP—is at an all-time high. But at the other end, the share that workers have—wages relative to GDP—is at a low. Reflecting this, in the United States the ratio of the average wage to the value of the stock market is at a multidecade low. In practical terms, this shows why many people face greater financial difficulty in building up their pensions. At a grander level, this contrast between Wall Street and Main Street sets out a stark conflict between capital and labor. With wealth inequality worldwide at a high, this tension will begin to play on people's expectations.

In developed markets, expectations of income, life expectancy, and social mobility are flattening out and in some areas falling. This creates generationally rooted disappointment, which in turn drives political attitudes and leads to a poverty of expectations. In contrast, emerging countries face a dilemma of expectations—in emerging markets people expect more: higher incomes, better consumption choices, and more interesting lifestyles. The 2018 film *Crazy Rich Asians* is an extreme illustration of this. The film captures the rise of the new wealthy in Asia and shows how that rise has conditioned lavish consumption habits and attitudes to the West. I am tempted to say that, like the 1987 film *Wall Street*, *Crazy Rich Asians* has a dangerously totemic air to it. Though wealth creation across Asia is on an upward trend, any falloff in this growth will translate into political volatility. Globally, wealth inequality between countries is also shifting, though it is improving as emerging countries catch up on the wealth levels. For example, from 2002 to 2016, wealth per adult increased by three times in India but by only 50 percent in the United Kingdom.

In general, the more one interrogates the way the world has developed under the steam of globalization, the more we see that extremes are emerging, that new stress factors and risks are touching the lives of ordinary people, and that these contribute to a sense of a "world turned upside down." To make matters more complicated, the tide of easy prosperity is going out. The further it retreats, the more it exposes fault lines that were hidden by the onward march of globalization.

In this context, the aim of this chapter is to set the scene for the rest of the book by sketching the consequences of the tide's going out: showing that the world has run out of breath economically and run out of patience politically, and that in places the long-term expectations of wealth and income are tapering downward and the established rules of the road for our world are being undercut.

"The Pace of Change Has Never Been This Fast"

The reader might respond by asking, Won't technology solve all of these problems? Today, there is such a dazzling array of new problem-solving technologies—from gene editing and digital health care to sleep masks to cryptocurrencies to lifestyle apps—that we might consider most of our material problems to be solvable. For instance, French author Nicolas Santolaria has written a book, *Comment j'ai sous-traité ma vie* (How I outsourced my life), in which he describes his attempt to outsource as many chores and lifestyle tasks as possible to apps, including dating apps that let him pay to have someone "pre–chat up," if that's the right phrase, partners he is interested in dating.

My rejoinder is that technology, when gushingly described by flashy futurologists, seems breathtaking, but for the majority of ordinary people it can prove confusing, intimidating, and vexing. For example, at the 2018 World Economic Forum, Canadian prime minister Justin Trudeau said, "The pace of change has never been this fast, and yet it will never be this slow again."[2] This will have delighted "Davosians," but it is also the kind of statement that strikes fear into most ordinary people. My feeling—supported by the way people vote and by the rise, for instance, of new mental-health disorders such as video game addiction and acute attention deficit disorder—is that the majority of people are experiencing more change than they are comfortable with and would rather slow down than accelerate the pace of change. For example, many executives will testify that there is an enormous gap between the promise of technology for corporations and the willingness of workforces to adopt new technologies.

I do not want to sound too old-fashioned, but the reality is that many people will increasingly feel that things are not the way they used to be. This sense of dislocation seems to be pervasive in the political debates across Europe and the United States and may be the result of economic angst having reached the bounds of people's patience for change and of the perceived side effects of globalization.

This feeling of anomie comes from different sources, though there are a few common threads. One is a widely expressed sense that political processes are not working well in Western countries. Another, to parse much of the media, is a growing impression of existential threat: terrorism, the fate of the euro, climate change, and disease. For instance, in 2014 the onset of the Ebola crisis in western Africa led to a surge of mentions on social media, reaching six thousand mentions per minute, which in turn in the United States led to a wave of people being tested for the disease, even though the number of positive cases in the United States was ultimately miniscule.[3] In many countries people feel they are losing touch with the values and behaviors that shaped their societies, a sort of loss of *heimat*. (*Heimat*, very simply and I hope uncontroversially, refers to a place or society that a group of people find familiar, trustworthy, and consistent with their culture, a place where people feel at home and at ease.) In certain cases, loss of *heimat* is not a bad thing— consider how Western societies have become more tolerant and open, or how the place of women is changing. However, in other cases, a loss of *heimat* leads people to lose their bearings and then to instinctively act against the forces they perceive to have disturbed them, such as technology and immigration.

Let me give a personal example: for much of my life I have been a passionate supporter of Manchester United, a football club with a unique history and with what used to be a distinctive attitude and a squad of players with cultural roots in Britain and Ireland. The club's history is marked by both poignant moments (such as the 1958 Munich air disaster, in which over half the team died in an airplane crash on takeoff from Munich Airport) and dramatic moments, and for a long time the club had a never-give-up attitude. Following the retirement of longtime manager Sir Alex Ferguson, all of this has now changed, and, like many other football clubs who used to express the ethos of their local regions, Manchester United has now largely become a consumer brand, with a global base of supporters and a set of players disparate in background and spirit. It has lost touch with its roots, its culture, and its winning ways. What is most galling is that the old United was much better than the current, made-for-TV version: under Ferguson they won two European Champions Cups, five Football Association (FA) Cups, and thirteen UK Premiership Leagues, while under his successors (up to José Mourinho) they have a total haul of one FA Cup and a Europa Cup.

I have titled this chapter "The Tide Goes Out" because there is a sense that, as with Manchester United's form, more and more negatives—social, economic, and politic—are coming to the surface. As the saying goes, it's only when the tide goes out that we can see who's swimming naked. So as globalization ebbs, its discontents become more obvious. For the rest of the chapter, I want to emphasize three things: First, globalization has been a force for good but is now receding. Second, as it retreats we become more aware of its perceived side effects, such as inequality, the changes in our lifestyles and our diets, and generally "the way we live now," to borrow Anthony Trollope's words. Relatedly, the aftermath of the global financial crisis and the responses to it have left a range of imbalances in place. Third, people are now reacting to these imbalances and side effects. This is manifest in growing political volatility, which in my view will bring about a revolution in politics as people search for more accountable and responsible forms of governance.

As it stands, many people like to place blame for the ills of specific countries at the door of globalization. Radical political leaders—such as Nigel Farage, formerly of the United Kingdom Independence Party (UKIP); Marine Le Pen, formerly of France's National Front; and the Five Star Movement in Italy—and media pundits like Sean Hannity of Fox News have spoken out loudly against globalization. The notion that everything is the fault of globalization is very convenient. It makes for an expedient culprit, and it is so pervasive that we have lost sight of its meaning and implications. In some respects, the world is now so well connected in its financial and information flows that globalization is everywhere, so much so that we have become much less conscious of it.

Globalization has few defenders, as it is now unfashionable and politically unprofitable to show support for it. It has no outright owner, though some international research bodies and thought leaders like the Organisation for Economic Cooperation and Development (OECD) and the World Economic Forum (WEF) are closely associated with it. Similarly, many economic, political, and social stresses, such as inequality, poverty, and the decline of agriculture, are ascribed to the evils of globalization, regardless of the true origins of those stresses (in fact, during globalization the world poverty level has collapsed from 35 percent of the world population in 1990 to 11 percent in 2013).[4] In addition, the public understanding of globalization is not strong. Understandably, few people take the trouble to sift through trade reports or examine the flow of labor around the world. Thus, as with the issue of "Europe" in British politics, where few politicians have said or can say anything positive about Europe, globalization is vulnerable to becoming a catchall for the negative aspects of economic growth and so functions as a sort of political doormat.

There is, however, a strong case to be made that globalization, the most powerful economic force the world has witnessed in the past twenty years, has been a force for good. It is now so pervasive in its effects and has produced so many startling outcomes—for example, the rise of Dubai, the successes of small states like Singapore, growing wealth in emerging economies (from 2000 to 2010 wealth per adult in Indonesia increased sixfold), the emerging-market consumer, and fast-changing consumer tastes (as I write this in late 2018, yoga mats are replacing smartphones as a must-have item)—that we risk taking it for granted. What is material today is that globalization is slowing, and in many instances its side effects are now more obvious.

Good-Bye to All That

In 1929 the English writer Robert Graves published his book *Good-Bye to All That*, with which he achieved acclaim and some notoriety. The book deals largely with his experiences as an officer in the First World War (during which he was injured so badly that his family were incorrectly informed of his death). More broadly, the book is a wry reflection on the passing of the British Empire, a very specific way of life and moral framework. Its title keeps coming to mind today, and it seems a good starting point from which to reflect on a period marked by Brexit, policy mishaps over world trade, and the disintegration of the world order.

These events are just a few of those leading us to say good-bye to globalization. A growing number of stress points—trade, political, institutional, and corporate—now undercut globalization. Unfortunately, there is not yet a deep debate on the future of globalization. Many writers and periodicals such as *Foreign Affairs* seem fixated on the choice between slightly different flavors of globalization "as we know it" rather than a radical departure from it. This is an enormously complacent error. Many of the success stories of the last thirty years have been driven by globalization. If it halts, then so too will many of the things people have come to rely upon and enjoy.

Yet data relating to many of the trends underlying globalization warn that an inflection point has been reached. We can see this in various ways. The component parts of globalization—flows of trade, finance, ideas, services, and people—have ebbed since 2015,[5] and while some of them (i.e., services) are still at historically high levels, it is hard not to have the impression that globalization is on the verge of a downward path, especially once we consider some of the underlying dynamics such as trade protectionism and regional exceptionalism.

The most basic representation of globalization is trade, which after plateauing in recent years is now dipping. From 2011 onward trade had rebounded from the relative lows of the global financial crisis and had again attained the level reached in 2008–2009, which historically is the highest level in at least fifty years. However, from 2016 to today and in the context of an upturn in broad economic activity, the openness of the world economy (ratio of trade to GDP) has fallen sharply, and this measure is back down to the level seen in 2011. Indeed, in late 2018 the OECD reported that the level of trade between G20 nations had dipped sharply.[6]

Another way to consider the pace of globalization is to look at the aggregate activity in the world's most open, globalized economies. If we add together the GDP for the likes of Ireland, Switzerland, Belgium, Singapore, and the Netherlands—small, open economies that in many respects are the canaries in the coal mine of the world economy, in the sense that they are the first to pick up a new trend—we see that their trend growth is slowing and is below the average level of growth enjoyed over the past twenty years.

Trade Wilting

There are several reasons why trade openness has diminished. For example, a shift in economic structure in China means fewer capital-expenditure-driven goods are traded. In addition, habitually weak demand from the eurozone has removed an important support for world trade. The rise of new technologies in manufacturing and supply-chain management has meant that many goods require less capital investment, and the trade dispute between the United States and China is fracturing international supply chains. Here technology has enabled some Western companies to relocate operations back to their own countries.

Other indicators of globalization paint a more negative picture: cross-border flows of financial assets (relative to GDP) have continued downward from their pre-financial-crisis peak, probably because of the effects of regulation and the general shrinking of the banking sector. Foreign direct investment has recovered in the past two years, but it too is now well below the levels reached in 2009, according to the World Bank. Restrictions on foreign (mostly Chinese) investment in the United States and Europe, together with capital controls in China, have also sharply curtailed cross-border investment flows.

Similarly, the profits of multinational companies—which, though not strictly an indicator of globalization, are a useful gauge of the health of the actors who have driven globalization—now look as if they have peaked. Profit margins for large US companies are very high historically, at close to 10 percent, but are now slowly contracting. In China, profit margins are not as grand as those in the United States and are also contracting, and furthermore, they are vulnerable to an economic correction.

At this stage, proponents of globalization might well conclude that it is pausing for breath or that it is in a transitional phase while new technologies and new economic actors emerge. This may prove to be the case. But data suggest that we should be more worried by rumblings in the engine room of globalization, which hint that the plateauing in globalization may be more structural than cyclical, and to an extent these rumblings are reminiscent of some of the behaviors seen in the early twentieth century.

The sense that globalization and trade have stopped growing is bolstered by a narrative claiming that the globalization pie has stopped expanding. The rise of protectionism means that the debate on globalization taking place today is really about who gets the slices of the globalization pie and how large and tasty those slices need to be. Some of this concern not to be left with too small a piece is justified, but it does introduce a beggar-thy-neighbor element to the conversation on globalization. It may also help explain why politicians who vocally stand up for their constituencies or "corners" in trade-related debates are being rewarded by electorates. For example, in the United States, senators approaching an election tend to take on a more protectionist stance on trade and immigration, especially where they are not certain of being reelected.[7]

What is troubling about the current narrative on globalization is that instead of proposing ways it can thrive or can grow in a more sustainable way, many countries, politicians, and commentators propose ways in which to borrow, reclaim, or take over somebody else's slice of globalization. Trade policy is becoming the proving ground for this hypothesis, and the trade dispute between the United States and China, a dispute that has also embroiled most of America's allies, is emblematic.

Few genuine trade agreements have been struck over the past ten years (the United States–Mexico–Canada Agreement [USMCA] is simply a cosmetically scrubbed-up version of the original North American Free Trade Agreement [NAFTA]), and in some cases, opportunities for better trade relations between countries have been spurned. Neither the original Trans-Pacific Partnership (TPP) deal between the United States, Japan, and a group of Asian countries (notably, China was not included) nor the Trans-Atlantic Trade and Investment Partnership (TTIP) between the United States and the European Union (effectively a partner deal to the TPP) gained approval, which means that there has not been a major international trade agreement since the General Agreement on Tariffs and Trades (GATT) Doha Trade Round in 2001. Before that, the 1990s were replete with trade-friendly agreements: the establishment of the WTO, the European Union single market taking effect in 1993, and the creation of the euro.

From an American point of view, the TPP would have been an ideal starting point strategically, as it would have presented China with a united front made up of the United States and a number of Asian economies. Its aim was to construct a trade alliance between the United States and a group of Latin American and Asian countries, notably Japan. Besides lowering trade tariffs between those countries, the objective of the deal was to create a trade alliance around and excluding China. Negotiated during the administration of Barack Obama, the partnership was rejected by the Trump administration.

Against this backdrop, the Trump administration's haphazard and ill-thought-out approach to trade relations with its neighbors, allies, and China has for the first time in decades elevated international trade to the top of the economic policy worry list. The administration's handling of trade relations has sowed distrust, suspicion, and risk aversion on the part of America's many trade partners. The uncertainty created by trade-related rhetoric has already had an economic impact, on inflation, profit margins, and investment.

There are other concerns for trade. In areas where there is scope for gains in efficiencies of scale under the auspices of existing trade agreements, some countries are holding back on implementation. There is also a creep toward more overt, traditional protectionism. One of the authorities on the matter, the Global Trade Alert center, launched in 2009 to monitor the extent to which cross-government policies liberalize and restrict trade in the aftermath of the global financial crisis, notes that trade-defense measures and bailouts or state aid are by far the most popular measures implemented to "protect" trade, followed by import tariffs and trade finance.[8] Trade liberalization has been declining since 2009 and is now at its lowest level since then (for example, in 2018 there were over three times as many trade-discriminatory as trade-liberalizing measures announced internationally).

Interestingly, it is the United States that implements the greatest number of trade-protectionist measures (outnumbering trade-liberalizing measures by a factor of nearly nine to one), followed by Russia and India. It is also worth commenting that the United Kingdom, Spain, Germany, and France have each implemented more traditional trade-protection measures than China, though China does have more discreet ways of tipping trade relations in its favor.

Luddites Awaken

With the growth of trade so limited, it is inevitable that trade, its consequences, and its side effects will be live political issues. Trade in goods, in particular, is an attractive target for politicians, conjuring tangible images of cars, fridges, and phones crossing borders—unlike financial transactions and data flows. Reflecting this, in the first televised debate of the 2016 US presidential race, the words "trade" and "NAFTA" were used twenty-four times. The current sensitivity of American politicians to trade with China may reflect the fact that as China develops its own goods and consumer brands (China crafted a "Made in China 2025" plan to produce its own high-end consumer goods and technologies and to effectively become self-sufficient in these areas), it becomes a tougher market to sell into, and at the same time, the barriers to trade with it, such as technology sharing, remain high. At a deeper level, there is of course now a realization in Washington and beyond that China is drawing level with the United States as a geo-economic player.

That China or other countries can apparently supplant American manufacturing capacity must be bad for American jobs, or so the logic goes. There is some evidence to support this. For instance, a leading academic on the intersection of technology, trade, and labor markets, David Autor at the Massachusetts Institute of Technology, has undertaken work on how falling wages and rising joblessness in parts of the United States are linked to the inflow of goods from China. He and his colleagues have produced wonderful graphics that show the areas of the American economy (mostly the Southeastern states) that, according to their analysis, have been negatively affected by the switch in manufacturing capacity toward China.[9]

Similarly, Peter Schott and his colleagues find that economic areas of the United States that are subject to greater competition from China via a change in US trade policy tend to be more politically "agitated."[10] Those areas exhibit relative increases in voter turnout, increases in the share of votes cast for Democrats, and a higher probability of being represented by a Democrat. The researchers point out that the historic tilt toward Democrats (over Republicans) is consistent with the fact that Democrats have been more likely than Republicans to support legislation limiting import competition or favoring economic assistance. This historic bias has now changed, perhaps as a result of the perception, or even the cultivation of the view, that American jobs have been exported and that Democratic politicians have allowed it to happen. President Trump exploited this view through 2018 in the run-up to the midterm elections, not to mention during the 2016 presidential race, notwithstanding the costs of the tariffs to the US economy.

Academic studies, however thorough, will only tell part of the story about the link between competitiveness, trade, and politics. To add greater color here, I highlight J. D. Vance's book *Hillbilly Elegy*, which does a superb job of synthesizing the forces and influences that have led many lower-middle-class Americans to change their allegiance from the

Democratic Party to politicians on the right. I find myself recommending his book to anyone interested in American politics today. It is honest and charming, though I am somewhat suspicious of the way it was received and lauded by Washington, DC, elites for apparently showing that large segments of the American population were "falling behind" and that traditional Democratic voters turned toward Donald Trump. Accounts of the demise of the white lower-middle-class and lower-class population are plentiful in social science, literature, and music in the United States, but few policy makers and corporate leaders appear to have paid attention to this demise.

In his book, Vance tells how he turned his life around through enlisting in the Marines, seeking an education (Ohio State and then Yale Law School), and playing golf (his grandmother had advised him that playing golf would help him understand how wealthier people socialize and do business). Importantly, he also lays out the reasons why relatively poorer white Americans feel neglected economically and politically. In my view, what his book achieves in this regard is to show the socioeconomic decay associated with small government and, to a degree, with the regional and distributional economic consequences of globalization. In that respect, the risk for America is that globalization will be replaced by something far less bountiful, and far less prosperous, so that the social problems outlined by Vance go neglected. To step back and take the long view, globalization has been the driver of high growth for the last thirty years and has recently lost momentum. My sense is that globalization is beginning to eat itself as countries and companies compete for what they now perceive to be a fixed pie of economic growth. The narrative on globalization is dominated by two, perhaps three positions.

The first is what could lazily be termed the position of the global elite, who rightly point out the dangers of protectionism but, in my view, refuse to recognize that globalization may simply have run its course and, in the course of geopolitical change, will be replaced by something else. The second position is that of a vocal commentariat that strives to underline the downsides of globalization and, mischievously or deviously, gives it as the cause of more everyday economic ills.

And third, though the vast majority of people understandably have no fixed, clear, or explicit position on globalization itself, they will feel the detailed ways in which it touches them in their everyday lives (e.g., the price of coffee, the attractiveness of global brands, and the ways in which employment is changing). It is very difficult to synthesize all of globalization's component parts in a balanced way without the benefit of a few hours' study of the websites of the likes of the OECD, which contain reams of data on trade, employment trends, and education quality.

Taken all together, this means that the debate on globalization takes place largely in the international press, is subject to wild distortion, but, perhaps most importantly, needs to be much better grounded in terms of its impact on households. The view that households have of globalization and of what the world is evolving into is colored by the many social, cultural, and economic changes that are materializing. Chief among them is inequality.

Is It Really Inequality?

Inequality is rightly a prominent policy issue, though the link between it and globalization is only partial because inequality depends on many different factors. Inequalities have strong structural causes, and in most cases they emanate from social policy choices within countries—for example, decisions about access to education, taxation policy, and the ways in which mortgages are structured—rather than from the impact of globalization on economies and societies per se. In fact, there is a weak correlation between the extent to which a country is globalized and its level of inequality, and many of the more highly globalized countries have decent social welfare systems that mitigate inequalities. For instance, Ireland is more globalized than its close neighbor England but has a lower inequality score.

The most commonly used measurement of inequality is the Gini coefficient, which measures how skewed or unequal the distribution of income is across a society. It has a value of zero if there is complete equality and of one if a single household has all the income. Typically, a score of above 0.31 signals higher inequality. According to the OECD website, the United States has a score of 0.39, which is very high compared to other countries. Mexico has a Gini of 0.46. In contrast, Canada has a lower inequality score (Gini coefficient of 0.31) partly because it has a very different approach to policy making.

Inequality is a concern in the developed world because it is persistent. In the context of low growth in incomes and wealth, the tensions associated with inequality are exacerbated. In emerging countries, inequality in income seems to be much less of a political and social issue, because with incomes and wealth growing at a relatively fast pace, people continue to expect to do better in the longer run, which is not the case in developed countries. Also, in emerging countries there is the sense that once the economy becomes less underdeveloped, inequality will drop as a result (i.e., a middle class will form).

In this regard, attacks on globalization appear to stem from the simple fact that its winners have largely been in developing countries and its relative losers have been in countries like the United States. The notable trend is that the middle to lower classes in the West have in general seen stagnant real income growth.[11] According to the McKinsey Global Institute, from 2005 to 2014, over 90 percent of the working population in Italy, 80 percent in the United States, 70 percent in the United Kingdom, and on average 75 percent of the working population of the twenty-five advanced economies saw stagnant or falling real incomes.[12] As a consequence, those people feel that politics, globalization, and perhaps governance in general are not working for them.

Thus, to put it very generally, the beneficiaries of globalization have been the lower to middle classes in emerging countries like China and Indonesia and the wealthier classes in the developed world. These uneven benefits are reflected in a World Economic Forum survey's findings

THE TIDE GOES OUT 39

that over 70 percent of people in the Philippines, Vietnam, India, and Thailand thought globalization was a force for good, whereas only 40 percent of respondents in America and France felt the same.[13] Emerging countries are now in the process of levelling out the distribution of wealth globally relative to the likes of the United Kingdom and the United States. Infrastructure is an example. Consider the rapid rise in the wealth of the United Arab Emirates—the jewels in the crown of globalization. The high quality of their infrastructure has been part of this rise, and in many cases, transport infrastructure in emerging countries is far better than that in the "old" world.

Other survey evidence also confirms the divide between the perceived winners and losers of globalization. For example, a Pew Research Center Spring 2016 Global Attitudes Survey showed that 50 percent of people in Western economies (Japan, France, the United States, and the United Kingdom) believed that the economic situation in their own country was bad,[14] though the vast majority of respondents in the two most populous countries in the world (China and India) held that the outlook was positive.

The reality that there are winners and losers from globalization has exposed the narrative of the upper echelons of Western society, for whom inequality is now a preoccupation. For example, the IMF, the World Bank, and the McKinsey Global Institute all profess alarm that inequality is too high. This newfound sympathy for the less-well-off may have several motivations, not least the popular reception of Thomas Piketty's book on inequality, *Capital in the 21st Century*, which has managed to stir interest in an arcane topic.[15] In general, the lion's share of evidence shows that inequality is at historically very high levels, especially in the larger economies of the world such as the United States and, to a growing degree, China.[16]

In recent years, inequality has not risen sharply (though the number of news reports on it has done so), but it has been persistently high. This persistence is perhaps the key link to sociopolitical tension in that continued inequality conditions people's long-term expectations of the world around them. The political consequence is that people form a view that the system is against them and vote against the system.

Evidence from a range of sources—the World Bank, OECD, and Branko Milanovic, a leading academic in the areas of development economics and inequality—shows that across the developed world inequality is high, with the United States and South Africa in the lead in this respect, followed by Turkey, Chile, Israel, the United Kingdom, and Spain.[17] Among other countries, Sweden has become slightly less equal though its Gini coefficient is nonetheless at a very low level, close to that of France, the Netherlands, and Canada.

There are other ways of examining differences in income distribution. For example, according to the Economic Policy Institute,[18] income inequality as captured by the share of income of the top 1 percent is now back to levels not seen since the 1920s. In New York, the ratio of the income of the top 1 percent to that of the other 99 percent is 45 to 1. A good portion of this gap is driven by high executive pay, which across the range of industries in the United States averages three hundred times the pay of the average worker. It is hard to find such an extreme relationship at any other time in history. In Rome in AD 14, for instance, the income of a Roman senator was one hundred times the average income, and legion commanders received an income of forty-five times the average!

Against this backdrop the political sensitivity to inequality has heightened for a number of reasons: conspicuously high salaries at the top end of the labor market, lower overall economic growth, and persistently low income growth. Such persistent inequality causes people to form permanent views about the state of the world and its relative justice. Real incomes have until very recently (in the United States at least) stayed low, which has manifestly hurt purchasing power, and many people have not participated in the rise in asset values seen in the postcrisis era. In fact, with large pension deficits mounting, inequalities may now be carried into the future.

Another striking way of examining how average people are faring compared to previous generations is to measure their real incomes compared to what they might have been ten years earlier to get a sense of how incomes are growing. In the United States there has been a sharp decline in real per capita income relative to where it was in 2008. In fact, between 2010 and 2017, growth in per capita real income was easily the lowest in over sixty years. This is a useful way of picking up the sense that people feel much less well off, especially those who may have been working long enough to recall periods of stronger income growth.

In the developing world the picture is somewhat different, reflecting Branko Milanovic's assertion that though inequality has in many cases increased within countries, it has narrowed when between-country relationships are accounted for. Here the positive effects of globalization are the clearest: it, together with national growth dynamics, has lifted hundreds of millions out of poverty into relative prosperity.[19]

More generally, in the last twenty years wealth and incomes have exploded in many emerging countries so that sensitivity to inequality is lower. For the moment, household expectations of prosperity across emerging markets are rising, despite stark inequality in some cases. If these aspirations are checked, as has happened in Mexico and Brazil, then other emerging countries may witness the same political volatility seen in the developed world.

Wealth of Nations

However, income inequality is only half the picture. Wealth is a more important metric, because it is the key factor that motivates people's large-scale purchasing decisions. When someone wants to buy a new car, she doesn't necessarily think of the expected GDP growth of her country; she tends to think in terms of the stock of their wealth. Wealth inequality, compared to income inequality, is important because shifts in wealth are typically slower moving but longer lasting in their effects on consumption behavior. Arguably, income inequality can be fairly easily affected by tax policy and redistribution by governments, but wealth inequality is harder to tackle across the board. Though the likes of Piketty and Milanovic have grabbed headlines for their work on income inequality, the internationally recognized experts on wealth are Professors Tony Shorrocks and Jim Davies, who have worked at institutions such as the United Nations and the London School of Economics.[20] Their research is noteworthy because, unlike the study of income inequality, the examination of wealth, and by extension wealth inequality, is hampered by the lack of detailed data across countries. However, Shorrocks and Davies have compiled the most comprehensive data set available.

Recent trends in wealth inequality are stark and show that globally, with a focus on the United States, wealth inequality remains close to a multidecade high. In fact, the share of total world wealth (financial assets plus property less debt) held by the top 10 percent of wealthy people has risen steadily to levels not seen since the 1930s. The top 1 percent of wealthy people now own over 47 percent of the world's wealth.

At the country level, the United States is joined by Switzerland and Hong Kong in having very high wealth inequality (top 10 percent own over 70 percent of the wealth). Switzerland differs from the United States in that although its wealth inequality is high, its income inequality is low and it scores very well on social stability factors such as health-care availability. In the developing world, Argentina, Brazil, India, Turkey, and South Africa all have similarly high wealth inequality scores. China, where the top 10 percent hold over 60 percent of wealth, also has relatively high wealth inequality. It currently has over sixteen thousand individuals with a net wealth of over USD 50 million,[21] which is more than the number of individuals with wealth over USD 50 million in Germany, the United Kingdom, and France put together. In contrast, many European countries—France, Italy, the United Kingdom, Ireland, Spain, and Greece—have what academics would consider moderate levels of wealth inequality (top 10 percent owns over 50 percent of wealth).

My own sense is that the vast majority of wealth is generated by entrepreneurship, the success of family businesses and property markets. In recent decades there may be two new factors in wealth creation. First, in some emerging markets, the early stage of wealth creation has allowed individuals and families with close ties to governments or ruling structures to profit to an enormous degree. James Crabtree makes this point with respect to India in his book *The Billionaire Raj*. Second, senior executives in large companies and financial institutions are able to gain enormous wealth through generous equity-based compensation. Unsurprisingly, the Anglo-Saxon countries—that is, the United Kingdom, the United States, Canada, and Australia—feature prominently here.

The picture of wealth inequality broadens if we take in other data sources. In the United States, wealth is also unevenly divided between generations. According to the Survey of Consumer Finance, which is produced every three years by the Federal Reserve to shed light on the quality of household balance sheets, 30 percent of households have no wealth, and the vast majority of wealth is held by those over forty-five years of age. Several Pew studies reflect this also. The report "American Middle Class Is Losing Ground" highlights the "squeezed middle" and reports that the number of people considered to be middle class (roughly 120 million people) is now outnumbered by the combined lower and upper classes and that, importantly, the share of total income of the middle class has fallen from 62 percent in 1970 to 43 percent in 2015.[22] In fact, America's wealthy middle class (close to 92 million people, with net wealth of USD 50,000 to USD 500,000) is now surpassed by China's middle class (over 102 million people, who, in relative terms, have wealth of USD 20,000 to USD 200,000).[23]

The trend toward greater inequality is clear. What is more difficult to measure, though arguably less demanding on intuition, are the many other ways in which inequalities reinforce and manifest themselves. A great many of them are deeply rooted in socioeconomic networks, such as access to professions, justice, and education. These are the factors that typically differentiate the insiders/elite from the rest. One could build a picture of a (Western) world where class mobility is slowing and where access to education, capital, and health care, to name a few, is increasingly restricted. Each of these sustains inequalities in different ways.

Access to capital is one route by which wealth inequalities are perpetuated and around which sociodemographic changes occur. In more recent years, those with access to capital have been able to take advantage of low interest rates and the flatteringly positive effect of quantitative easing on asset prices, while also being less exposed to some of QE's negative consequences (such as rising pension deficits).[24] This has fueled explosive growth in property prices in prestigious metropolitan areas, which, among many other things, now means that middle wealth / middle income households are being forced out of city centers. One example appears in a letter of resignation written by Kate Downing, a Palo Alto, California, transport and planning commissioner,[25] whose salary did not enable her to live in the area she was responsible for overseeing. In fact, if she were to buy the apartment she rented, the mortgage payments would amount to her entire before-tax salary. The same is true in many other cosmopolitan cities around the world, from Sydney to Tel Aviv to Hong Kong to Boston, and many readers, especially younger ones, may have faced this acute problem of affordability.

Education is another area where emerging inequalities show themselves. In most countries, the educational experience is often as valuable for the social networks and conditioning it provides as for the knowledge and skills it produces, and free online courses have little to offer in this regard. The difficulty and cost of accessing the best schools in global cities such as London and New York are extreme examples of this educational inequality. And the same thing may be coming for people in other cities and countries who do not yet have to confront this kind of contest in their everyday lives. In France, for instance, there is a growing divide between the relatively large number of decently educated middle-class students, most of whom achieve good international test scores, and an underclass of students who—for a variety of reasons—struggle to attain a basic level of education.[26]

Yet another vital manifestation of inequality is uneven health care. An important paper by Anne Case and Angus Deaton, "Rising Morbidity and Mortality in Midlife among White Non-Hispanic Americans in the 21st Century," highlights the deterioration in health conditions, especially those relating to mental health, for middle-aged white men and women in the United States. The mortality rate for this cohort has increased sharply owing to drug and alcohol poisoning, suicides (the United States is seeing a sharp rise in suicides, according to the Centers for Disease Control and Prevention),[27] and related diseases such as cirrhosis of the liver. Groups with lower levels of education saw a sharper rise in mortality. Deaton, a professor at Princeton University, won the Nobel Prize in Economics in 2015 for his work linking topics like welfare, health, and poverty.

The worsening of health conditions is a sign that politicians should pay much greater attention to health care in public policy, especially in the United States, where life expectancy is on average four years below that of other developed countries such as Canada, Germany, France, and Spain. There is also evidence to show that in other countries with arguably better or more widely available health-care systems (such as France), health-related inequalities (such as in infant mortality) are much lower than in the United States. Janet Currie, also at Princeton University, has, together with other researchers, shown that public policy can make a difference to health- and mortality-related inequalities.[28] Effectively, an American from a disadvantaged background would be healthier if he or she moved to France at birth (or before!). In coming years health-care inequality in the United States may get worse. One particularly troubling development is the opioid crisis, which is claiming tens of thousands of lives and is estimated by the Council of Economic Advisers to have cost 3 percent of US GDP in 2015 alone.[29]

Another more detailed example of health-care inequality is in dental care. Mary Otto's book *Teeth* shows the startling differences in dental health across social classes and reports that they spring from differences in education, diet, and upbringing. In her book Otto tells of a boy who died when a tooth infection, undetected because his parents had no dental-care insurance, spread to his brain. Another trend she highlights is the growing lack of attention by dentists in the United States to basic dental hygiene, in favor of higher-paying procedures such as dental surgery.

Technology is another factor that may help cement existing inequalities. For example, in her book *Automating Inequality*, Virginia Eubanks describes how automation of welfare services through the growing use of algorithms to sift welfare recipients, and in areas like medical insurance assessments, can lead to institutionalized inequalities (the algorithm throws out the more needy welfare applicants) and injustice. She describes a regime of data analytics that, through design or error, denies assistance to those in poverty, with low education levels or poor computer literacy, or with a history of mental health issues. Minor glitches in computer databases or overlays by algorithms (such as circuit breakers for suspected fraud) have the effect of cutting people off from benefits—which happened to Eubanks's partner and alerted her to this potentially systemic problem.

The computerization of welfare benefits also allows more detailed monitoring of recipients and their lifestyles. One example Eubanks mentions is the Allegheny County (Pennsylvania) Family Screening Tool (AFST), which is designed to screen 131 variables that help predict whether children in a family are in danger of abuse. The tyranny of this system is that disadvantaged families receive high AFST scores because of their regular interactions with social services, and they are denied assistance as a result. Eubanks's overriding fear is that algorithms are designed to reinforce existing prejudices within the US system, where many people presume that people are poor because they have made bad choices rather than because they are disadvantaged. The same process is probably increasingly true in more commercial applications such as credit screening and access to education. It has the effect of hardening inequalities and making social stratification more rigid. Another example of technology-driven inequality comes from Joy Buolamwini, the founder of the Algorithmic Justice League, whose research initially discovered that facial recognition software was much more accurate at recognizing white faces than black faces. Inaccuracies in algorithmic-based identification can translate into denial of access to social welfare, or misclassification of an innocent person in criminal records.

Inequality is deeply rooted, and in the United States it is pushing extreme levels. A valuable data resource here is the National Longitudinal Survey of Youth, which tracks the lifestyle of a control set of young people across America. It details the rise of obesity, of incarceration (showing that one-third of Americans have been arrested by the age of twenty-five), of interracial relationships, and of health-care issues.[30] Inequality is a recurring theme in the research based on this data set.

These blockages in social advancement and behavior are important because they condition people's expectations of their future and of the world around them. If people are faced with a reality in which income and wealth growth are capped, and in which educational and professional advancement may no longer be as fluid as they have been historically, it can produce a sense of disappointment that is then manifest in political attitudes.

Trends in social mobility also reflect a sense that the "American Dream" is less attainable than it was historically. For example, one academic study identifies a "grandparent effect" in the United States, meaning that people's roots, or the socioeconomic position of their grandparents, determines their standing in society.[31] The study uses long-term generational data going back to the 1910 census (so it includes data on grandparents and great-grandparents) and asserts that US society is less mobile than many think. Another fascinating study based on Italian data—but one that makes me think of the Gore, Bush, and Kennedy families in US politics—uses tax records for family dynasties in Italy going back to 1427 (twenty-four years before Christopher Columbus was born).[32] Broadly speaking, the top earners in Italy today are found to have already been at the top of the socioeconomic ladder six centuries ago. This is striking and shows that despite the changes brought about by the Renaissance and upheavals such as two world wars, family prosperity in Italy has carried through the centuries. As an aside, family businesses have a particularly successful track record in Italy.

Still, inequality itself may not explain the degree of change in political attitudes displayed across a range of countries. There is a greater sense of a world turned upside down, or a sense that something is not right. One startling place where the world we are used to is slipping away is in our bodies. The last ten years have probably seen the biggest change in human body/skeletal form since the nineteenth century. On balance people exercise less, and when they do employ their body in work it is often in the hunched form of the "texter," which is producing a multitude of new skeletal and repetitive-strain injuries.

Obesity rates are a clear manifestation of these bodily changes: the OECD notes that in some countries (such as the United Kingdom, Mexico, and the United States), obesity rates are close to 30 percent (with Korea, Japan, and India having among the lowest obesity rates) and that, more broadly, in the United States and the United Kingdom between 60 and 70 percent of the population qualify as being over-weight or obese. In China, the prevalence of overweight or obese people has shot up from 20 percent in 1991 to 45 percent in 2011.[33] A driver of this is sugar consumption, which in many countries has spurred a rise in conditions such as diabetes. In tandem with this, calorie consumption in the United States has risen from 3,200 calories average per day in 1981 to 4,000 in 2005 according to the US Department of Agriculture (USDA). Other ailments are also telling, such as high levels of hip and knee osteoarthritis because of sedentary lifestyles.[34] Similarly, arthritis-related repetitive-strain injuries are on the rise in the United States.[35]

The behavior of the climate is another area where change is becoming more alarming and extreme. In the last fifteen years, there has been a rising magnitude in international temperature anomalies, on a scale not seen since the 1880s (when temperature anomalies were to the downward/cold side). In particular, in the last one hundred years, nine of the hottest years on record have come in the twelve years from 2006 to 2018, and there are growing numbers of climate-driven disasters and accidents. With flash fires and droughts (from California to Chad to Sweden) now more commonplace, NASA satellite-based research shows growing extremes in the displacement of freshwater around the world.[36] This research—illustrated by some interesting graphical representations—

shows that climate change and human behavior are causing wet areas to become wetter and dry areas to become drier.[37] This hydraulic shift will affect cities, economies, and agriculture and in extreme cases—as is now being seen in Africa, where there are freshwater-based tensions between Egypt and the Sudan and between Kenya and Ethiopia—could lead to wars.

Irregularities in the flowering of plants and trees and in the migratory patterns of animals and birds help confirm the sense that all is not as it should be. For instance, the World Bank estimates that in and around the United States there are 250 threatened species of fish and that there are 100 threatened species of birds in China. There are also a growing number of accounts of ecosystems that are destabilized.[38]

Old World Recedes

The way we communicate is also changing. In 1990 close to 270 million letters passed through the US Postal Service on a daily basis, but this had dropped to close to 150 million by 2014.[39] At the same time, the number of email accounts globally has risen from close to 3 billion in 2011 to nearly 5 billion in 2017. On a similar trajectory, social media users have grown from fewer than 1 billion in 2010 to 2.5 billion in 2017, and the average time spent on social media has risen from 96 minutes daily to 118 minutes daily in 2016.[40]

Attitudes toward marriage are also changing. Pew surveys show that, in 2006, 52 percent of Americans felt it very important that a male/female couple be legally married, but this had dropped to close to 40 percent by 2013. This reflects changing demographics: nearly 25 percent of men and 17 percent of women aged over twenty-five have never been married, compared to 10 percent and 8 percent, respectively, in 1960s America. Views of relationships are changing in other ways. In 2004, according to the Pew Research Center, 30 percent of US adults favored allowing same-sex marriage and nearly 60 percent opposed it, and by 2016 this had changed to 55 percent in favor and 35 percent against. There is quite a bit of difference in attitudes between age groups on the question of same-sex marriage, with millennials strongly in favor and older generation (grandparents) against. In addition, technology is dramatically changing the ways in which people meet each other and interact romantically. One interesting outcome is that dating through social media appears to be producing more couples with disparate backgrounds.[41]

The pattern of the average day may also be changing. According to the US Bureau of Labor Statistics, Americans spend roughly three hours a day watching television and less than thirty minutes on sports and other recreation-related activities.[42] In many countries wasted time is also increasing. According to the TomTom Traffic Index, travel time during peak traffic hours in the United Kingdom and China takes nearly 40 percent longer. Chinese people waste the most time in travel congestion, on average losing 161 hours per year (in 2015), with those in the United Kingdom losing 149 hours and Americans losing only 117 hours.

A very contentious political issue is migration, which surfaces as one of the changes people are least comfortable with. In some countries, the number of international migrants living in a country as a proportion of its total population is high. Switzerland has a migrant stock of close to 29 percent, making it one of the most migrant-intense countries in the developed world, according to the World Bank (Canada has 21 percent and Singapore 45 percent, for instance). In the United States and United Kingdom, the percentage of migrant stock has steadily increased in recent years, from 9 percent in 1990 to 14 percent in 2015 in the United States, and from 6 percent in 1990 to 13 percent in 2016 in the United Kingdom. In some cities—Brussels, Toronto, Sydney, and Los Angeles—the proportion of the population that is foreign born is very high (close to 30 percent). One reason for this is that fertility rates in most developed countries are at historically very low levels. For example, Catholic Italy is now at the bottom of the European fertility table, with a rate of 0.7 children per family (in 1960 it was 7). To a certain degree, people's decision to have families or not is a statement about their long-term views on the future and the relative pessimism over the costs of living (e.g., young people still live with their parents) and to an extent is also a statement by women regarding their role in society. In addition, the low birthrate may reflect the way in which social media and inflexible work practices in countries like Japan have diminished social skills, to the detriment of physical relationships between men and women (according to the BBC, the proportion of virgins among single Japanese between the ages of eighteen and thirty-four is 45 percent).[43] As a result of low fertility, the Japanese population is expected to drop from 128 million today to 86 million in forty years.

What Do People Think?

Having laid out the retreat of globalization, the problems that retreat exposes, and the ways in which people's expectations and their sense of calm are being disturbed, it should be no surprise that disillusionment is marking political choices. My line of thinking here is that tectonic trends in economics—such as inequality and very low, inflation-adjusted increases in wages—shape the ways in which we view the world and, as such, filter through to political choices.

In the United States, the first inkling of discontent came in 2014 with the shocking unseating of the House majority leader Eric Cantor by the Tea Party in the Republican primary ahead of the congressional elections by a relatively unknown economics professor named Dave Brat. Then the drift of blue-collar voters from the Democratic Party to the right and the appeal of nonestablishment candidates like Bernie Sanders to younger voters became new political trends. We can now say, without controversy, that Americans have lost faith in politics and politicians. For example, Gallup polls show that Americans rate members of Congress at the very bottom of professions (only 7 percent believed members of Congress had high ethical standards), just above car salespeople and well down in the ranking from nursing, the top profession.[44] It is also worth mentioning that in the United States, according to Gallup, nearly 45 percent of voters now identify themselves as independents, and two groups of close to 25 percent each identify with the Democrats and Republicans, respectively.

In Europe there is also a growing literature on political dislocation. When the late Peter Mair, an Irish political scientist and professor of European Politics at the European University Institute in Florence, started to write his book *Ruling the Void* in 2007 before the global and European financial crises, there was already a tangible sense that democracy, and in particular party-based democracy, in Europe was atrophying. Voter turnout was falling across a range of countries; voter behavior had become more volatile, with voters shopping around fringe and smaller parties with larger, more established political parties seeing a corresponding drop in membership and loyalty.

By the time Mair's book was published in 2013, after his death, these trends had been exacerbated by financial crisis, though he had still been ahead of his time in declaring that the era of "party democracy has passed." Another trend identified by Mair was the "Europeanization" of national politics, which he took to mean the penetration of "European rules, directives and norms into the domestic sphere" as individual states increasingly adopted laws "made in Brussels" to replace domestically agreed ones.[45] Brexiteers are known to complain that the Europe Union regulates the size of British cucumbers, sausages, and pints of beer. This trend probably prefigured the counterreaction of British voters toward the European Union in the Brexit referendum. Even as Brexit passes, it looks like Britain will still be beholden to European law across a range of fields such as trade and services. Getting out of Europe is well-nigh impossible in practice.

If we update many of the tables and data in the Mair book, the trends he described have become more pronounced. Voter sentiment remains poor, to put it lightly. Opinion polls and surveys show that close to 80 percent of Europeans distrust political parties and that about 40 percent are pessimistic about Europe. Comparing EU citizens' attitudes to the European Union between 1993 and 2016: in Greece trust in the

European Union has dropped from over 60 percent to 22 percent, and in France and Germany it now lies in the mid–30 percent range. In many European countries, however, especially in eastern Europe, people trust the European Union more than their national political parties.[46]

Pessimism

Correspondingly, pessimism in the European Union has risen sharply in the past nine years. In 2007, less than 20 percent of people in European countries were pessimistic about the European Union, but this has now risen to close to 35 percent, led by Germany and France. Nearly half (49 percent) of Europeans felt that their voice doesn't count in European affairs. That said, Eurobarometer polls show that the majority of citizens in eurozone countries would stay in if they were offered a United Kingdom–style referendum. Europeans are more cynical or less trusting when it comes to politicians. In 2000, 65 percent of Europeans declared that they distrusted political parties. This has now risen to close to 90 percent in France, Greece, Spain, and Portugal. The Danes and the Dutch still have a modicum of trust in politics, and Swedes and Finns have become modestly more trusting of political parties than they used to be.

Internationally, we see the same picture. For example, the 2018 Edelman Trust Barometer outlines the crisis in trust around the world.[47] It shows that two-thirds of the countries surveyed are "distrusters" in the sense that less than 50 percent of voters trust the mainstream institutions of business, government, media, and nongovernmental organizations (NGOs) to do what is right. The sharp change in the survey results in recent years has been the steepest decline in trust in the United States on record for the Edelman Barometer, with Italy and Brazil also seeing drops in trust. In more detail, it found that only 15 percent of the general population believed the present system is working, 53 percent do not, and 32 percent were uncertain.

Distrust in the system breeds volatility in the behavior of voters. In most European countries political stability is now increasingly rare.

Voter turnout is falling in many countries, precipitously so in the last ten years, with that in France falling from 80 percent in 1945 to below 60 percent in 2011, though more recently it rose to 74 percent in 2017.[48] In Italy, Greece, Germany, and Spain, voter turnout is the lowest it's been in the past sixty years, having dropped discernibly in the past twenty years. In the last European Parliament elections, average turnout has dipped from the mid–60 percent level to the low 40 percents. Reinforcing these numbers is a generalized sense of disinterest in mainstream politics across European countries. Voters also show less allegiance to established parties. Reflecting the rise of issues like immigration, they are specifically attracted to right-wing parties, which are garnering 25 percent of the vote in many countries.[49]

My own experience observing elections in countries like France and Ireland suggests that when it comes to mainstream politics, there is a great deal of apathy on the part of voters, disbelief that they can influence election results. In France, the election of Emmanuel Macron, widely and I think correctly seen as someone who can reinvigorate France, took place in the context of a historically low turnout because many voters had thought the result was a foregone conclusion. Two other trends are worth mentioning: First, radical parties are attracting both ideologically committed voters and, it seems, voters who would not ordinarily have voted in elections. And in Ireland, two recent referenda on gay marriage and abortion have mobilized very large turnouts, suggesting that, second, when it comes to single-issue votes, many who do not ordinarily vote (i.e., in this case, younger voters) are politically very committed. In addition, in the Brexit referendum, three million people who had not voted in the prior three general elections came out to vote in the referendum.

The practical consequence of dissatisfaction with the old political order in the developed world is that it causes apathy (as evidenced in lower turnout), rage, or political entrepreneurship. Reflecting this, the last five years have seen a jump in the formation of new political parties across Europe, from five in 2010 to fourteen by 2015. Of these new parties, several are emerging on the right of the political spectrum, joining other established right-wing parties such as the Front National (now rebranded as Rassemblement National) in France and the United Kingdom Independence Party (UKIP), effectively European versions of the Freedom Caucus and the Tea Party Caucus, and contributing to a new political phenomenon whereby right-wing parties are garnering a rising share of voter support. It is now not unusual for right-wing parties to have 20 percent or more of the vote across a range of European countries. For example, in the Swedish general election in September 2018, the far-right-wing Sweden Democrat Party won 17.6 percent of the vote. More broadly, an interesting study from Ray Dalio, the founder of the world's largest hedge fund, Bridgewater Associates, in 2017 showed that the populist vote (at 35 percent in developed countries like the United States, Italy, the United Kingdom, and Germany) has today almost equaled the previous peak, 40 percent in the mid-1930s.[50]

The rise of the Right, the budding of the New Left, and the disillusionment of the many are now the norm in politics. Some cultivate these trends for darker ends. Many more are in denial and hope that political volatility will disappear. This is unlikely. The fracturing of the political system in the developed world is just the beginning of a new, deep-seated trend. The aim of this book is to stand back and examine the tectonic forces acting on the world and to try to plot a way forward. Globalization, which has carried so much forward, is in retreat and will not return. Peace, in the form of the end of communism, the reunification of Germany, and the opening up of many former communist emerging economies, provided the basis for the wave of globalization we have experienced. Globalization has arguably been the most prosperous period in the history of humanity. Remarkably, it has been a period of relative calm during which there have been few wars, and no wars between democracies.

As the tide of globalization goes out, it leaves more and more socioeconomic imbalances exposed. Some of these imbalances are caused by globalization; others are simply blamed on it. Some occur within countries, others happen between countries. Geopolitically, societies and political leaders in the old world will have to become accustomed to the rise of new countries and to the impact that rise has on relative wealth, trade, and immigration and on the shape of world institutions. Consider that in the mid-seventeenth century, India and China made up approximately 50 percent of world GDP.[51] China, at least, has still not gotten over the shock of losing its perch. Voters, unlike politicians, it seems, realize that the world is at a turning point, and their behavior at the ballot box is betraying a nervous sense of foreboding.

THREE

WHAT'S NEXT?

Déjà Vu All Over Again

W E NOW LIVE IN A FRAGILE WORLD—ONE WHERE MANY SOCIAL, TECHNO-logical, and physical changes are happening before us. Voters are beginning to react against the established order that has grown up over the past thirty years; imbalances like indebtedness and obesity are slowing growth; and, most importantly, globalization, the magic sauce that has made the world prosperous and relatively peaceful over the past three decades, is beginning to wither. Very soon we will want to know what comes next.

We can turn to history for some help in thinking through an answer. For some, globalization today still has a shininess and appears very new. Many of the technological aspects of globalization are so glittering that it is hard to imagine that it has occurred before or, indeed, that we could now do without its fruits—the iPhone X, bitcoin, or artificial intelligence. But globalization does have a precedent, and it is a cautionary tale at that. Though the current wave of globalization is coming to an end, we can get a glimpse of what might happen next by going back in time to the first wave of globalization, in the period 1870 to 1913.

Economic Consequences of the Peace

At the turn of the twentieth century, the first wave of globalization was in full swing, and London was its epicenter. It was gripped by a consumer culture not seen before. John Maynard Keynes captured its spirit in his 1919 book *Economic Consequences of the Peace*:

> The inhabitant of London could order by telephone, sipping his morning tea in bed, the various products of the whole earth, in such quantity as he might see fit, and reasonably expect their early delivery upon his doorstep; he could at the same moment and by the same means adventure his wealth in the natural resources and the new enterprises of any quarter of the world, and share, without exertion or trouble, in their prospective fruits and advantages, or he could decide to couple the security of his fortunes with the good faith of the townspeople of any substantial municipality in any continent that fancy or information might recommend.... Most important of all, he regarded this state of affairs as normal, certain and permanent except in the direction of further improvement, and any deviation from it as aberrant, scandalous and avoidable.[1]

The world Keynes described bears a striking similarity to our own. One can imagine a twenty-first-century Keynes, sipping his morning tea in bed, speculating on commodities with iPad in hand, booking a flight to South Africa, and remotely running his stockbroking business.[2] If Anthony Trollope were to find himself in our world and if he were to try to rewrite *The Way We Live Now*, it might very well focus on technology. His central character would be not Augustus Melmotte but an Asian woman, wearing a designer T-shirt rather than a morning suit, and she would speculate on bitcoin rather than railway stocks. Technology today is the great creator of new wealth and the primary force changing human behavior—socially, politically, and economically.

Technology's role in the zeitgeist is manifest in many of the more intriguing economic puzzles that confound us. It reveals itself in the role of algorithmic and computer-based trading in financial markets, in the massive changes it has enabled in how we work, and in the structure of the labor market. Moreover, technology has manifestly been the enabler of enormous structural changes in retail and consumer goods and in the rise of new financial assets from exchange-traded funds (ETFs) to cryptocurrencies.

Keynes's snapshot gives a sense of what globalization is: the increasing interdependence and integration of economies, markets, nations, and cultures. It also shows up the parallels between the world of the first wave of globalization and the world of today. In this respect, it is worth journeying back in time to see how globalization first formed and—importantly, given the threats to it today—how it ended and what lessons we can learn.

Déjà Vu All Over Again

One of the defining markers of the nineteenth- and early-twentieth-century period of globalization was the way in which prices of the same goods in different parts of the world converged. Take commodity prices as an example: London to Cincinnati price differentials for bacon fell from 93 percent in 1870 to 18 percent in 1913, the London to Bombay cotton price spread fell from 57 percent in 1873 to 20 percent in 1913, and the London to Rangoon rice price spread fell from 93 percent to 26 percent over the same period.[3] Other parts of the world saw similar balancing out in prices. Ronald Findlay and Kevin O'Rourke's exceptional book on trade, *Power and Plenty*, notes, "Between 1846–55 and 1871–79 the price of raw silk rose by 50% in Japan, where it had been relatively low, but climbed by just 19% in world markets, while the price of cheap tea rose by 64% in Japan and just 10% elsewhere."[4] Findlay and O'Rourke's book is a life's work from two top-level economists and should be required reading for those pondering how the rise of nations is intertwined with trade flows. Memorably, they note, "The greatest expansions of world trade have tended to come . . . from the barrel of a Maxim gun, the edge of a scimitar, or the ferocity of nomadic horsemen."[5] Ominously, so have the greatest economic contractions.

Echoing this, thanks to advances in technology (especially transport via boats and trains), during this early period of globalization costs fell dramatically in much the same way as communications, travel, and business process costs have been disrupted over the last twenty years. Consider a few examples: the process of surfacing roads developed by John McAdam meant that it took thirty-six hours to travel from Manchester to London in 1820, compared to five days in 1780; the expansion of canal networks across the world greatly facilitated transportation by steamer; and the opening in 1869 of the Suez Canal, over one hundred miles long, "brought Asia 4,000 miles nearer to Europe."[6]

Against this backdrop, the level of world trade surged, so that by 1913 merchandise exports as a share of GDP in Western European economies reached a level of 17 percent, up from 14 percent in 1870 (subsequently falling to around 6 percent by 1938 and rebounding to above 17 percent again in the 1990s).[7] Similarly, the fantastic power that capital markets seem to wield today makes it difficult to appreciate that the financial world could have been anything as developed as it is now. Yet a number of countries (especially those outside the United States) were more financially developed in 1913 than they were in 1980.[8] For instance, in proportion to GDP, the market capitalization of the French stock market was nearly twice that of the United States in 1913 but had fallen to a quarter of it by 1980. Stock market data for the past hundred or so years also shows how the fortunes of various countries have changed: in 1900 the UK stock market made up one-quarter of the value of all equities globally, with the United States making up 15 percent. Today the United States is 51 percent of world equity capitalization and the United Kingdom is only 6.3 percent. In 1900 Belgium made up 3.5 percent of world equities and France had 13 percent; today, in late 2018,

France has dropped to 3 percent, and Belgium is barely visible.[9] Today China has 3.1 percent, and if in the twenty-first century its financial markets develop like those of the United States in the twentieth century, the size and depth of its financial markets will grow quickly.[10]

Generally speaking, the development of financial markets over the course of the last hundred years reached its nadir in 1980, from which point it has increased toward and beyond the levels of development seen at the turn of the last century. Yet a lesson to today's highly globalized countries (like Singapore and Ireland) is that the countries that were the most financially developed in 1913 (such as Argentina) did not necessarily remain so. Argentina is an interesting country, not least from the point of view of its economic history, having defaulted on its debt eight times since independence in 1816. In 1924 the GDP per capita of Argentina was seven times that of Brazil (today it is 1.5 times Brazil's) and three times that of Japan (it is only 50 percent of Japan's today). It was one of the richest countries in the world, a center for finance, trade, and agriculture. Many of the buildings that still adorn Buenos Aires, such as its Opera House, date from that period. However, Argentina did not follow the lead of other economic powers in diversifying its economy toward manufacturing, nor did it make its agriculture sector competitive and open. As a result, the onset of the Great Depression exposed its structural weaknesses (meat exports to Europe collapsed by over two-thirds from 1924 to 1930) and the rigidity of its political system.

Seen It All Before

There are many parallels between the first wave of globalization and the current one, the most important being the rise in trade, the growth of financial systems, and the rapid diminution in the cost of doing business as transportation and communication costs dropped. It is also interesting to note that stock market bubbles arose during both periods of globalization, driven by the advent of new technologies. In the early twentieth century it was primarily the railway, telephone, and radio stocks that led the rise in share prices. In 1900, over 60 percent of the market capitalization of the US stock market and 50 percent of the UK market was made up of railway stocks, which have all but disappeared today. In 1999 information technology was the chief culprit, followed by the financial sector in 2008. Cryptocurrencies are the new "railway stock" in that respect.

Still, there are crucial differences between the two periods. Chief among them is the fact that today more countries and more people are touched by globalization, and in most cases they are better off as a result. The roles of multinational corporations and foreign direct investment (FDI) have been much greater since the late 1980s than they were in the late nineteenth century. In general, the period 1870–1913 saw foreign direct investment flowing mainly from developed countries to other developed countries, whereas now more FDI has flowed from developed to developing countries. In addition, the state of the world before the first period of globalization was different from that before the second: Before the first period of globalization, the entire world was poor and agrarian. When the second wave began, it was sharply divided between rich and poor nations. Globalization today has a much greater reach. This is partly due to the facts that, compared to the early twentieth century, more people than ever before enjoy electoral franchise of some form, and people are much better connected in terms of telecommunication and social media penetration and related factors, such as the rise in urbanization.

Advances in technology now occur more rapidly and, in fields like telecommunications, they have sped up the transfer of ideas and information and made globalized forms of production more feasible. Corporations have grown in size and influence over the last hundred years, to the extent that corporations are the dominant force behind globalization today. As a result, there are now far many more global products or brand names than there were in the period 1870–1913. Fiat, Hoover, General Electric, and Sunbeam were established then, and Gucci, BMW, and Ford were only getting started.

A final difference between globalization now and in the nineteenth century is the growth of institutions and transnational governance.

Though the nation-state is still very much a viable entity, power is increasingly placed in the hands of unelected policy makers. This shift is reflected in a number of quarters, such as the standardization of banking regulations and of accounting and financial measures. Institutions have taken over the role played by the gold standard, the Pax Britannica, and the ideological consensus that prevailed in the nineteenth century, which gave structure to the world order and acted to channel its various geopolitical and economic crises. Until recently this sense of structure has been manifest in bodies like the WTO, the Federal Reserve, the United Nations, the European Union, or the IMF and has, broadly speaking, been beneficial in preventing and resolving crises, and in particular in placing a premium on negotiating skills rather than military power. These same institutions are now under scrutiny in a changing world, and in many cases (e.g., the WTO) they are becoming less relevant as countries like the United States circumvent the procedures and rules they themselves have put in place.

Against this cheery backdrop, the really important lesson of nineteenth-century globalization is how it came apart. In 1909–1910, the writer Norman Angell published a book entitled *The Great Illusion* in which he argued that the world was so intertwined economically that war was unlikely (i.e., it would be too costly). He was wrong on this front, though his warnings about the growth of great navies in Germany and Britain resonates today. However vibrant globalization was at the turn of the twentieth century, burgeoning levels of trade, finance, and technological advances (in transport and communications) soon led to imbalances in the European, Latin American, and American economies, which in many cases were dealt fatal blows by poor policy making.

Economic openness quickly gave way to protectionism and the application of tariffs. The rise in poverty and unemployment that was brought about by inflation in the price of goods and deflation in asset prices forced an eventual response from governments that had come to fear the greater say the poor had in politics because of the expanding electoral franchise. Whereas small government had previously been in vogue (in 1912 government expenditure in developed countries was about 13 percent of GDP), governments were now expected to spend and protect their way back to prosperity. Thus, protectionism, economic decline, nationalism, and finally war brought down the curtain on the first period of globalization.

In many corners of the world, the Great Depression that followed the end of globalization ushered in an economic dark age that only ended with the fall of communism and the resurgence of globalization as we now know it. Some of the political trends we see today—the apparent rollback of liberal democracy, the rise of populist nationalism, and the emergence of strongmen leaders—creates a tension that has many fearing a repeat of the 1930s. Is this—the Great Depression, its international political consequences, and yet another world war—to be our fate?

Overreaching

The global financial crisis of 2008 did not end in an economic depression, though neither has it produced a true economic renaissance. Many of the factors that caused the crisis in the first place—indebtedness, corporate risk taking, and poor governance—have simply been in abeyance, hibernating, and are now again emerging into the daylight. A consequence of these persistent economic fault lines is that we are in a political depression. In this light, some respected commentators—notably, Madeleine Albright in her book *Fascism: A Warning*—draw parallels between political figures today and those of the 1920s and '30s.

Today there are certainly economic and political parallels with the late 1920s. For instance, there are already many who compare Donald Trump, the US president as of this writing, to Herbert Hoover (president from 1929 to 1933). Hoover distinguished himself in various ways, notably in his humanitarian work in Belgium, with the US Food and Drug Administration, and in Central Europe in the aftermath of the First World War. In other ways, he has several things in common with President Trump: German/British parentage, a business background, and a mastery of new communications channels, in Hoover's case the use of radio (rather than Twitter) to reach voters and the introduction of the press conference as a regular political event.

Furthermore, the trade dispute between the United States and China has excited commentators who fear that Trump may repeat the mistakes of the Hoover government. Even the *Wall Street Journal* editorial team has warned that the Trump trade team is like Senator Reed Smoot and Representative Willis Hawley, promotors of the disastrous 1930 Smoot-Hawley Tariff Act that aided and abetted the onset of the Great Depression with the introduction of tariffs of up to 60 percent on twenty thousand types of goods imported into the United States.[11] The net effect of the act was to squash any hope of an economic recovery in the aftermath of the Great Depression and to cut world trade by 33 percent.

In addition, readers might tremble to know that Hoover took office with US equity valuations at very high levels. Robert Shiller's excellent database highlights that the US long-term market's price to earnings ratio was at 32 in January 1929 (the highest it reached was 44 in December 1999) and that it reads 28 today, which is 69 percent higher than the historical average of 16 and thus puts the market in expensive territory from a valuation standpoint.[12] Eight months into Hoover's term the Wall Street Crash occurred, and the United States lurched first into recession and then into the Great Depression.

One of the lessons from the Hoover period, which has been pored over by the likes of Ben Bernanke,[13] is that the erection of trade barriers and tariffs is not an effective way to fight an international recession because they tend to quench any burning embers of economic recovery by causing a retrenchment in risk appetite and investment. That the world did not lapse into protectionism after the global financial crisis period has much to do with the fact that policy makers like Bernanke have digested the lessons of history.[14] Other people, it seems, have not.

To a large extent, the 2008 global financial crisis was caused by the steady buildup and overreach of financial globalization. That the world economy and international political system did not lapse into protectionism and generalized hostility is testament to the ongoing lure of globalization, the mind-set of key policy makers, and international institutional arrangements. Yet there is a sense that the way in which the crisis has been addressed provides the basis for the next economic crisis (as with the title of Keynes's book *The Economic Consequences of the Peace:* Keynes argued that the harsh treatment of Germany laid the seeds for the next conflict). In fact, one can argue that the true economic crisis has simply been postponed, and that the methods employed (and those not employed) to stave off the financial crisis have simply bought time. In doing so they have exacerbated fault lines, replenishing financial wealth but not leading to a broader recovery in prosperity and human development.

Any book that looks forward and projects economic and political trends must indulge in the dark arts of forecasting and prediction. In my view, it is always best not to record predictions lest their inaccuracy be later uncovered. I have spent a good deal of time both building frameworks that produce forward or future-focused investment views and predicting economic trends. In that respect, I know enough about the process not to disagree with the view—attributed by some to John Kenneth Galbraith—that one of the few functions of economic forecasting is to make astrology respectable. As an aside, a relatively recent paper in the National Bureau of Economics Research (NBER) Working Paper series shows that fertility is a useful lead indicator of the business cycle, especially with the onset of recessions.[15] So "animal spirits" of some sort can help with forecasting. Indeed, Galbraith's books, notably *The Great Crash*, skillfully capture the wild manner in which economic animal spirits can sway markets and economics and can undermine the conventional wisdom of policy makers.

There are plenty of biases and temptations inherent in the forecasting process. Notably, for those writing books on economics or finance, it is now almost obligatory to christen a publication with a bold proposition or a headline-grabbing prediction, often one that foretells an economic or financial crash. Often the amplitude of the prediction is inversely proportional to the quality of the analysis. Exaggeration is not the preserve of economics alone. In his book *The Future of War*, Lawrence Freedman notes Major General Bob Scales's views on the think tanks, industrial conglomerates, and lobbyists who ply the government with solutions to "the next war" and says he holds that "the least successful enterprise in Washington DC . . . was 'the one that places bets on the nature and character of tomorrow's wars.' . . . 'Virtually without exception, they get it wrong.'"[16]

My own sense is that long-term trends tend to evolve rather than materialize suddenly. I am reminded of the German economist Rudiger Dornbusch's overshooting economic model, which helps explain how economic trends take longer than expected to turn but when they do turn, they do so faster than expected.[17] Financial markets tend to amplify trends in economics, often in an exaggerated way where banks create financial products to reflect those trends. For example, one of the more profitable investment strategies in recent years has been to buy low volatility ETFs, whose value rises as market volatility falls. Billions of dollars poured into ETFs until a rise in market volatility in February 2018 caused them to unwind their positions, ironically resulting in one of the biggest spikes in volatility historically and in the collapse of the "low volatility" funds.

It is often the case that once a new trend arrives, it is christened by the forecasting community. Many of them will have failed to spot the emergence of the new trend but are quick to align themselves with it (which tells us more about the labor market than about anything else: people align their careers with hot trends). For instance, the December 2017 spike in the price of bitcoin was accompanied by a raft of new research opinions on the cryptocurrency from new cryptocoin brokers and large banks. For what it is worth, my own view on cryptocurrencies is that the future will be characterized as "Blockchain everywhere, bitcoin nowhere"—that is, the distributed ledger technology behind bitcoin will become more pervasive across economic sectors, but bitcoin will fail to prove itself as a currency proper and will live out an existence as a lurid, speculative asset.*

To return to the business of forecasting, I am also often struck by the number of times that bodies like the IMF and central banks follow up a crisis or market event with a downward adjustment to their GDP forecasts. In doing so, they succeed only in giving the impression that the policy fire brigade is late to the scene or behind the curve, following a crisis rather than getting ahead of it. In many ways, sharp changes to GDP forecasts are a sort of rite of passage for new economic trends. Forecast downgrades mark the end of one phase, and optimistic forecast upgrades signal the arrival of a new phase. Yet by the time the forecasters have reacted, the event is already well underway.

Why Did Nobody Notice?

So to an extent, forecasting is a code that says more about the forecasters and their relationship with the subject of the forecast than it does about the future outlook. The failure of the economics profession to foresee the global financial crisis has tarnished it in the eyes of many, and, famously, Queen Elizabeth demanded about the debt bubble, "Why did nobody notice it?" during a visit to the London School of Economics in November 2008.[18]

There are many culpable parties here: markets, politicians, and economists, to name the usual suspects. Take markets first: I often explain the ability of financial markets to ignore obvious risks by making an analogy either to Jekyll and Hyde or to a personal favorite, Elio Petri's 1970 film *Investigation of a Citizen Above Suspicion*. In this movie a police inspector kills his girlfriend and then provocatively leaves clues to his culpability for his colleagues to find. They never suspect him. Then he confesses to

---

* Distributed ledger technology "allows simultaneous access, validation and record updating . . . across a network spread across multiple entities or locations. [It is] more commonly known as the blockchain technology.""Distributed Ledger Technology," Investopedia, https://www.investopedia.com/terms/d/distributed-ledger-technology-dlt.asp.

the crime, but his bosses ignore him. The film, to stretch its meaning a little, is a good metaphor for how markets sometimes behave. Quite obvious risks can build—such as asset bubbles and indebtedness—but markets are not sensitized to them.

In the run-up to the global financial crisis, there were few telltales that markets were prepared for the magnitude of what later transpired. One widely cited system failure was that the majority of academic economists were blinkered by a consensus that valued restrictive mathematical models of how economies and markets operate.[19] In the United States, the job market for academic economists, and the fact that the Federal Reserve System is the largest employer for trained economists, helped produce a very conformist economics field. Indeed, there continue to be blistering attacks on this approach to economics from such experts as former World Bank chief economist Paul Romer, author Nassim Taleb, and former Federal Reserve governor Kevin Warsh. In their own ways they highlight the shortcomings in the socialization and groupthink of academic economists. Romer states, "As a result, if facts disconfirm the officially sanctioned theoretical vision, they are subordinated." Taleb more provocatively holds, "Beware the semi-erudite who thinks he is an erudite. He fails to naturally detect sophistry." And Warsh criticized the Federal Reserve: "Its models are unreliable, its policies erratic and its guidance confusing. It is also politically vulnerable."[20]

A more conventional critique of economics by Oxford University's David Vines and Samuel Wills continues to support many of the conventional economic models but criticizes their failure to, say, fully incorporate financial market variables.[21] Today, the failure of such dry models may be to not take into account the kind of social and political behavior we are now seeing (e.g., the impact of social media on productivity or the impact of populism on asset prices) and the impact that behavior can have on consumption and investment patterns.

To be unkind, another problem with forecasting and economic forecasting in particular is that economists as a species are not well socialized. A US-based PhD program involves over four years of being locked away writing code, papers, and equations, and that is maybe not the best training to understand the world of humans. My own experience, having started off my professional life as an academic and having then spent the lion's share of my career in the rough-and-tumble of financial markets, is that an enormous amount of academic research (at least in economics and finance) is not representative of the more practical ways in which economies function and does not sufficiently aim to tackle real-world problems. If I had to return to academia, my approach to research would be very different from what it could have been if I had remained in the university.

Economists and analysts may in the future be better served by taking more the approach of a sleuth than of an econometric modeler. Specifically, they should employ a wider variety of skills, ferret out facts and use firsthand experience to better understand them, and be more wide-ranging in their choice of the factors they choose to study. For instance, anthropology and sociology can sometimes better help understand the behavior of bankers and markets than can finance theory.[22] If the pendulum of the economics profession is swinging away from a modeling-based approach, better that it swing toward development economics, for instance, which very often requires a more granular appreciation of how policy formulation works in practice.

Development economics is also the field where we can study the impact on economic growth of a relative change in the quality of institutions or in rule of law, simply by virtue of the fact that the potential incremental change in both variables is much larger in developing than developed countries.[23] In more detail, the policies, actions, and actors that affect development in emerging nations are complex, both individually and in the ways they interact with each other. In the Trump/ Brexit/Macron age, politics and institutional quality are exerting a very significant role on markets and economies, and a multipronged, more bottom-up approach may be required to open the black box of how policy decision making is undertaken, how it might be improved, and, as I will discuss later in this book, how politicians can make good use of it.

The failure of mainstream economics to foresee the arrival and path of the global financial crisis should also be a warning to the many critics of unexpected events like Brexit and the election of Donald Trump. Far too much time is devoted to lamenting such events rather than trying to locate them as part of a process of change and then trying to come up with better alternatives, moving beyond the "shock and awe" of recent political events and plotting a course for the future. The idea of levelling enables us to frame unexpected and new political events as part of a new process or phase in history. It is a consequence of the tide of globalization, the buildup of imbalances, and a sense among ordinary people that the array of technological, health, and social challenges they face is overwhelming. The focus should be not on the events but, rather, on the process.

The process philosophers and scientists call a "paradigm shift" helps explain how the levelling is unfolding. In science, the paradigm shift describes how scientific revolutions have come about. Established ideas and theories held by consensus are broken down by dissent from outsiders. Then processes of rebuttal and falsification break down existing frameworks. This examination does not often accomplish the task of constructing a better alternative early on. It usually takes time and experimentation, but ideally it produces better ideas and better frameworks.

This is a very shorthand way of describing the formal structure of the creation of new ideas (principally in science) that was outlined in *The Structure of Scientific Revolutions* by the American physicist and philosopher Thomas Kuhn in the early 1960s. He outlined the process through which ideas are established, identifying several stages. In the preparadigm stage, a theory is held by consensus. But then anomalies appear, and soon a crisis of truth and belief occurs, prompting a reexamination of the concept. This process of reexamination produces a paradigm shift, which is as much about the changed reference points and models that scientists use to interrogate the world as it is about producing a new model of the subject of their debate. Innovation, in the form of new ideas and new technologies, is a key part of the passage from the old paradigm to the new. (The scientist Geoffrey West, who is in fact eminent across a number of disciplines, underlines the importance of innovation in his excellent book *Scale*. From an economic point of view, he makes the point that innovation is especially urgent where the sustenance of growth is concerned.) Then, as the new theory of reality gains acceptance, the postrevolution phase begins.

Other philosophers, notably Karl Popper, sought to overlay more stringent rules that would help prove or disprove the new models resulting from paradigm shifts (he introduced the idea of falsifiability or "black swan" principle, which states that the test of whether something can be called scientific depends on whether it can be proven to be false). Indeed, Kuhn's paradigm shift is as badly abused and misused as Popper's notion of black swans. Both phrases have become popularized and have fallen into the vocabulary of management consultants, and as a result they have lost their meaning. For example, many people today refer to a risky scenario (e.g., could the stock market fall by 5 percent?) as a black swan event, though the original meaning of the term is quite different.

The idea of the levelling fits into the frame of a paradigm shift. Think of the levelling as a series of waves or reverberations of change. The global financial crisis was the first rupture, when the slowing of growth and the revelation of the shortcomings of globalization sent early tremors. Many social trends—such as obesity, the overuse of social media, and the reemergence of developed-world poverty—are raising the level of concern that human-specific factors, to put it as dryly as that, are being neglected. In politics, cracks are appearing in the system as voters begin to act, gravitating toward radical parties and sanctioning extreme events. Geopolitically, the idea of the liberal world order is under attack, and China is now a clear rival to the United States. American foreign policy is seen as aggressive, whereas it was once seen as benevolent. More change will come. Another recession or geopolitical crisis would only compound the sense of confusion. We are still simply at the early part of the paradigm shift, when the existing or consensual order is crumbling and slowly being rejected. This will continue.

In the framework of the levelling, the next stage is for the debate to move away from the ruptures and toward a realization and acceptance that change is afoot, and toward a sense of what the future may look like economically, politically, and diplomatically. Then this skeleton world-view can be filled out by ideas, frameworks, and new institutions that can revitalize society.

The writings of Kuhn and especially Popper are useful in that they set out the template for paradigm shifts and also conceive ideas that are useful today. Specifically, Popper developed the idea of the open society. For many people, this is the basis for modern liberal democracy in the postcommunist era. An open society is one characterized by freedom, by transparent and active government, and by an absence of what philosophers call domination. It is surprising in the light of today's political dislocation that the idea of the open society is not more widely debated and used. This may be because it lacks a tangible and practical framework, and also because it is associated with a liberal worldview that is increasingly being rejected. In this light, it is worrisome that in countries like Poland and Hungary, the idea of the open society and its proponents, such as George Soros (a pupil of Popper), are being rejected. As with many political ideas, Popper's development of the concept of the open society came as a reaction to darker forces—in particular, the totalitarianism of Nazi Germany and Stalin's Russia.

This helps remind us that new ideas, and more so the impetus for them, are often born out of crises. A neat way of seeing the progression of ideas and how they shaped history is to follow the chapters in the Foreign Affairs book *The Clash of Ideas*. It is a collection of essays that mark the passage of events and mind-sets through the twentieth century, opening with Harold J. Laski's 1923 essay "Lenin and Mussolini," progressing through, among others, Erich Koch-Weser's "Radical Forces in Germany" (1931), Alvin Hansen's and Charles Kindleberger's pre–Marshall Plan thoughts in "The Economic Tasks of the Postwar World" (1942), and Charles Kupchan's "The Democratic Malaise" (2012).

In keeping with the pattern of a paradigm shift, new ideas rather than scorn and social media noise are what can distinguish the period ahead. The philosopher Isaiah Berlin referred to the search for new ideas as man's most elevating experience.[24] Though the concept of the paradigm shift gives a sense of how new ideas are forged, the manufacture of ideas and their dissemination also deserve attention, not least because, as recent history has shown, bad ideas can travel faster and farther than good ones. This discrepancy in the dissemination of ideas is, of course, important because for the levelling to be positive it must be based on good rather than bad ideas.

Therefore, in the context of a paradigm shift, we need to understand how good, constructive ideas can percolate to the surface of public debate. Dan Drezner, in his book *The Ideas Industry*, describes how the formation of ideas has moved beyond universities to think tanks, consultancies, and investment banks. The creation of new databases and data sources is part of this, as is the use of social media to amplify ideas. Many people feel that social media has damaged both the democratic and intellectual space by allowing noise and rancor to overcome good ideas and, equally, by boosting bad ideas and negative sentiment. What many feel about social media reminds me of the 1976 film *Network*, whose protagonist, a newscaster, is driven mad by the demands that network TV places on him and who, in an on-air rant, declares, "I'm as mad as hell and I'm not going to take this anymore."

Another element in the development of ideas that deserves more attention is the rise of cross-disciplinary research that mixes insights into, say, biology and anthropology with insights in economics, for example. This mingling of disciplines is critical because, to reiterate a point made earlier in this book, the forces operating on our world—financial, scientific, social, economic, and diplomatic—are intertwined. A useful example of the multidisciplinary way we need to think about the world comes from the Santa Fe Institute, which is unique because of the eminence of its researchers but also in the way they bring together perspectives from very different fields of study to try to better understand complex, adaptive systems.[25]

The nub of *The Levelling* is that the world is entering a transition phase moving toward a state of being that will be different from what we have enjoyed in the past thirty years. The early phase—ranging from the financial crisis to the democratic recession—where we now find ourselves looks noisy, chaotic, and directionless. And the disruption is not simply a developed-world problem: look at the contests in Turkey and in African countries like Kenya and South Africa between dominant individuals and institutions such as the media, the judiciary, and constitutional law. Noise, chaos, and a search for direction are characteristics of the early phase of paradigm shifts. Our future could be a grisly repeat of 1913, the last time globalization came to an end.

One could conjure up a nasty, dystopian vision of a society that looks like a scene from a painting by Pieter Bruegel (I'm thinking of *The Fight between Carnival and Lent* or even *The Triumph of Death*) or of the kind of future set out in the television series *The Handmaid's Tale* (based on Margaret Atwood's book of the same name). Imagine societies cleft by inequality, where racism is again institutionalized, where, with echoes of the 1920s, sterilization and euthanasia are spoken of as policy options (the critical backlash from the scientific community against Nicholas Wade's *A Troublesome Inheritance*, in which he links natural selection, race, and genetics, underscores the sensitivity to such proposals),[26] where Chinese Americans are purged from jobs in Silicon Valley and in government, where fiscal paradises are replaced by ethical paradises,* where the trend rate of growth worldwide drops from 3 percent to 1 percent, and where humans serve technology rather than the other way around. I will stop there. But it is not hard to paint a picture in which some of the trends we are now experiencing in the world run out of control.

A less extreme, more realistic scenario is that the majority of people will come to firmly believe that the world around them is changing

---

* What I have in mind here is that some countries condone and accept practices in areas like genetic editing that are not commonly or legally accepted around the world.

dramatically and that their needs are not well represented or under-stood by politicians. The logical extension of this is that new policies, new frameworks, and new ideas need to shape an outlook that is more constructive and better balanced. These new ideas cut across politics and democracies, economics, finance, and diplomacy, all of which are inter-connected. I emphasize four problems in particular.

I will start with economics, and having mocked forecasters and avoided the flimsy science of forecasting, I will now boldly forecast what will happen to the international economic political order over the next five or so years, through the mid 2020s. The chief risk is of reces-sions in the United States and China. The Chinese economy is replete with fault lines (debt, low productivity, the effects of environmental damage on the slowdown of the economy). The US expansion, already the second longest since 1870, is running out of steam as inflation rises, central bank stimulus reverses, and both debt and the fiscal deficit rise to historically high levels. An economic crisis, or two, that severely tests policy makers is on the horizon. Worse still will be the realization that the average or trend level of growth for the next ten years, through the 2020s, will be lower than that of the past thirty years. Over the past thirty years, global economic growth has averaged 3.5 percent, but ma-turing emerging economies, aging populations worldwide, the need for debt levels to contract, and low productivity all mean that it could fall to closer to 2 percent. This may seem like a manageable downshift, but assumptions of a generous level of economic growth is hardwired into financial markets, policy bodies, government spending assumptions, and corporate strategies, so that a step change lower would provoke a painful and long-lasting correction.

From the point of view of the levelling, this means a number of things. The first is that politicians will be tested to an even greater degree to produce balanced growth. Following nearly two decades of economic growth being enabled by rising debt and the overlordly influence of cen-tral banks, there is an urgent need to rediscover the formula for organic growth. My contention is that the source of organic growth is to be found in the quality of the rule of law, institutions, and investment in humans (through education and technology). In addition, the idea of human development as a central pillar of economic growth needs to be given much greater credence.

The second problem is that before organic growth can flourish, the imbalances created in the world economy and financial system over the past twenty years need to be dealt with. There has been a scandalous degree of complacency over the facts that debt levels internationally are higher than ever before, that central banks, in their efforts to rescue the world economy from the global financial crisis, have simply encouraged more debt issuance by companies and governments, and that this has led to inefficient allocation of capital. Unless central banks can fully disengage from quantitative easing and unless world debt levels are pared down, it will be impossible for growth to flourish again because the burden of debt on government spending, company balance sheets, and households will prove restrictive.

The third problem relates to geopolitics and what has come to be known as the "world order"—the way power is distributed among the players on the global stage. The levelling will see an emerging multipolar world dominated by at least three large regions that do things (e.g., democracy, economics, and religion) increasingly distinctly. New rules of the road and new institutions will need to be crafted, and old ones will fade. The idea of the rise and fall of nations will gain prominence: post-Brexit Britain will have to reinvent itself, India will have to decide whether it wants to be a superpower, and Russia will have to generate economic power. New constellations of countries will spring up, and the way we look at the relationship between democracy and development will change as it becomes clear that in many countries, democracy was not a prerequisite for economic growth (notably China).

Fourth, and perhaps most important, the levelling makes a demand and asks a question. The demand is that economic policy must focus more on people: on curbing the side effects of new technologies and lifestyle problems such as obesity and on recultivating the ethic of human

development as a core economic policy. Most of the major economies—
the United States, China, and the United Kingdom, for instance—do
not do this. The question is to the public themselves and it is simply
this: What do you want? Let me forestall readers from responding with
answers like "a yacht," "lots of money," or "a nice holiday home," by saying that my question is a challenge to the public at large to express in a
coherent and practical way what they want from politicians and their
political systems. I fundamentally believe that electing politicians with
extreme views or extreme modes of behavior, together with inchoate
parties on the extreme left and right, will not fix political systems, and
neither will it shape them for the twenty-first century.

This will soon become clear in the United States, the United Kingdom, and further afield. At some stage, protest voting, the seductive
attraction of strongmen and strongwomen, and the lure of nationalism
will prove unsatisfying in terms of their policies and consequences. The
previous chapter showed that there are many pressure points acting on
societies, minds, bodies, and wallets. The logical question is, What do
people expect to be done about this, especially those who vote for more
extreme political outcomes? There could be many competing answers
here. The one that seems plausible to me is that people want more accountability from their elected representatives. By this I mean that they
want their elected representatives to better understand their fears and
needs, to be answerable where possible, and to react to those fears and
needs in a constructive way. For example, harassing, threatening, and de-
porting immigrants is not a solution to the issue of immigrant flows, an
issue that needs to be resolved across a range of policy areas: diplomacy,
social services, housing capacity, and education, to name just a few.

There are several reasons why more accountability (which I define
as taking responsibility for issues and acting to resolve them in a way
that adds to long-term socioeconomic stability) is desired by voters. To
start with, the era of globalization has seen power ebb away from elected
officials. Companies have grown bigger than countries, and they exploit
differences in laws across nations. The global financial crisis saw policy

makers and governments in many countries struggle for a long period of time in the face of financial market chaos and economic breakdown.

Central banks then moved into the economic policy space normally occupied by politicians. In Europe, power is increasingly seen to be concentrated in the hands of the European Commission and large countries such as Germany rather than in the hands of smaller, individual nation-states such as Finland or Greece. New technologies have risen up (social media being a prime example) with little corresponding cybersecurity, safeguards for consumers from cyberbullying, or guarantees of authenticity of content. Together they have opened up an entirely different world where concepts of trust, truth, and social interaction are being challenged. These are just a few examples to show that much of what happens in our world carries on in a space that is above the heads of most elected officials and the broader policy-making community.

This concern that policy makers are out of their depth might also explain the popularity of strongman-type leaders, or at least of politicians who project themselves as pragmatic, can-do types in countries as disparate as Turkey, the United States, the Philippines, Hungary, and Poland. Similarly, we witness the rise of politicians who demand that political power become increasingly concentrated in and associated with a single individual (i.e., China, Russia, Saudi Arabia, and maybe even France).

One of the key reasons for stressing the notion of accountability/ responsibility as part of the levelling is that it speaks to the very large gap in power between the public and many of those in positions of power. This gap reflects an emerging narrative around politics in the developing and developed world that states that politics is less about left and right and more about insiders and outsiders. This gap is the reason why the example of the seventeenth-century battle between Levellers and Grandees is so relevant today. This tension is also captured in a number of recent books; David Goodhart's *The Road to Somewhere* is an example. He splits British society into two value blocks: "Anywheres" and "Somewheres" (his thesis arguably also applies to the gaps between the communities in, say, New York or Boston or Los Angeles and middle

America). The Anywheres, who make up about a quarter of the population, according to Goodhart, are involved in running the country, or they work in the knowledge economy. They are well educated and value mobility and autonomy, they can adjust to social change, and their view of the world is not rooted in any particular place ("Anywhere").

In contrast, Somewheres are less well educated; are rooted in specific geographies (i.e., they still live near where they were brought up); value groups, tradition, families, and communities; and are more troubled by immigration and ethnic change. They are the social group most vulnerable to changes in labor markets, as they neither inhabit the upper echelons of the job market nor are under pressure from technology, process redesign, and immigration in the lower tiers of the job market.

A related, strange development, which might reflect the Somewhere/Anywhere division, is that the personal characteristics of politicians have become less traditional, less family-centric. In Europe, nearly half the leaders of the European Union's twenty-seven states, plus Britain, have no children, and a rising number of politicians are gay. This suggests that the intensity (and perhaps cruelty) of the political game makes it increasingly difficult to enjoy both a family life and a political career. If this is the case, it is a pity, and the burdens on politicians (from the media and social media) should be shifted. However, from a sociopolitical point of view, this new type of politician is increasingly distant from those who vote for them, at a personal and a social level.

These trends add up to the need to reassess politics. Donald Trump has shown that he can beat politicians at their own game by upsetting the conventions on which politics has been based. My objective is not to obsess about President Trump and his modus operandi but to look for new ways of narrowing the gap between people and those who are given the privilege of governing them. The starting point in this challenge is for people, rather than their leaders, to decide what they want from politics. One of the best examples of how this can be done lies with the example of the Levellers.

FOUR

THE LEVELLERS

Agreements of the People

St. Mary's

Let's rejoin the first pages of this book where I introduced the site of the Putney Debates. If you follow my steps south on the way out of London, across the busy and congested Putney Bridge, there lies St. Mary's Church in Putney, somewhat hidden and dominated by newer, neighboring buildings. It is likely that most of those who pass St. Mary's do not realize its significance in the history of democracy.

Entering the church, it is hard to miss the nave inscription: "For really I thinke that the poorest hee that is in England hath a life to live as the greatest he."[1] It comes from Colonel Thomas Rainsborough, an officer and military hero in Oliver Cromwell's New Model Army and a prominent member of the Levellers. It gives a clue as to the kind of sentiment that once flowed from the Levellers.

Those sentiments were born out of England's First Civil War (1642–1646) between the Royalist supporters of Charles I (Cavaliers) and Cromwell's Parliamentarians (Roundheads). The leaders (Grandees) of

Cromwell's New Model Army captured Charles and attempted to negotiate a settlement with him. However, and unusually for the time, this faltered amid opposition from the rank and file of the army, who had more ambitious aims than the mere fashioning of an understanding with Charles. This substantial faction in the army (the Levellers) wanted what we would recognize today as democracy and equality. Ostensibly in order to hear their views and to help inform a new constitution, Cromwell held the Putney Debates, principally on the location of St. Mary's Church on the Thames.

This was an unprecedented undertaking in that it gave rank-and-file soldiers a voice in the aims of the army and the future English Constitution. Viewed against the long run of history, this kind of debate was radical and to many represented the beginning of a world turned upside down. Such a departure was in many ways testament to the power of the Levellers. They had become the predominant group among a number of movements that grew up in mid-seventeenth-century Britain in response to growing questioning of the power of the king, grievances over the ownership of land, and a budding sense of equality.

In the chaotic post–Civil War period (1642–1649), people were exercised by a sense that the poverty and deprivation of the ordinary man were unjust, that they were badly represented by corrupt politicians who ruled over them, and that the people merited at the very least some voice in the affairs of the country.

In common with many new movements through the ages, the Levellers were initially dismissed as a lunatic fringe. The term "Leveller" was a term of abuse, casting the Levellers as "hedge cutters," or yokels, and ignorant rabble, betraying the negative light in which they were seen. But the Levellers themselves saw the term as meaning a levelling of the law and political power to produce equality across people.

Rosemary and Green Ribbons

Socially and politically the Levellers stood in contrast both to the Crown and to the Grandees who controlled the army. The early Levellers were more of a mongrel, grassroots movement than an organized political party in the sense of today's parties. There was a significant degree of homogeneity across the movement, whose members were predominantly army men, laborers, and or tradesmen in and around London. Unusually, and significantly, there was also a large group of female Levellers. They were, as John Rees, the author of *The Leveller Revolution*, notes, roundly abused as "Mealymouth'd Muttonmongers wives," "a company of Gossops," and "Levelling sea-greene sisters." Nonetheless, the Leveller women did much to advance the cause: approximately ten thousand women Levellers signed a petition to Parliament in 1649, which Parliament refused to accept. This was a revolutionary move: women stepped out of the subservient role that society had prescribed for them. In putting forward their petition their aim was to support the male Leveller leaders but also to "claim an equal share and interest with the men in the Common-wealth." The reaction in Parliament was not kind; the Leveller women were told to go home and wash their dishes, to which some replied that they "had no dishes left to wash." Yet the involvement of women in the Leveller movement is one illustration of the reach of their network, much of which sprawled across central London.[2]

Physical social networks—such as the coffeehouses, alehouses, and churches of the City of London—played a role in the transmission of their message. In John Rees's book, there is a wonderful map of the main locations in London where the Levellers used to gather. Today, it constitutes a very good guide to the City of London, and readers should, if they have half a day to spare, follow it, taking care to visit some of the backstreets of the city and the pubs found there.

The behavior of the Levellers also resonates with movements today. They wore symbols—clumps of rosemary and green ribbons—to underline their identity. Also, just as today's political movements use social media, the Levellers were adept at using the printing press to spread their message, and at times they produced print runs of pamphlets that ran into the tens of thousands.

So to a very large extent, the Levellers became an organized movement that through discussion and debate produced a set of aims and
principles. There is some academic argument as to the extent to which
they constituted a political party, but the manner in which their movement dissipated following the arrest and execution of some of its members, and in particular following the funeral of Colonel Rainsborough,
suggests that the movement was not as well structured as some think.[3]

What Did They Want?

That we know much of the Levellers' thoughts and creed owes to the
prevalence of printing at the time, to the recording of the Putney Debates
by Sir William Clarke and a team of stenographers, and, it should be
said, to a large amount of luck.[4] The transcripts of the debates were lost,
mislaid, or hidden for well over two hundred years until they cropped
up at Oxford in 1890. The accidental absence of the transcripts of the
debates also helps explain why they have not figured more prominently
in analysis, commentary, and the history of the seventeenth century.

The miracle of how the manuscripts were rediscovered is expertly
told by Lesley Le Claire, a historian and librarian of Worcester College,
Oxford, from 1977 to 1992.[5] She relates that at the age of twenty-four,
Clarke, who was a junior army secretary, scribbled down the proceedings
of the debates, though he properly transcribed them only fifteen years
later, in 1662. Four years after that, by which time Clarke was a well-off,
senior army administrator, his leg was shattered by a cannonball during
a naval battle with the Dutch, and he died soon after. As his young son
George grew up, the late Clarke's wife entrusted his papers to his son,
who later became a senior academic at All Soul's College, Oxford. Upon
his death, George Clarke bequeathed his money and library to several
colleges in Oxford University, with much of his library going to the relatively new Worcester College. Over 150 years later, the Clarke manuscripts lay unread in Oxford, until an eccentric librarian of Worcester
College, Henry Pottinger, recommended them to a young historian of the

English Civil War, Charles Firth. Firth studied and published the manuscripts, though in a very dry way, but failed to promote them. It was only with the publication in 1938 of A. S. P. Woodhouse's book *Puritanism and Liberty* that historians noted the significance of the Clarke papers.

The various texts show the Levellers as distinct in their desire for equality and in the detailed, practical way in which they expressed this. The basis of the Levellers' political code was the concept of natural rights, that is, that there should be freedom and equality among men or "freeborn" people, a principle that was developed by John Locke and Thomas Paine (Paine's famous work *Rights of Man* was once derogatorily called "a levelling system")[6] and that carried through from the Levellers to the American Declaration of Independence. We might also tie natural rights to Montesquieu's *The Spirit of the Laws* because a core principle of the Levellers was the honest, unbiased making and application of the law.

Another pillar of the Levellers' demands related to the workings of the law, which in their (justified) view was often applied in an arbitrary way and with deference to wealth and social standing. The Levellers called for a transparent expression and implementation of the law in a way that was fair and comprehensible to the ordinary man.

An important document that precedes the publication of the Agreements of the People is Richard Overton's *Remonstrance of Many Thousand Citizens* ("A remonstrance of many thousand citizens and other freeborn people of England to their own House of Common . . . ").[7] Overton was a prominent Leveller and a passionate pamphleteer. The *Remonstrance* was sparked by Overton's indignation at the state's attempt to control and censure the publication of pamphlets and at the imprisonment of fellow Leveller John Lilburne.

Overton's text is full of rage and speaks to the way people today feel about political accountability and competence. For instance, he often refers to the breakdown in trust between members of Parliament and those who elected them: "They chose rather to trust unto their policies and court arts—to king-waste and delusion—than to justice and plain dealing."[8] He explicitly draws on a number of important distinctions, such as that between "principals" and "agents" and the separation of powers between those who make laws and those who implement them.

His reproaches to Parliament could well come from citizens in a post-financial-crisis country today: "Have you shook this nation like an earthquake to produce no more than this for us? Is it for this that ye have made so free use and been so bold both with our persons and estates?" And when he aims at their detachment: "For we must deal plainly with you. Ye have long time acted more like the House of Peers than the House of Commons."[9]

Many people today can empathize with Overton's focus on corruption, duplicity ("Forsake and utterly renounce all crafty and subtle intentions; hide not your thoughts from us"), and statecraft. Overton is underwhelmed by what members of Parliament have done with the power invested in them and sets out remedies, such as frequent elections and a separation between the power to make laws and to implement them, and he demands, "You must deal better with us." He demands equality for the "freeborn" and equal treatment in law: "Nor is there any reason that they should in any measure be less liable to any law than the gentry are."[10]

Overton's *Remonstrance* gives a strong impression of the ethic of the Levellers. In the context of his later influence within the Levellers, it helps make the point that they were more classical republicans than socialists, as some see them. They were more interested in developing a largely political rather than social levelling, based on the autonomy of the public. A good portion of the Overton texts and parts of the subsequent agreements hang heavily on the notion of defending the people against tyranny and against arbitrariness in the application of law and state policy—for example: "We must therefore pray you to make a law against all kinds of arbitrary government as the highest capital offence against the commonwealth."[11] This idea and the texts of the agreements chime with the philosopher Philip Pettit's definition of a civic republic as one in which citizens are free from domination.[12]

Again, most likely with Lilburne in mind, Overton claimed, "Ye now frequently commit men's persons to prison without showing cause," and he complained of a tradition of judges and lawyers "who sell justice and injustice."[13] There is also a sense that the political class had distanced itself from the people (bear in mind that at this time the notion of equality was still a revolutionary one).

Reading through his pamphlets one might even detect a sense of prophecy, or simply of a cycle come full circle in regard to Brexit and Scotland: "When as we see apparently that this nation and that of Scotland are joined together in a most bloody and consuming war by the waste and policy of a sort of lords in each nation that were malcontents and vexed." Some British people reading this will consider the prosecution of Brexit a waste, and many will think of their leaders as "malcontents." Overton also has much to say on how Parliament spends the state's money, especially on wars and on the negative effects of conscription. On this topic, he warns members of Parliament that using war as an excuse to avoid other issues will not do: "If ye could excuse yourselves as ye used to do by saying it has been a time of war, that will not do."[14]

Well-Being of the People

Overton was joined at the head of the Levellers by Rainsborough, John Lilburne (whose wife, Katherine, also organized women's Leveller groups), William Walwyn, John Wildman, and Thomas Prince. They were the primary signatories of the agreements. The first Agreement of the People was prepared at the end of October 1647, just at the beginning of the debates.[15] This agreement focused on political equality and has a claim to being the first written constitution in democratic history. It carries some striking epithets, such as a terse definition of equality and good law: "that in all laws made or to be made, every person may be bound alike" and "that as the laws ought to be equal, so they must be good and not evidently destructive to the safety and well-being of the people."[16]

A second agreement was rushed into print in mid-December 1648 as some of the Leveller leaders were threatened with arrest, and the third and final agreement appeared in May 1649.[17] Against a political background colored by a despotic king and an overbearing Parliament, the aim of the Levellers was to flatten the power structure, restrain government, and end "domination" of the ordinary man—or, in the words of the Levellers, "Agree to ascertain our Government, to abolish all arbitrary Power, and to set bounds and limits both to our Supreme, and all Subordinate Authority, and remove all known Grievances."[18] The second agreement contains a few more references to policy than did the first agreement, such as the establishment of a Council of State and a sensible and fair approach to the taking on of debt.

The third and final agreement (supported by one-third of the population of London) was fashioned by John Lilburne, William Walwyn, Thomas Prince, and Richard Overton, all prisoners in the Tower of London, in May 1649. It is the most complete of the three agreements and touches on topics, such as trade, that earlier documents do not treat. It strikes a doleful note that electorates in many countries might appreciate today: "having for some yeare's by-past, drunk deep of the Cup of misery and sorrow."[19]

The Cup of Misery

We can boil down the arguments of the Levellers and try to express them in today's terms. They wanted a simplification of the law in plain English, an end to onerous indebtedness procedures, suffrage for most males, religious freedom, and political and electoral reform.[20] They demanded an end to corruption in politics and within the judiciary. They wanted integrity from those in office but pessimistically warned (in the third agreement) that they had "by woefull experience found the prevalence of corrupt interests powerfully inclining most men once entrusted with authority."[21]

Practically, we can translate their wishes as more-representative parliamentary reform, measures to curb corruption, an ending of privileges and exemptions for members of Parliament and the Grandee classes, and measures to reduce politicians' time in office. Furthermore, the Levellers signaled a preference for local or community representation and democracy (i.e., there should be no imposition of candidates or officers), probity in office, and civil behavior (the agreement was against disorder, rioting, and destruction of property).[22] Legally, the state would uphold natural rights, affirm religious freedom, enforce a transparent rule of law (in "plain English"), and enact progressive legal reform.

In terms of foreign policy, they prescribed a stance based on commerce, a vigilant sense of security, and the absence of antagonism (i.e., "Don't do stupid stuff," to quote Barack Obama, or the former Turkish foreign-policy maxim of "Zero problem with neighbours"). The Levellers were for trade on fair terms, stating in a petition to the House of Commons in 1648 that there should be "freed all trade and merchandising from all monopolizing and engrossing by companies."[23]

Again, the third agreement is the clearest on these points, committing to "the conservation of Peace and commerce with forrain Nations," stating on free trade, "That it shall not be in their power to continue to make any Laws to abridge or hinder any person or persons, from trading or merchandising into any place beyond the Seas, where any of this Nation are free to trade," and cautioning Parliament that "it shall not be in their power to excise Customes upon any sort of Food, or any other Goods, Wares or Commodities, longer than four months after the beginning of the next Representative, being both of them extreme burthensome and oppressive to Trade." Financially the state would run a sensible budgetary policy and households would pay their debts, though not with their liberty ("you would have considered the many thousands that are ruined by perpetual imprisonment for debt and provided their enlargement").[24]

Saddles on Their Backs

The ethic of the Levellers was, in the terms of the political thought that followed them, classically republican. Some of their political ideas later crept into American politics, from Jefferson's deployment of the Leveller quotations ("mankind has not been born with saddles on their backs")[25] to parts of the Declaration of Independence. Other Leveller texts reek of French republicanism before its time.[26] In the emerging political and intellectual spectrum of the age, the Levellers were constitutional republicans of the center, flanked on the left by the True Levellers and by groups such as the Diggers, who would be seen as left-wing environmentalists in today's politics.

The Levellers were modern and innovative in their thoughts, in the constitution they presented, and in the way they conducted their debates. Yet one aspect of the Leveller texts and discourses that remains rooted in the mid-seventeenth century is the way in which religion (Christianity) informs them. Both the Levellers and Grandees like Cromwell were infused with the teachings of the Bible. Notably, unlike Cromwell, the Levellers preached tolerance for all religious beliefs.

The religious aspect of the Leveller texts may make them seem dated to modern readers, and it is worth mentioning that the strong religious element in the Levellers' thought process is very un-British compared to Britain today, though it would still resonate with the political debate in the United States. Religious participation rates across Europe are also low—perhaps 10 percent or less of people attend a weekly religious service—and in many instances religion is a taboo topic, with the debate on religion colored more by prejudice against Muslims or Jews or by the role of the Catholic Church as an actor in debates on abortion and *mariage pour tous* (marriage for everyone, or same-sex marriage).[27]

Though I feel that I am now straying beyond the bounds of this book, it is worth remarking that there is relatively little mention of religion in terms of people's everyday lives (in Europe especially) in the context of voter discontent with political institutions. It may well be, and some survey evidence backs this up, that dissatisfaction with religious institutions (consider the scandals surrounding revelations of child abuse by Catholic priests in Boston and Pennsylvania and other parts of the Americas) is just another piece of a larger sense of frustration with the lack of leadership in public office.

The Levellers also had a sense of history and of their roots. Throughout the agreements they are keen to root their approach to law and equality in ancient ways of doings things that stretch back to the pre-Norman period of England, before the eleventh-century conquest and the Magna Carta. They value indigenous traditions, and in this way they leave a sense that the English Civil Wars had disrupted the cultural context in which the law was interpreted.

In the end, though, the idealism of the Levellers did not pay off. The Levellers were a threat to the statecraft and desire for power of the Grandees. Having probably held the Putney Debates as a means of drawing the ire of the ordinary soldiers, Cromwell and the other Grandees of the army soon headed off the passion of the Levellers by delaying the debates, then by changing their nature (only officers were allowed to participate in the later rounds), and then by controlling the agenda and the recording of the discussions.

The Grandees' humoring of the Levellers provoked further anger in the ranks, and at some points the army was on the brink of mutiny, but it soon drew together following Charles's escape from Hampton Court Palace. In the aftermath of this minicrisis, the spirit of the debates and that of the Levellers themselves begun to falter. In 1648 Rainsborough was murdered by Royalist soldiers. Although his death initially served as a rallying cry for the Levellers, it sapped their power and the movement faltered, with some of its members migrating to America. The Levellers briefly rose again following the death of Charles but were routed by Cromwell and his forces in various skirmishes.

Rainsborough's death and the command that Cromwell and the Grandees took over the process of the debates have a sense of "everything needs to change, so everything can stay the same."[28] We can wonder what might have happened for the Levellers, Britain, and maybe even Europe. However, the longer-term implications and relevance of the Levellers movement are profound.

The Leveller movement could ultimately be judged a failure because of the manner and the speed with which the Leveller flame was quenched. However, against the longer run of history, the Leveller movement is a beacon in the practical, popular development of democracy and of a concept of equality. In many ways, it was the movement that pioneered these ideas across the Western world. In the context of the seventeenth century, the fact that the Putney Debates were held, that the agreements were published, and that a democratic political system grew from the New Model Army and the Levellers is significant.

The Levellers are also interesting because they may offer a guide to how political sentiment and ideas evolve today. There are some parallels between the times of the Levellers and today: both are periods of economic dislocation, change, and creativity.

Economically the late 1640s were stark. Extreme weather conditions marked the middle of the seventeenth century. Poor harvests and resulting high taxes led to poverty, hunger, and unemployment. As with all revolutions, empty bellies were one of the key motivating factors for unrest in England. In 1647 there was a sense that an era was ending as the place of the monarchy was threatened owing to the unpopularity of the king and as the progress of the New Model Army through the country gave a glimmer of a potentially different system.

In addition, the period when the Levellers came about was one of fascinating intellectual creativity and significant geopolitical change and was ripe with a sense of social and political shifts. In the mid-seventeenth century, English society was abuzz with the tingle of change rippling across public life, or to quote the historian Christopher Hill, of "great forces at work in society," as he describes the impact of Thomas Hobbes's *Behemoth* and James Harrington's *The Commonwealth of Oceana*.[29]

The Levellers are also relevant to the current debate on politics in that they represent a move beyond populism because their ethos is bottom up and constructive rather than demagogic and destructive. Unlike many of the protest groups that arise today, the Levellers did not simply want to tear down the existing system; rather, they wanted to improve it and build a system or democratic architecture worthy of their ideals. Yet another quotation from Overton emphasizes this: "That if a leveller be one, who bears affection to anarchy, destroying propriety or government, then I am none. But if upon the account of New–market and other engagements, for the setling of a well-grounded government, redress of grievances; civil, ecclesiastical, or military, or inflicting condign punishment upon capital offenders, if this be levelling, I was and am a leveller."[30] Echoing this, the Levellers did not want a levelling of wealth; they rejected "childish fears" that their aim was to "make all men's estates equal."

It may well be that the various new sociopolitical movements that are springing up in the United States and around Europe are just the very first, fragmentary signs of a political system revolution and growing civic engagement. In this context, the Levellers should serve to remind many of the critics of populism (or, more precisely, the intended victims of populist politics) that budding political change, and in particular the formation of new parties, is not simply a blunt attack on elites or on the liberal order as conceived by them but, rather, an authentic response to a world gone awry.[31] The example of the Levellers focuses more on some of the solutions to what might follow populism.

At the same time, no matter how attractive their story is, admirers of the Levellers should avoid making too idealistic comparisons between them and modern political developments. What does make the comparison with events in today's world relevant, however, is the disillusionment and detachment of very large proportions of the population in a number of developed countries from their respective political establishments and structures, and the growing sense that the world is divided between Grandees (we could make a very long list of Grandees today: most members of Trump's cabinet, Dick Cheney, the Bush and Clinton families, Nancy Pelosi, and Chuck Schumer are just a few who come to mind) and Levellers (who want to restart the system in a more equal way).

In the previous chapter I traced the passage of new ideas through paradigm shifts and specifically mentioned Karl Popper's idea of the "open society," which shares a common ethic with the Levellers. Their project was perhaps the first attempt at an open society in the sense that the Levellers militated against the total powers of the monarch and Parliament with an aim to create a liberal democracy.

The deeper parallels with classical republican texts lie in the way in which the Levellers embodied a change in sociopolitical views, which they then sought to formalize through legal, political, and economic reforms. In his work, Popper treats the rise of the "dictator Oliver Cromwell" and poses the question, "How is the state to be constituted so that bad rulers can be got rid of without bloodshed, without violence?"[32]—a question that in the context of today's world is highly apt. Another testimony that is relevant here is that of A. D. Lindsay, master of Balliol College, Oxford, in the 1920s, better known as "Sandie" and later formally as Lord Lindsay. He held that the agreements of the Levellers were the starting point of "modern discussions of democracy."[33] This is significant because in 1938 Lindsay stood as an independent candidate in the general election, in opposition to the Munich Agreement, which he viewed as appeasing Adolf Hitler. Lindsay's election slogan was "A vote for Hogg [Quintin Hogg, his opponent] is a vote for Hitler."

The foremost contributions of the Levellers were that they provided the bedrock for the growth of democracy and constitutional republicanism, for the development of a coherent sense of the rights of the citizen in Britain, and for the spread of such ideas to France and America. For instance, members of the Rainsborough family left Britain for America and joined the Puritan movement. Notably, some parts of the 1776 US Declaration of Independence could be seen as a Leveller text in their ethos and roots. Also, an important conduit of Leveller thought to countries like France, Ireland, and America was Thomas Paine, author of *Common Sense* and *The Rights of Man*. Elsewhere the work of writers associated with the Levellers, such as the work of Gerrard Winstanley (a religious reformer and founder of the Diggers, whose political philosophy was to the left of the Levellers'), found their way to Amsterdam and were later picked up by radical thinkers such as Spinoza, the Dutch Enlightenment philosopher.[34]

This is why the Levellers matter today. Not only were they a popular movement that militated for political reform, but they did so on a principled basis that remains relevant. In this way they are not only a point of reference for political protest movements but a guide to how the codes, policies, and identities of new parties can be structured. The Levellers formulated how they wanted the world around them to change and set out both principles and tangible policies as to how this could be achieved. They desired a democratic form of government that was representative, accountable, and responsible. These goals may sound obviously desirable today, but that was not at all the case in the mid-seventeenth century. Professor Martin Loughlin writes, "They nevertheless managed to formulate a set of ideas that can now be recognised as the first clear expression in European thought of the basic precepts of constitutional democracy."[35] They resonate with our time because they represent a bottom-up approach to revitalizing politics, public life, and a sense of equality. At a time when so many people seem to disagree (bear in mind that in March 2017, *Foreign Policy* magazine asked readers if another US civil war was likely), the notion of an "agreement" is something that turns heads.[36]

The Levellers' agreements have several modern applications. First, the agreements are practical. They are based on common sense and revolve around concrete measures that can be put in place. They are neither too idealistic nor so specific as to cause splits. Second, the way the Levellers organized themselves may be a useful example to groups today in showing how a more streetwise approach to politics can work better.

The Leveller Code Today

In essence, the Levellers wanted a political system that fostered responsibility to the people on the part of their leaders, one where those leaders or representatives were more accountable. Their aim was a sociopolitical-legal environment where there was no uneven distribution of outcomes. Given the resonances between the Levellers' political climate and what many people today feel is a broken political contract, we can ask, What would they want if they existed today?

If the Agreements of the People were to be couched in the terms of how the world will look in, say, five years' time in 2024, they might strike the following points. The first would probably center on tangible political reform, specifically on reducing corruption, on bringing political representatives closer to those who vote for them, and on permitting new blood to enter the political system. Tangible measures could take the form of term limits, restrictions on officials' passing political positions on through their family, the use of information technology (even blockchain) to reduce corruption in procurement, a broad use of technology to reduce clientelism, public information on the funding and remuneration of political parties and individuals, and public monitoring of political mandates and programs. Importantly, this could take place at local- as well as national-level politics.

The Levellers also had a no-nonsense approach to institutions. To put it concisely, they wanted institutions that were strong and fair and executed the law in a transparent way. The classical republican ethos of many of the Levellers is a pillar of the agreements, especially the last one, where there is a sense that institutions should be the bedrock on which the state operates.

The second point is equality, where the Levellers had in mind equality between all "freeborn" men (as highlighted earlier there was also an active women's Leveller group). Today, the desire for equality is urgent and can take various forms, but an end to discrimination on the basis of gender, sexuality, color, and religion is a cornerstone. Economic equality can be expressed in many ways, but one might specify it as the provision of decent public goods (education, health, legal representation). Related to this, in some countries the legal system is a source of domination, violence, and intimidation. In others, it is more a case of the crafting of laws and regulations taking place far away from the people, with lobbyists involved in crafting the fine print of laws baked both in Brussels and on Capitol Hill in Washington.

The Levellers were also keen that the law be written and applied in plain English so that ordinary people might understand it. Today, legal and financial systems are complex and willfully beyond the apprehension of many people. Improving financial literacy and, for example, making banks better communicate financial statements and products in a clear everyday manner might be one specific demand here.

In terms of economic policy, there is less recorded about the thoughts of the Levellers on economics than about their views on politics, but from what we know they were against the running up of large amounts of debt and the arbitrary resolution of indebtedness. In this respect they might well feel threatened by the very high levels of debt in today's world and, to use the example of the eurozone crisis, by the very different and somewhat arbitrary way in which bad debts were resolved.

Condensing some of these thoughts, we might presumptuously make a first stab at a modern agreement, which could run as follows:

AGREEMENT OF THE PEOPLE TWENTY-FIRST CENTURY

This agreement is made with the aims of repairing the broken contract of trust between elected representatives and their electorates, of offering a constructive alternative to negative political and public debate, and of providing an expression of what we believe people want their societies to look like. Our goal is a world where people are not dominated by technology, by the food and goods they consume, or by finance and science; where societies are democratic; and where countries build high-quality institutions to support them. We want political systems that encourage responsibility and that focus decision making on long-term problems. We want laws that are enforced for everyone. Leaders—be they in business, politics, or other fields—should be responsible for the risks and imbalances they create. Human development as a central pillar of economic growth needs to be given much greater credence, and public goods such as privacy and education need to be cherished.

Public goods are the fabric of societies and the makings of econ-omies—too many of these are privatized; more still are run with no greater sense of purpose than cost cutting. We advocate that they be rejuvenated and taken seriously as part of the debate on public life.

Our societies live in a tyranny of imbalances: environmental dam-age, debt, obesity, low productivity, and the domination of our time by social media. We want this to end, and we want politicians to act to rein in imbalances.

In public life, responsibility is actively evaded. Complacency and moral corruption are eating away at the body politic and must be stopped. We want politicians who are accountable but who exercise their power in a way that does no harm.

We want accountability in politics to be encouraged by term lim-its, limits on family monopolization of political positions, and the creation of incentives and supports for new blood to enter public life.

Representatives should be encouraged to take actions that are re-sponsible. Public institutions like central banks should permit stability and be active in crises without fostering imbalances or diminishing the responsibility of elected bodies. Individual entities—be they compa-nies, countries, or cities—should bear responsibility in a measurable way for the risks they create.

As countries grow larger and the problems they face grow more complex, governance must change so that regions and cities have more power to tackle problems at a local level and specifically at a city level. Immigration must be recognized as a major challenge and dealt with as a contract of integration and assimilation between migrants and hosts.

We favor greater transparency and the use of technology to make clear the involvement of politicians and their associates in procure-ment and public contracts and to make effective the policing and transparence of payments to and through political parties and to elected representatives themselves.

The law and its application has drifted far away from ordinary people in its complexity, in people's ability to access legal advice, in the costs of being involved in legal action, and in the way in which legal systems can be more advantageous to companies than to individuals.

The law should be clearer and, in terms of its clarity and cost, should be equally applicable to all people and not favor companies over individuals. Exceptions to the law should be limited, redrafts of laws and the insertion of loopholes should be minimized, and legal costs should be reduced. Literacy regarding such areas as legal advice and financial products should be encouraged.

New questions in the law and philosophy—such as the role of the state in surveillance, robots as economic and legal actors, new forms of war, and ethical issues surrounding DNA-based innovation—should ideally have high global standards, be grounded in historical and religious principles, and be made on the basis that they maintain equality among people.

Human well-being should become a greater policy focal point in terms of the impact that diet, pharmaceuticals, and environmental pollution have on it and also in terms of the role of mental health in health care. Mental health is the root cause of many social, medical, and justice-related problems. It must have a much more prominent place as an element in health care, justice, and social welfare systems.

Technology has always been a force in societies and economies, but it is now pushing economic, ethical, and philosophical barriers in areas like gene editing. Technology should be used to enable transparency in public life, and its impact on education and social cohesion should be managed by states. Social welfare systems and state infrastructure can benefit from technology, but the way they support society may need to change to reflect the way technology displaces people.

The intersection of technology and economics leads to imbalances in power, of governments over citizens, of data gatherers over data subjects, and of owners of technology over the rest. Ownership of technologically generated data must rest with its subjects, some technologies must be public goods, and there must be clear limits to governments' use and holdings of data on their citizens. Ownership and transmission of personal data rests with individuals, and the right to use this data should rest strictly with them.

That is a first, rough draft of what a twenty-first century agreement might look like. I say rough, because I do not think I can do this alone and will in time need the help of many others, and, indeed, readers may have their own versions. Trying to reimagine and refit the Agreement of the People to today's world is difficult. First, it is hard not to superimpose one's own beliefs, prejudices, and biases. Second, it is harder still not to be overly moralistic and idealistic as well. In avoiding idealism, there is a need to, as the Levellers did, ground the agreement in the concerns of people and in so doing to make tangible, workable solutions. An additional level of complexity comes from our interconnected world, so that if the modern "Levellers" concept is to spread, it needs to cut across common concerns. Furthermore, it needs to be relevant to people in developed and developing countries and touch points that are common to them.

If Overton, Rainsborough, and the other leading Levellers were dropped into today's world, they might recognize the growing sense of agitation around politics, public life, and the direction of the world economy. Many facets of society today, such as the rising culture of consumerism, might at the same time confuse them. However, they would recognize several traits: frustration with political classes, shifting views of society and economies that are not yet reflected in policy, and disenchantment with corruption, lack of transparency, and closed political systems. Economic uncertainty and the changes provoked by technology add to the worry list. Finally, they might comment that the breakdown of incumbent parties, the apparent rise of populism, and the selection by voters of apparently extreme electoral options mark the beginning of a wholesale change in the political-economic landscape but that this needs to be followed by a more constructive, bottom-up framework.

The purpose of revisiting and recrafting the Agreements of the People is to provide a vessel or structure for people in various countries to shape their needs and political wants. The aim is to carry the current political debate beyond noisy populism. One of the striking passages in Jan-Werner Müller's book *What Is Populism?* is a quotation from Turkish president Recep Tayyip Erdoğan to his critics: in typically populist form he states, "We are the people, who are you?"[37] My response is that now is the time for the "people" to think, to take on the method and constructive approach of the Levellers, and to set out what they want from politics, public life, and democracy.

FIVE

CAN THEY DO IT?

Equality, Accountability, Responsibility

THE LEVELLERS SHOULD BE AN INSPIRATION TO DISAFFECTED VOTERS TODAY. Their success came in creating a popularly conceived, coherent template for what the people want. Their agreements were a first and have become a lodestone in the history of constitutional democracy. What the Levellers wanted—equality, accountability, and responsibility—are also what voters today want. An Agreement of the People Twenty-First Century should strike this chord. However, the shortcoming of the Levellers was in the statecraft of politics: they were not structured and well-organized enough, they were naive, and they were outfoxed by the Grandees. With new entrants to the political world in mind—such as the many new political faces on the US electoral scene in the November 2018 midterm elections—we should also recall the weaknesses of the Levellers and try to learn from them. In this light, this chapter looks at the ways an agreement might come to life and at innovations that, in the context of a changing world, might bring people closer to politics.

A first step is to recognize that politics is the crucible where many forces play out, and it is usually only when these forces become intense that political change occurs. The extent to which the political landscape changes is determined by economics, finance, geopolitics, and social trends. Previous chapters have highlighted real wage growth, immigration, and inequality as some of the factors to keep an eye on. A more extreme example, from the Arab Spring, is the way in which inflation in basic food prices can, in the context of a repressive political regime, lead to unrest and revolution.

Another painfully digested lesson from the global financial crisis is that for things to get better, they must get worse. It is only in the darkest hour that policy makers take the necessary action they could easily have taken in calmer times. Numerous Latin American economic crises, the global financial crisis, and the many chapters of the eurozone crisis show that politicians only act when financial market pain (as measured by volatility) and the prospect of economic collapse are acute. For instance, Germany only adopted a 500 billion euro rescue package for its banks in mid-October 2008 following a meeting of international leaders (who confirmed the gravity of the global financial situation to Chancellor Angela Merkel), despite the Deutsche Bundesbank's having earlier proposed such a move.

My own benchmark is to expect a policy intervention and a market rebound only when volatility has approached record levels (almost every move by EU politicians during the euro crisis was preceded by a high in market volatility), when emergency summits are called, and when the media declare that the end of the world is coming. The reason I use this example is that I suspect that the life cycle of political ideas is similar. The reality is that for new political ideas and structures to become relevant and to pass through a true paradigm shift, they must enter into the ideological vacuum left by a crumbling consensus. New, constructive ideas only arise out of a political or economic crisis—many political revolutions are examples—though the great challenge is in sustaining them and allowing them to evolve and develop.

The Rise of the Right

My view is that the current topsy-turvy political climate, where the forces of discontent have been bubbling for some time, will eventually provide the space for a fresh approach to politics. Today's political recession is plausibly the echo of the global financial crisis and the solutions, or lack of them, deployed to resolve it. The economic crisis has not been resolved in that it has not prompted a thorough rethinking of economic policy, and few of the architects and engineers of the crisis have been put in prison or otherwise taken to task. In responding to the crisis, central banks have staved off a complete collapse in the world economy, but at the cost of a new set of financial risks. Economic fault lines such as inequality and indebtedness are more precarious now than in 2007. Many economies in Asia—notably that of China—look the way Spain, Ireland, and the United States did in 2007. My view is that ordinary people sense this, sense that in many countries the policy response to the crisis has passed them by, and sense that in the future, prosperity will be hard to come by.

To back this up, a number of academics—such as Klaus von Beyme, one of Europe's most prominent political theory experts, and Cas Mudde, an academic who writes on political extremism and populism in the United States and Europe—have shown a link between economic and political ruptures.[1] They have a tendency to echo with each other through history. Independently, three German social scientists have also examined how politics changes after financial crisis.[2] Using data going back 140 years, they chart a sharp rise in support for (usually new) politically radical (usually far-right) parties in the aftermath of financial crises, finding that on average far-right parties tend to see a 30 percent rise in their vote following a financial crisis (though apparently this effect fades five years after the crisis). The rise of Sweden's New Democracy Party after the 1990 banking crisis and the popularity of Italy's Northern League during the same period are examples, as are the rises of the alt-right in the United States, the Five Star Movement in Italy, the Podemos and Ciudadanos Parties in Spain, and the True Finns in Finland.

They also find that incidents of unrest (riots, street protests) tend to be higher after a financial crisis. Unsurprisingly, there has been a rise in political violence in the United States, for example (mostly from the Far Right), according to the University of Maryland Global Terrorism Database.[3] I would speculate that one contemporary departure from history may be that today much of the violence or protest associated with political unrest is found not on the streets but online. Another interesting element here is that the rise in far-right parties is also much stronger in the aftermath of a financial crisis than of a normal recession, potentially because the causes of a financial crisis are often seen to emanate from government policy or the lack of it, because the policy responses to the resolution of financial crises are unpopular, and because financial crises can have sharp redistributive consequences.

In a way, this is consistent with the fact that globalization and democracy have risen together over the past thirty years. As globalization unravels, then so too, unfortunately, does liberal democracy. The Economist Intelligence Unit's 2017 Democracy Index report showed that the quality and prevalence of democracy have declined significantly in recent years as media freedom and freedom of speech have come under attack.[4] Other surveys echo this. The Bertelsmann Stiftung transformation study shows that the quality of governance and democracy worldwide has fallen to its lowest level in twelve years, with over forty governments perceived to have debased the rule of law in the recent past.[5]

Unsurprisingly in this context, many new parties have both antiglobalization and anti-liberal-democracy credentials. Judging by their manifestos, most far-right and radical left-wing parties share antitrade, anti-immigration, and antiglobalization stances as consistent policy threads. Generally, the radical right-wing parties place much greater emphasis on noneconomic issues in their manifestos than do established left and right parties.[6] In Europe, at least, there is much anti-elite criticism from euroskeptical, smaller, new parties.[7] In the

United States, criticism of the mainstream parties comes from above (the White House) and increasingly from the grass roots, where mainstream incumbent politicians (such as the Democratic congressman Joe Crowley) are being supplanted by new, previously unknown candidates (in the 2018 primary, by Alexandria Ocasio-Cortez, now congresswoman).

The rise of protest-oriented parties is amplified by social media. Media and communication strategies have always conditioned politics. Ronald Reagan's television performances (notably his 1984 "Morning in America" television ad) and the duel between John Kennedy and Richard Nixon in the 1960s are good examples of the power of media in politics. Radio had the same effect in the 1920s. Nor is Europe immune from the impact of media. Tony Blair probably prevailed over Gordon Brown as the leader of New Labour because of his media and communication skills, and in Germany in the late 1990s Oskar Lafontaine ceded the Social Democratic Party (SPD) leadership to Gerhard Schröder as the latter was apparently better on TV.[8] Schröder then went on to become German chancellor from 1998 to 2005.

Of course, the Levellers themselves showed their grasp of communications with the effectiveness of their pamphleteering, in a way reminiscent of George Soros's efforts to smuggle photocopiers into communist Eastern Europe so that texts on democracy could be copied and distributed. It is often taken for granted in, say, the United States that people know what democracy is, where it comes from, and how it can be nourished. In communist Eastern Europe, as in some parts of the world today, people had a very jaundiced view of democracy, its aim, and how it could be achieved. The spread of literature on freedom, democracy, and the limits of totalitarianism through smuggled photocopies helped build the pressure on communism. Today, the pamphleteering of the Levellers also strikes a chord with the reality that in many nondemocratic countries the flow of ideas is increasingly stifled, with control of social media replacing the seizure of printing presses as the means of suppression.

Twitter Is the New Radio

Social media have disrupted the functioning of many grassroots political organizations, though, as in the world of business, the more successful parties are combining social media with more traditional approaches. Social media first radically affected politics during the Arab Spring when it enabled the coordination of protest movements, the rapid spread of messaging, and the creation of an international consciousness of events in Egypt, Tunisia, and Libya. However, as social media have permeated mainstream politics, their effects have become much less unambiguously positive. In some respects they have amplified extreme views. For instance, in the European Parliament, the two groups at the respective left- and right-wing extremes have close to 11 percent of seats but over 40 percent of Twitter followers. In this way, social media is excellent for mobilizing voters, though perhaps less so in representing them.

Partly as a result of the grip the social media have on politics, many commentators restrict themselves to describing and marveling at political circuses on both sides of the Atlantic. Relatively few propose solutions. One interesting contribution in this regard is David Van Reybrouck's *Against Elections* (Van Reybrouck is strongly in favor of democracy despite his title!) in which he highlights the large number of Europeans who appear to have lost faith in the European Union, as signaled by low turnout and high turnover in voter affiliations. He further makes the point that the formation of coalitions is taking longer. True to this view, the lengthy establishment of governments in Belgium, Ireland, and Spain in recent years has if anything been an advertisement for "undemocracy," that is, technocratic rather than democratic governance. In the United States, some well-respected academics have made the point eloquently—notably Alan Blinder, the former vice-chair of the Federal Reserve and an economist at Princeton University, who in 1997, with some foresight, spoke of the estrangement between Americans and their politicians and expressed a view that the process of government has become "too political."[9] One specific remedy he suggested was that policy areas such as fiscal policy should be driven more by economists than by their political masters.

Van Reybrouck also notes a growing feeling of hopelessness on the part of Europe's citizens, referring to "the powerlessness of the citizen in the face of government, the government in the face of Europe and Europe in the face of the world."[10] This strikes me as a very Leveller type of problem in the sense that people feel that politics is far from them: it doesn't tackle the problems they have, politicians devote time to global rather than local issues, and in some cases the actions of politicians are self-interested rather than in the public interest. One useful approach employed in the Van Reybrouck book is to provide pyramid-based diagrams of where power has rested in different sociopolitical systems through the ages. In the period before and up to 1800, which in many countries was characterized by a feudal system, power was concentrated at the very top of society in the hands of a sovereign (supported by the nobility), with a wide gap in the space that would now be occupied by parliaments and political parties.[11] It is this gap that the Levellers briefly occupied.

Van Reybrouck's book is interesting in that he proposes a practical solution to the apparent degradation of democracy. Casting his mind back to ancient Greece, where the notion of a political career did not yet exist, he describes the use of "sortition"—very simply, randomly appointing people to decision-making positions or committees. The Greeks cast lots to generate the sortition. This has value in that it ensures that the common man has a direct involvement in the political process.* Van Reybrouck proposes different, practical forms of sortition-based involvement in the process of democracy, such as review panels (that compile legislation according to the input of interest panels), rules councils (that decide on rules and procedures of legislative work), and agenda councils (that compile the agenda and choose topics for legislation).

---

* In contrast to the epistocratic school, which holds that only those who are educated and well informed can vote.

Sortition arguably also ensures more focus on decision making and policy rather than on the publicity and political energy generated by those decisions. This approach, of nonelected governance, has appeal in limited circumstances: it is unlikely that non- or less-democratic countries would opt for this system, and it is also unlikely that democracies would embrace sortition in more than a limited number of cases. However, in a rising number of cases, sortition's role and effectiveness are clear, notably in Iceland, the Netherlands, Canada, and Ireland's Citizens' Assembly. This last body has played a growing role in Irish democracy, most recently in helping craft the referendum on abortion rights. Members are drawn from all social groupings and devote weekends to discussing long-term policy issues from climate change to an aging population. For a society that is apparently fed up with politicians (the Irish political spectrum has become increasingly fragmented), the Citizens' Assembly has achieved a number of perceived successes. One is the civilized way in which policy is discussed, which I can say is in contrast to discussions between Irish politicians in the media and in the Dáil (Parliament). The second is the way testimony from experts is gathered and assimilated, and a third is the way the assembly engages with ordinary people in taking assessments of the potential impact of policy changes on them.

Sortition is at best only a partial solution. For politics to reform, it needs not only new ideas but new parties and new people. In the context of our consumerist and brand-driven societies, the next phase in the political earthquake undercutting the United States and Europe will be the arrival of new political parties. Europe has already seen the highest rate of political entrepreneurship in some time. Fifteen new parties have been created across the European Union in the past two years, many of them at the extremes of right and left. Three are particularly successful: Syriza, originally a radical left-wing party formed in Greece in 2004, came to power in 2015 amid the IMF-led bailout program for Greece and is now potentially replacing PASOK as the establishment party on the left. La République En Marche, formed in 2016 as the political vehicle for now-president Emmanuel Macron, is a centrist, liberal party that now dominates the French Assemblée nationale. And the far-right euroskeptic party Alternative für Deutschland (AfD), founded in 2013, after surviving a number of leadership changes, now has 12 percent of the seats in the German Bundestag. The popularity of Bernie Sanders and the appeal of Donald Trump are also manifest proof of the demand for new political forces.

A countervailing, generally more positive and more recent trend is the emergence of new political candidates. One powerful case is the rise in the number of women entering politics in the United States (in 2018, 23 percent of the candidates contesting congressional primary elections were women, mostly Democratic and many of them political novices). In more detail, 257 women stood for congressional seats in 2018, as compared to only 48 in 1978. These new candidates so far are disparate, mostly suburban-based, and with a "pop-up," social media–driven quality. They represent both frustration at the current political system and the first stages of a response to it through political entrepreneurship.

Disruption

Innovation and disruption characterize many industries and many walks of life. There is no reason why politics should be exempt. Take business as an analogy: new companies and ventures often succeed because of a new technology or a shift in consumer behavior. Of the top ten companies by market capitalization in the United States, eight did not exist twenty years ago. However, in politics, many of the political parties prominent today have been around for a very long time. To take this analogy further: if the French Socialist Party, the Democratic Party in the United States, or the Tory Party in the United Kingdom were stocks, they would trade at a sharp valuation difference from their peers. If they were companies, their sales would be falling and talk would grow of a takeover.

In many ways, political parties have it easy; they are not subject to the same stresses as companies. Indeed, political parties are also lucky in that unlike, say, consumer goods companies, their "consumers" are much more loyal in their preferences. This stickiness is under threat. Persistently lowered income expectations, demographics, immigration, and the influence of social media all tend to lead many voters to be less anchored by party heritage and identity. Allegiances to parties tend to be built through families and communities and are only broken by the deepest of crises. In this way they are like football clubs: there is always a sense of place, of roots, and of an identity even though players come and go and the level of support ebbs and flows too.

Another reason established parties are drifting from their political moorings is that many of them are associated with events and individuals in history (Mustafa Kemal Atatürk, Éamon de Valera, Ronald Reagan, Helmut Kohl, and Charles de Gaulle are examples). As time passes, events foundational to their rise have less meaning and relevance for younger generations. In this respect, political parties may also follow a life cycle: an initial enthusiastic start-up phase, growth and government, entering the establishment, and then in some cases decline. These life cycles operate around strong and decisive leaders. When these leaders are gone, parties spend time in the political wilderness, where they may slowly change and in some cases die out and be replaced by new ones. Intuitively, parties whose identity is tied to ideology (mostly on the left) will find it harder to adapt than will those tied to concepts of culture and nationalism (more on the right).

Applying this to the developed world, it is possible to imagine that fractures in large, mainstream parties in Germany, the United Kingdom, and the United States will produce new parties. In both the United States and the United Kingdom, for example, factions and splits are developing in the main political parties, and in the United Kingdom new movements like United for Change are emerging. In the United States, we have the Trump Republicans versus the Bush country-club Republicans and the Sanders/Warren Democrats versus the Clinton Democrats. In the United Kingdom, the Tories are split between Brexiteers and Remainers, while Labour is cleft between hard-left-wing Corbyn socialists and a moderate New Labour faction. In this context, full-scale splits are likely. On a more speculative level, there are already subgroups with specific interests within the Chinese Communist Party, though it is difficult to see it being rent apart.

Heimat

New political parties can rise up for several reasons. Social change is making many established parties redundant, especially those with strong ideological roots. Changing demographics, the better representation of women, a recognition of the importance of mental health as a variable in health-care spending (one of the biggest spending items in most countries), the impact of multilateral institutions on the spending decisions of individual states, the impact of technology on society and work, and the sense of dislocation that people in many countries appear to feel are some of the emerging political issues.

Historically, political parties have tended to fit the configuration of their societies: the divide between the Left and the Right and the extent to which nationalism, religion, and liberty are invoked in public life. Some of these axes are being reinforced; others are withering. One important change is the perception that the Left-versus-Right debate is no longer a valid basis for the differentiation of political parties. There are several reasons for this; mainstream parties on the right have in general not managed to boost economic growth, and those on the left are politically vulnerable to new trends such as terrorism and immigration.

The new trend in politics will be the rise of new parties. Some of these parties may base their manifestos on cross-border appeal (e.g., green parties or Steve Bannon's Movement, which seeks to connect far-right groups in the United States and Europe). New parties may begin small, but some of those small parties will become mainstream parties, and they may be built up on principles and issues that existing parties do not address well. For instance, many existing parties eschew the role of religion in public life, few of them can craft and communicate a sense of homeland, or *heimat*, without seeming right wing, others struggle with how to frame the role of technology in societies and economies, and most have failed to address fault lines in public health provision.

Other, new axes and grand questions may also become part of the political geometry. In addition, the view that, in both developed and emerging countries, the new divide is between insiders and outsiders—or better, between Grandees and the rest (Levellers, perhaps)—leaves both the Left and the Right in an isolated position.

Moreover, if we assume that the world is levelling in terms of how many socioeconomic variables have reached their limits, incumbent parties may simply not be equipped or willing to deal with such challenges.

Since the aftermath of the global financial crisis, some of the economic and sociopolitical changes that have come about and that can be tied to the levelling have left some mainstream political parties struggling—both the Republicans and Democrats in the United States, the Tories in the United Kingdom, the SPD in Germany, the Socialists in France, and PASOK in Greece, to name a few. Weak leadership has played a role in these cases, as has a shifting political landscape. It may also be that these parties have traditionally operated in two-party systems, which have now been disrupted by the advent of new parties and new political questions. Parties in multiparty systems tend to be more adaptive. (The Netherlands is an example of such a system: six parties have 9 percent of the vote or greater, coalition governments are the norm, and there has not been a single-party government since the Second World War.)

To continue the analogy between political parties and companies: the evidence on the success of new political parties also resembles that of corporate success. New parties tend to be successful when they can co-opt or take over the social network of an existing party (its grassroots candidate-selection process, funding, and general savoir faire). As with a company, building all of these up from scratch takes time and can be error prone. Often the takeover of an existing support base comes in the wake of the collapse of an existing party.

A somewhat self-evident research finding shows that, as with business start-ups, achieving a good showing in its first election is also a marker of success for a new party, though many new parties still miss a businesslike focus on the mechanics of elections (e.g., the failure of the Party of Hope in the 2017 Japanese elections is an example of potential turned to withering defeat).[12] One approach, whose appeal has been strengthened by the rise of social media, is for smaller, new parties to be radical in their ideology and in the way they communicate because in an age of social media, radicalism translates into greater marketing impact. As in many other walks of life, technology is disrupting politics: hacking, the concept of "fake news," social media, and the pressures of constant media interaction are some of the factors that have accelerated the rise of new parties and causes and left others behind. For instance, the 2018 Edelman Trust Barometer showed that seven in ten people internationally are worried about fake news.[13] A related trend—and one that is also part of the rise of a globalized, consumer culture—is the extent to which people are attracted by and attached to brands. Brands and politics are increasingly linked, the best illustration of which was speculation that Oprah Winfrey would run for the office of US president.

New parties will also have to navigate the complexities of electoral systems. In some countries, such as Germany, small parties need to get above a threshold vote in order to be allowed to take up seats in the Bundestag, and this can dissuade voters from voting for new, smaller parties. This is referred to as "Duverger's Law," named after the French sociologist Maurice Duverger, who observed that "first-past-the-post" electoral systems tend to foster two-party systems, whereas double-ballot-majority systems and proportional-representation systems tend to foster multiparty landscapes.

Much of the evidence on the formation of new parties comes from Western democratic countries. Parties are less consequential in one-party systems or in nations where individuals and their families and close supporters rule. This does not mean that new political parties do not matter to emerging countries. Quite the opposite.

Outside the older, developed countries in the world, there is, broadly speaking, an absence of anger simply because in many emerging countries expectations of income are still positive, and especially so in Asia, where the Asian economic miracle has managed to spin along for so long.[14] But there is growing discontent with corruption and with environmental and labor issues, though perhaps not yet a level of agitation that would suggest a political paradigm shift. To a growing extent there is now a perception in emerging countries that an elite has formed, not simply at the political level but also at the level of elites based on family dynasties ("princelings") who monopolize wealth, influence, social standing, and access to power. This "Grandeeization" may prove to be the basis for a levelling-led discourse in some emerging countries, such as Turkey, Nigeria, and Brazil.

Aspirations and expectations are the key political elements for emerging markets. Aspirations for better income, consumption, and social status are rising, and in many cases a natural tandem trend is a desire for ideas and a more open society. To an extent some countries can curb this by overlaying nationalism, for example, on the political debate. The burden of rising expectations is also dangerous for emerging countries if those expectations are checked by a recession or a financial market event. A realization that the future will not be as bright as the past twenty years may encourage some political and intellectual entrepreneurship.

How to Succeed in Politics

The central theme in *The Levelling* is the passage of the world from a state of growing disorder toward a new order in politics, economics, finance, and geopolitics. In politics, a key element of this passage is the successful development and passage of constructive new ideas and new political initiatives. However, new ideas and initiatives are not always successfully implemented. The Levellers in the seventeenth century were stymied by the Grandees. So before we rush off to set up new, start-up political parties, let's bear in mind a few cautionary tales. At least two stand out. The first, which confirms much of the academic evidence on new political initiatives (which shows that a takeover of existing political structures works well), is the speedy rise of Emmanuel Macron and his new party, La République En Marche. It is instructive in the sense that it shows the way successful revolutions can be driven from the inside rather than the outside of the political system. In terms of his education, background, and formative experiences, Macron is a stereotypical insider of the French model, adhering to the profile of a system insider: middle-class (father a neurologist, mother a doctor), well-educated (École Nationale d'Administration and assistant to a philosophy professor), employed by a pillar of the private sector (Rothschild Bank, like former president Georges Pompidou), and widely supported by the French business establishment.

Moreover, we might say that Macron was as much chosen by the French establishment as by the people. Some suggest that he has simply replaced an incumbent elite with a younger one, though this view ignores the energy and intent of the French president and those around him who assiduously prepare each policy move. His arrival on the political scene was well timed because the French people were highly dissatisfied with the two previous presidents and with their sense of where their country was going. An open path to power and a welcoming establishment helped create the perception of a revolution. The structure of the presidential system in France also permitted Macron to use his personal standing to form a personalized party structure that soon co-opted parts of the Socialist and Republican Parties. The lesson here is that using the system rather than breaking it can be productive.

In contrast is the second standout cautionary tale, the Arab Spring, which failed, though it was greeted with great hope in the developed world and across North Africa. That failure was a disappointment, given the broad base of the initial protests, given that hunger, corruption, and inequality had motivated millions of people to protest, and given that they were quickly enabled by social media. A number of factors complicated the Arab Spring revolutions: brutal intervention by armies and police forces, the complexity introduced by religious groups, the threat of outright Islamification in countries like Egypt, the often less-than-discreet intervention by outside governments, and the consequences of ensuing economic meltdown. Another factor relates to the structure of the countries involved in the Arab Spring. Few were resilient, most were riddled with corruption, and their economic structures were relatively basic. As a result, when governments fell, there was, beyond armies and police forces, very little by way of institutional apparatus that could sustain the running of countries like Egypt.

A few more examples help illustrate the complexity of accomplishing change, in different ways. In Chile after the fall of Augusto Pinochet and the restoration of democracy, a group of well-trained technocrats was able to stabilize the country and stave off the risk of a financial crisis. In addition, much is written about the ability of the Allies to run Germany and Japan once they had surrendered at the end of the Second World War. In both cases, institutions, laws, and technical skills remained in place, so the apparatus of the state was, to a degree in the postwar climate, intact. In post–Gulf War II Iraq, by contrast, once the Iraqi Army had been disbanded, there were few viable institutions or political infrastructures left to build a nation around, and chaos soon ensued.

The lessons here, in the context of the levelling, is that what makes states work and what makes them resilient are factors like institutions, skills, and established ways of doing things. Revolutions or events of political turmoil that disrupt institutions will therefore usually end in failure. So there are several lessons for political opportunists and revolutionaries. First, timing is important, because a crisis or a sharp shift in a factor like migration or economic activity will provide the circumstances around which people may be willing to contemplate a new party. Second, the institutional structure of a country is the avenue through which a new party can rise. Usually a new party needs to be adopted or co-opted by some element of the establishment, and more often than not the absence of such an establishment is as much a risk to new parties as it is an opportunity. This also suggests that for a new political initiative to be successful, it must be carried through by those who have knowledge of how the system works.

New Parties

The scene is set for new people, new ideas, and new parties in the major economies. The old political world is riven by cracks and fissures. The Democrats and Republicans in the United States are looking unsure of themselves and outmaneuvered on their flanks, Germans are starting to think of political life beyond Angela Merkel, England's Tories are divided from far right to right, and the Labour Party is split from center to far left. In addition, within existing party umbrellas in the United States, new left-wing candidates in the Democratic Party and right-wing candidates in the Republican Party are emerging, and this new political blood will stretch the divides within parties even further. We can imagine new political parties rising across the world into this vacuum as a response to the irrelevance of incumbent parties, and, it should be said, we can also imagine the uglier extreme, new parties whose only ambition seems to be to tear down the existing world order rather than contribute to the establishment of a new one. In time, the idea that people can continue to vote for parties who reject the existing world and who consider "no" a valid response to its problems will run out of steam. People, at large, will begin to demand long-term, workable solutions to the issues they face, and new party structures will be part of this.

In the next section, I speculate as to what new, fictional parties might look like, so as to guide how existing parties could be replaced. My new parties are the Levellers, a party of reform, equality, and accountable politics; the Diggers, a left-wing, environmental party; the Heimat Party, popular in Alpine countries, focused on tradition and customs; the Pilgrim Party, centered on the role of religion in public life, attracting both Christians and Muslims, for example; the Governance Party, focused on a citizenry tied to technology and favoring technological oversight of codes of conduct in public life, society, and business; the Atlas Party, favoring the right of individual freedom and responsibility for citizens; and the Leviathan Party, whose political bargain involves diminished personal freedom as the price for heavy state direction of the economy and society.

What might they look like in more detail?

The Leveller Party

The Leveller Party is understandably central to the process of the levelling. Its aim is to replace political disorder and economic imbalance with a new approach to policy making. The Leveller Party seeks to bring politicians—and in some cases policy makers—closer to the people they serve by making them responsive, responsible, and accountable for their actions. The core belief of the Levellers is that there should be equality of treatment for all citizens before the law and in policy making. They want to return the focus of policy making to individuals and to give much greater importance to human development as a central pillar of economic and social policy. They favor economic concepts such as resilience and country strength (i.e., a mentality that fosters the ability to withstand external shocks, achieve sustainable economic growth, and promote social stability and human development) over an outright focus on growth. The Levellers do not aim for an economic levelling; rather, they want a socioeconomic system that is open and generally unburdened by imbalances such as indebtedness, excessive wealth inequality, and differential access to health care. Correspondingly, they require that new developments in technology, ownership of personal data, trade, and demographics be balanced, or "levelled," by responses in the form of education, infrastructure in the broad sense, and institutional development.

The Heimat Party

The Heimat Party is a pan-European party, popular in Alpine countries like Slovenia, Norway, and Denmark, with growing links in the United

States on the East Coast and in the Northeast. There is now even a branch in St. Petersburg, Russia. The growing popularity of the party is based on its message that the only solution to a disordered world is a return to one anchored by tradition and heritage and a resetting of some of the aspects of globalization (e.g., immigration, excessively high pay in industries like banking and technology). The core value of the Heimat Party is a belief in the role of tradition and age-old customs in the equilibrium of daily life and as pillars of public life. It emphasizes cultural events, native European languages, and codes of behavior. In countries where the Heimat Party is in government, such codes are strictly observed, and those people who do not adhere to them are excluded or sanctioned. Immigrants are accepted to Heimat countries only on the condition that they assimilate quickly, using local languages and adhering to local customs, and Heimat countries provide stringent integration programs. The Heimat Party places a significant degree of emphasis on clear, detailed regulations and professional institutions. It disavows multilateral organizations like the European Union.

The Digger Party

The Digger Party is an active green, or environmental, party, with left-wing, redistributive economic policies. The aim of the Diggers in the context of the levelling is to reset environmental imbalances globally, and the party is cross-border in its reach and appeal, with candidates representing its manifesto in many countries. It favors a common international agreement between the significant cities of the world to undertake green policies, to drastically reduce automobile traffic, and to provide green city hinterlands. Economically it favors heavy carbon taxes and broad environmentally based taxes, such as emission taxes, and stiff penalties on pollution. Its philosophy is not simply a land-based one; it has equally serious aims on marine ecology and on the need to respect marine ecosystems. Another distinctive element of its policy range is that it advocates spending a relatively large proportion of health and social budgets on mental health. One interesting development in the rise of the Diggers is the party's popularity in China, especially in urban and suburban areas and especially with Chinese women and younger generations, who have increasingly reacted to the crippling health toll of the environmental damage to China's rivers, air, and land. The rise of the Diggers in China has been permitted by the Communist Party, on the strict provision that the party's goals remain tightly defined: to undertake actions to limit damage to the environment (e.g., by electricity use or transport choices), to act as responsible consumers, and to use social media to report environmentally damaging actions by others.

The contribution of the Diggers to the levelling globally is that the party provides a political vehicle and a reservoir of political capital for proenvironment policies across countries. It manages to join up political momentum on the environment across countries and in this way creates greater pressure for countries to act together and for countries to adhere to international environmental standards.

The Pilgrim Party

The Pilgrim Party started in Atlanta, Georgia, and grew quickly, drawing support from Christian voters in the United States and also from Muslim communities in Germany, the UK Midlands, and Spain. Its place in the new order is based on a belief that in a world turned upside down, order is best restored by incorporating religion into public life. This goes firmly against the idea of a classical republic, but in many countries, the party's message has helped fill the political void. The Pilgrim Party argues for the inclusion of religion as a guide to policy making and for the open consideration of religion as a factor in public life. The Pilgrims' underlying value is that the behavior of citizens and those who lead them should follow clear moral guidelines. In economic terms the party favors low taxes and low social benefits but encourages high levels of charitable giving. It is resolutely against the use of science in many aspects of human life and proposes to ban genetic engineering. Work is a virtue for the Pilgrims, and the party's policies in the fields of justice and security involve harsh punishment for most forms of crime.

The Governance Party

The Governance Party started life as a virtual or online party, inspired by debates among academics, bloggers, and tech entrepreneurs on the role of technology, data use, and government. The budding use of blockchain in health-care and social welfare systems opened up a whole range of new possibilities for the ways in which countries might be run, and the early promotors of the Governance Party, primarily from universities and the technology sector, were responding to those possibilities. They found that incumbent political parties had little by way of response to their ideas on how to use technology and data to better run countries. The Governance Party preaches that technology should not be feared and should be actively used by government. The party's early successes came in some European city councils, parts of India, and the West Coast of the United States and led to the formation of a fully fledged party. It believes in codes of conduct in public life, society, and business and that these can be overseen through technology. With this approach, corruption should be wiped out. Blockchain is the favorite technological modus operandi here. In addition, citizenry is closely tied to electronic-based identity systems so that nearly all forms of behavior—consumption, voting, contribution to pension plans, to name a few—can be monitored and optimized. In some countries a citizenship card ("Governance card") is in issue, and in certain countries citizens are awarded a Governance score.

The Governance Party believes strongly in equality and believes that it can be optimized through the use of technology in society and the co-option of large technology enterprises by the state. It has introduced two recent innovations: first, a proposal for a cybercurrency through which a central bank could optimize household and company balance sheets, and second, the use of artificial intelligence programs in the running of cities (e.g., in transport networks, police resource deployment, and environmental efforts).

The Atlas Party

The Atlas Party is popular in Chile, South Africa, Korea, Sweden, and parts of the United States, such as Missouri and Texas. Its manifesto enshrines the importance of individual freedom and responsibility for citizens, or "nationals." It favors generally low tax rates and has a functional, economic-policy-led attitude to immigrants, seeing them as "nonnational guest workers." The Atlas Party favors very low government spending (relative to GDP), preferring that individuals build up their own resources. It favors a muscular approach to foreign policy and has a penchant for military-based interventions, but only when absolutely necessary. The ethos of the Atlas Party is to favor individual responsibility over institutional obligation. One of its manifesto pledges is to work to close international institutions such as the United Nations, which it believes muddles world affairs. Nor does it favor bodies like the World Health Organization (WHO) or the IMF. It believes that science should be actively harnessed for social, economic, and technological betterment, and the Atlas Party aims to incentivize this through taxation policy.

The Leviathan Party

The Leviathan Party takes its name from Thomas Hobbes's book *Leviathan*, which proposes a society in which an all-powerful ruling force promises men (and women) order in return for the surrender of some of their freedom. The Leviathan Party is a futuristic construct of this notion in which citizenship and the idea of "freeborn men and women" are forgone in exchange for an overarching bargain that encompasses personal safety, robust control of economic forces by a central economic authority, freedom in the area of consumption and entertainment choices provided those choices fall within a quota of nationally produced goods and services, access to genomic programs, and domestic robotic services. The aim of the Leviathan Party is to neutralize imbalances, especially those in human behavior and social order, and, in the light of history, to demonstrate that robust central control can produce progress. The adherents to the Leviathan Party are mostly found in middle-sized Asian countries like Thailand and Malaysia. They invest heavily in state-owned enterprises in the areas of military and naval technology and in genetic engineering, in the hope that developments in these areas will help secure the future of their nations.

New Blood

With the familiar geometry of politics changing and with voters acting less loyally, this is a time of opportunity for new movements. One question is, Who will drive them? It is easy to have ideologues, extremists, and career politicians drive the political process. It seems to me much harder to get normal people involved.

Changing the intake of human capital in politics is a difficult undertaking. In a democracy everyone has the opportunity to involve him- or herself in public life, but the barriers to doing so are high and multiple. On several occasions I have asked groups of businesspeople in countries such as Britain and Belgium whether they, as successful people and leaders of their own enterprises, would enter politics. In most cases, they have created businesses, nurtured them through the last recession, and seen them expand. These people are avidly interested in politics and, for business reasons, preoccupied with issues like Brexit and trade relations. Yet, with very few exceptions, people bow their heads and shyly avoid the question. They cite many reasons: the long hours away from their families (family life, child care, and sexism are often cited as obstacles), the intrusion and hostility of the media, the negativity of social media—based debate, their frustration with the fact that normal political avenues achieve little by way of policy in any case, and the attractions of the more dynamic world of business. I have put the same question to American businesspeople, a significant number of whom felt that they would get nothing done as a politician, would be subsumed by the system, and would not being able to innovate and react with the same speed and flexibility as they could in business. It cannot be healthy for public life that so many people who are accomplished in challenging walks of life feel put off by a career in politics.

At the same time, extremely high ambition and a sense of personal importance very often drive the wrong people into politics while others who may be better qualified by their life experiences are put off by the tone of politics (a commencement speech at the Harvard Law School by former Arizona senator Jeff Flake underlined this when he spoke of a "poisonous politics" and the "base, cruel, transactional brand of politics"), the constant scrutiny by media, the tyranny of social media, and a sense that ultimately very little gets done in politics in any case.

So to an extent, politics and policy have a labor market problem. Of course, one might disagree and say that politics is a grueling game of survival, that it attracts and keeps survivors. My own view is that given the many social, health, economic, and geopolitical issues that are emerging in the world, while the existing order is at the same time being battered away, it is essential to have talented and serious people in public service.

The "Bio" Politician

The United States provides some examples of how the political system can be entrenched and also of how "outsiders" are allowed to access the levers of power. On the one hand, there are parts of the US system where political influence is deeply entrenched in networks and families. Several studies show that name recognition, especially of well-known political families, gives incumbent politicians an advantage. Reflecting this, in recent years the dynastic element in US political leadership has been clear (Hillary Clinton, the Bushes, Al Gore, the Kennedys, the Daleys, and Mitt Romney, to name a few, are all part of dynasties).

On the other hand, there is a notable trend of war veterans aiming to continue their service in politics and of academics and businesspeople being invited to serve in government. Robert Reich, the secretary of labor from 1993 to 1997 during the Clinton presidency, is an example, and he recounts the experience in his excellent *Locked in the Cabinet*. He gives several insights; one piece of advice that he received and employed in his Senate confirmation hearing was to answer every question with a phrase like "Thank you Senator, that's an excellent question and I look forward to working with you." Another more profound insight was his discovery of the way policy is really made. As an academic he had believed that policy stemmed from theory and research and that this could be translated directly into government action. As he begins to understand how power works, Reich is desperate to be "in the loop" but is ultimately not as successful at this as more seasoned Washington insiders.[15]

A further contrast in political types might help illustrate this point further. In July 2018, Boris Johnson resigned as British foreign secretary. Britain no longer has an empire, but the office of foreign secretary is still respected. During his tenure, however, Johnson made a number of gaffes and was generally seen to have damaged rather than advanced Britain's interests. Similarly, in the aftermath of the Brexit referendum, he was also seen as a natural leader of the Tory Party, but the way he has conducted himself since then has led many party colleagues to the view that, even by the standards of politicians, he is too self-serving, and he has lost support within his party.

The day after Johnson resigned as foreign secretary, the death of Lord Carrington (at the age of ninety-nine) was announced. Carrington had been British foreign secretary from 1979 to 1982. He was generally recognized as an exemplar of integrity in public life. Early in his political life, he had served in Winston Churchill's cabinet of the early 1950s; later he was defense secretary for Edward Heath and then foreign secretary to Margaret Thatcher. To cut a long and good story (of his life) short, he resigned as foreign secretary three days after the Argentine invasion of the Falkland Islands on the grounds that the invasion happened on his watch and was therefore his fault. As political resignations go, this one was seen to be selfless and principled and stands in contrast to the tactical maneuvering of some politicians today. Carrington, along with many contemporary central bankers (Paul Volcker, Ben Bernanke, Janet Yellen, and Mario Draghi, for instance), is a good example of sincere public service, and his behavior stands in contrast to that of successors like Boris Johnson.

The problem, then, is to attract more outsiders into public life and also to have them discover how politics works. The distinction I wish to draw is to have policy makers who are more responsible for and focused on policy making than on their own personal advancement. Advancing oneself is, of course, prevalent across all organizations and institutions, but the difference with politics is that people's lives are affected by bad policy making.

A new response to the apparent degradation in the standard of politics and the entrenchment of career politicians is to identify politicians in the same way we label foods and raw materials as "natural" or as "free" of potentially harmful ingredients. I am not quite proposing "sugar-free" or "lead-free" politics but, rather, a labeling that is more akin to that on "natural" foods. It would help distinguish between career politicians and those who are entering politics from a position of little experience of the "dark arts" of politics. One attraction of this approach is that it could be applied across countries, so that there might be a commonly understood benchmark as to what constitutes a "modern" politician and some accepted standards as to how he or she might conduct politics.

There is already some evidence of an influx of non–career politicians in the candidates who ran in the 2018 primaries in the United States, largely on the Democratic side. Independent candidate Evan McMullin's decision to stand in the 2016 presidential election is another example. His aim was to win Utah's Electoral College votes and thereby block Donald Trump's candidacy. A few other original politicians in the US races are worth noting: on the right there is Kentucky's Thomas Massie, and on the left, Alyse Galvin, a Democratic congressional candidate in Alaska, and now-Congresswoman Abigail Spanberger of Virginia caught my eye as examples of "biopoliticians." Another popular new entrant to the political stage is Robert "Beto" O'Rourke, who unsuccessfully took on Ted Cruz in the Texas Senate race, who managed to conduct himself in a dignified and constructive manner during the 2018 midterm campaign, and who supports the Pro-Truth Pledge, a project set up to promote fact-based discourse and civility in public life. A new, welcome trend is the growth in political entrepreneurship with a focus on special causes, such as the Rise of the Rest, which is a social-impact-oriented investment fund set up by Steve Case, the founder of America Online (AOL), to invest in start-ups in American cities beyond dominant regions such as Silicon Valley or cities such as New York and Boston.

The "biopolitics" idea is to attract people into politics who are not career politicians, people who have not so actively participated in established parties over time that they can be considered apparatchiks, who believe in certain standards of behavior, and who can demonstrate some accomplishment in nonpolitical walks of life. It may sound strange to want to reward those who have not spent time in political parties, where they may well have learned how democratic systems work and what issues concern people. My own rather cynical response is that immersion in political party life conditions them in a way that is not conducive to good problem solving and decision making, because of a lack of accountability and a culture where people are permitted to park policy problems for political reasons.

Under this biopolitics framework, political candidates would attest that they have not been active members of a political party for, say, much of the preceding ten to fifteen years, and they would outline a series of occupations and accomplishments that they believe have formed them as decision makers and as people who understand how specific facets of society work. There are already some similar though more specific initiatives. The 314 Action campaign seeks to get scientists more actively involved in politics in the United States; in Congress, lawmakers with science backgrounds are vastly outnumbered by those with legal backgrounds.

It may also be unrealistic to expect this, but a biopolitician may also sign up to a code of conduct guiding how they campaign, communicate through the media, and behave in office. Then, under the framework, they may be accorded different rules for funding campaigns (potentially with more public money), airtime on media and social media, access to a database of voter addresses, and the availability of public or state-owned media (TV and radio) as campaign points. If this sounds naive, consider the case of Brazil. The country is mired in political turmoil, and in particular its political system is rife with corruption. In the many public rallies and protests against corruption, one of the demands has been for a slate of candidates who have no background in politics. In general, and especially in countries like the United States, the United Kingdom, and across Europe, there are many good, experienced politicians who, in different countries, are trying to reenter the political fray. However, given the great appetite among the public for new political faces and ideas, it is better in my view for older political generations to support and coach new candidates instead.

Other factors that would support a move toward biopoliticians include placing a ten-year embargo on a politician's running for a seat that has been held by a family member and not allowing family members to stand for seats in proximity to each other. If applied at local as well as national level, such rules would vastly reduce the blockages to new entrants to the political scene. This has been attempted in the Philippines, but arguably the law was not crafted well enough to prevent some families (the Romualdo family in Camiguin Province) from gaming the system. More recently, in 2015, Indonesia has passed a law to prevent anyone with one degree of separation from an incumbent (by either marriage or blood) from running for office until a five year gap term has passed.

Term limits, at both national and local levels, are a similar measure, supported by the Leveller Party, that might have the effect of clearing the path for new candidates to come through national and local politics.

This is perhaps more important at local and regional levels where entrenchment can be pronounced.

There are probably other formulas that can be applied here. The primary objective is to learn from the Levellers, to avoid having new ideas and potentially new political blood being outmaneuvered by today's Grandees. One lesson we can learn from more recent episodes of change is that, more often than not, successful new entrants to a political system co-opt it rather than destroy it. At the same time, there is much that needs to be replaced. A new code or creed, new party structures, and new channels through which outsiders can become involved in policy decision making are vital. Political system change is only one part of the challenge of the levelling. What to do with power is the next test.

SIX

GREAT COUNTRIES OR STRONG COUNTRIES?
Katherine Chidley's Dilemma

I N THE 1980S, MARGARET THATCHER, BRITISH PRIME MINISTER FROM 1979 to 1990, would, together with much of the House of Commons, tune into a political satire called *Yes, Minister.* The series, which was Thatcher's favorite television show, ran from 1980 to 1984 and was then reincarnated as *Yes, Prime Minister* from 1986 to 1988. It was set in the office of a British cabinet minister, Jim Hacker, in the fictional Department of Administrative Affairs. Hacker's efforts to introduce change to his department and to enact legislation are skillfully thwarted by his chief civil servant (permanent secretary), Sir Humphrey Appleby. The aim of the series, delivered superbly by such actors as Nigel Hawthorne, is to show how in reality politicians are powerless in the face of bureaucracy and masterful civil servants.

Throughout the series, Hacker is skillfully guided into policy dead ends by his "mandarin," Sir Humphrey, whose role is to ensure that none of the politician's new ideas and initiatives ever become policy. The series itself is highly amusing, but it illustrates the bigger point that new politicians are often faced with a system and a way of doing things, or a technocracy, that is hard to change.

In the United States, top mandarins are less permanent than Sir Humphrey because the upper echelons of the civil service change as the government changes, but beneath the very top levels there is a sufficiently large mass of civil servants that bureaucracies in the Treasury Department and State Department have their own identity. If anything, in recent years, a lack of investment in these institutions has meant that they do not have enough top-quality staff (for example, in the first year of the Trump administration, the number of foreign affairs professionals at the State Department fell by 12 percent).

In the context, then, of the previous two chapters, where I discussed the need for new ideas, new parties, and new people in politics, what might a new, idealistic politician face when confronted with a formidable bureaucracy like that described in *Yes, Minister*?

To bring this to life, let's imagine someone politically committed but new to politics, elected (for the Leveller Party) and thrown into the position of finance minister. We will call this new politician Katherine Chidley—well educated, a successful businesswoman, author of a well-received book on politics, and a mother.[1] Chidley's aim is to find a formula for sustainable economic growth that will also lead to a balanced society. This sounds idealistic, but she is determined, and equally so to avoid creating imbalances in debt levels, asset prices, and trade. Minister Chidley has many obstacles ahead; the first is coming to grips with her department and with the nuances of economics and finance.

Chidley is undoubtedly an intelligent woman, even an intellectual, but she is not an expert in economics and finance. As the new finance minister she might, if not careful, find herself being quickly carried along in the jargon of economics, speaking in terms of deficits and the code of GDP forecasts. Like most professions, finance and economics have their own codes, rituals, and language. To the outsider, most of this is dull and hard to comprehend. And, again as with most professions, the fact that economics and finance are hard to comprehend is intentional, a barrier to entry to exclude the many from decisions about their future. In many cases, bureaucracies use these rituals and jargon to maintain the status quo. In the coming weeks Chidley will see economics and policy making from the inside and will make a journey of discovery, learning to distinguish cosmetic drivers of growth from longer-term, more meaningful factors. These meaningful factors—such as a focus on investment in human development—take time to show dividends but are ultimately the ingredients that make countries strong and resilient.

In her first few days on the job, she asks her "Sir Humphrey" to give her an honest view of the lay of the land: What is the outlook for economic growth, where does economic growth come from, and, optimistically, how can she improve her country's level of growth? An honest mandarin might point out that economic growth, as we have come to know it, is getting scarcer and more constrained. In order to soften that blow the mandarin might heave a great pile of research and policy papers from institutions like the IMF, the World Bank, and OECD onto the desk of Minister Chidley.

The End of the Road

The mandarin might add to the pile the reports of the many G20 and G7 meetings that dot the international political economic landscape. Ahead of these meetings, "sherpas" busily prepare serious statements that are then ordained by political leaders. In recent years, these statements say something like, "Economic growth is our priority, we are committed to growth, and we are ready to take action to achieve it." A search of the G20 website reveals all-encompassing statements such as "We will strengthen the G20 growth agenda to catalyse new drivers of growth, and open up new horizons for development."[2] What these statements mean in reality is that the G20 is worried about the lack of decent economic growth and can do little to speed it up or is not prepared to take the measures necessary to do so. G20 members should worry more about the consequences of a very low or no-growth world.

The point of the mandarin's lumping all these reports on Katherine's desk is to subtly warn her that the level of economic growth across the world is lower than it has been, is of generally poor quality (boosted by one-off factors such as tax cuts), and is likely to be persistently low. Since the global financial crisis, the trend, or long-term average growth rate, in the developed and developing countries of the world has slowed and is now at its weakest since the 1980s.[3] Recent publications from the World Bank and the Bank for International Settlements (BIS) confirm this and hold that global growth has peaked.[4] They cite a number of factors here: rising interest rates and central bank normalization, a maturing business cycle, and structural factors such as demographics. There is also a recognition in the work of bodies like the BIS that growth levels over the past thirty years have been very high, thanks to globalization and financial market liberalization, and that such boons for growth may not be repeated.

Already, Minister Chidley will see that a troubling pattern is emerging. At one level, we see the slowing and transformation of globalization. At another, the end of a very long economic cycle is in sight. There is also a sense of exhaustion, not merely on the part of households and businesses but also on the part of policy makers, especially central banks, who have gone to extraordinary lengths to sustain growth and prevent a deep recession. This exhaustion may be attributable to the fact that at no point since the late 1990s has there been a full-scale reckoning or clearing out of the imbalances in the world economic system. A clearing or reckoning involves the restructuring of debt and businesses, together with an assumption of financial risks by those who instigated them. Many of those risks have simply been swept under the policy carpet and still exist. As a result, policy makers continue to treat symptoms rather than underlying problems.

The view that the world economy has reached the end of a long period of globalization becomes clearer when considering the phases that drove the world economy after the Second World War. Starting in the 1950s, international growth rates were modest. This was a time when

North Korea still had a higher average growth rate than South Korea and when the United States worried that Russia might overtake it economically (in the late 1960s, Russia made up close to 14 percent of world GDP, not far off that of Japan in the early 1990s, when it contributed 17 percent of the world's output). Russia soon discovered that without advances in productivity, growth was limited.

In Europe, the 1960s was a period when economies thrived, with the French and German economies in particular driven by large state enterprises, infrastructure building, helpful demographics, and greater cross-border trade in Europe. In the 1980s, Europe's model of success was supplanted by success in the Anglo-Saxon countries, where economic reforms in the United States and Britain—principally in the areas of tax, deregulation, and financial services—spurred economic and social change.

The momentum of many of these forces carried through to the 1990s despite an international recession in 1990–1991. The beginnings of speedy growth in the emerging world, notably China, and the onset of full globalization following the fall of communism then further elevated world growth. With brief interruptions by the slowdown in the German economy in the early 1990s following reunification and the dot-com crisis in 2001–2002, global growth remained high up to the middle of the first decade of the twenty-first century. Yet much of this growth was financialized, in the sense that growth was created by the issuance of rising amounts of debt and the creation of financial market products on the back of that debt (the 2015 film *The Big Short* provides a good illustration).

As a result, instead of earnings growth coming from more organic and tangible sectors of the economy (e.g., manufacturing of aerospace equipment, recruitment agencies, luxury goods, or technology and telecom providers), it came from the use of financial products and services to leverage underlying economic activity. Formally, in national accounts, financial products are treated as activity, though in reality they simply involve the purchase and reallocation of risk, and by 2007, this risk was not well allocated. The housing crisis was a great case in point. Cheap money boosted house prices, high house prices boosted transaction leverages, and exotic and ultimately dangerous derivative instruments magnified the impact of the housing sector on the economy. All the while, banks made money at each of these turns, and by 2006 nearly 40 percent of all the earnings of corporate America came from finance (as an aside, technology now occupies this role, and potentially, from a regulatory point of view, technology may be the new banking sector).

Financialized growth ultimately came undone and led to the global financial crisis, whose stresses later triggered the eurozone crisis. For much of the postcrisis period, the world economy has been driven by risk and liquidity cycles in which sentiment and eventually economic activity have been driven by monetary infusions from central banks. The fluctuations that arose from these liquidity cycles have periodically upset markets, terrified central bankers, and made companies cautious enough that corporate investment has been slow to recover. These risk and liquidity cycles have distorted the economic cycle in grotesque ways, so that we now have what appears to be a recovery in GDP and in the stock market but no meaningful recovery in wage growth, investment, productivity, or equality. Compared to most other business cycles through history, this one has been odd and ugly.

How Long Is a Cycle?

The business cycle is a straightforward but boring economic concept. From the point of view of a politician, however, it lurks beneath many career successes and failures. Politicians elected at the beginning of a recovery can claim all the credit for it, and those elected at the start of a contraction struggle to distance themselves from its negative consequences. George H. W. Bush, for example, was elected president at the top of a long economic boom. As this gave way to recession in 1990, his 1988 pledge of "Read my lips, no new taxes" left him struggling politically, and he failed to win reelection. At times policy makers will feel they are masters of the business cycle, but most of the time they are simply its passengers. The good ones, at least, will adapt their rhetoric to it: upturns will be carefully managed to channel animal spirits, whereas downturns are caused by wild speculators who need to be reined in.

In seeking to understand business cycles, Minister Chidley might be interested to know that the NBER of the United States has a dedicated business cycle website.[5] To noneconomists, this may seem like a very quirky, specialized undertaking, but the business cycle can govern our lives and can make or break political careers.

The NBER has collected business cycle data going back to the 1850s and breaks business cycles into phases of expansion and contraction. Cycles have lasted for about five years on average (fifty-six months). Globalization has changed all that. The two business cycles that characterized this era of globalization (July 1990 to March 2000 and November 2001 to December 2007) are by a decent stretch two of the longest in economic history. (Those cycles spent 92 and 120 months in expansion compared to an average of about 30 months. The 1960s are the only other period to come close in terms of duration of economic expansion.)

The current expansion phase (the NBER has declared that the start of the business cycle came in June 2009) is so far closing in on the record length of expansion, with 120 months now under its belt, making it the second-longest expansion on record, though, importantly, the average level of growth during this expansion phase has been lower than the historic average. In the global setting, it is also worth noting that the length of the current Chinese expansion phase is an especially ripe 210 months, which raises the question of how long this miracle can continue.

The lengthening and, it must be said, enrichment of the business cycle by globalization has led to pondering on new economic models. In the later part of Bill Clinton's second term, the notion of the "Goldilocks" economy was invoked to mean an economy that was "neither too hot nor too cold" in terms of its mixture of growth and inflation. Then, famously, in September 2008 Prime Minister Gordon Brown talked of the idea of a "no boom, no bust" economy, only weeks before the onset of the global financial crisis.

When politicians and policy makers begin to marvel at economic miracles, it is often a sign that a long economic expansion is coming to an end. Economic expansions accumulate risks and imbalances as they mature, partly because long periods of expansion permit the layering of leverage and overinvestment. What can often happen is that toward the later part of a long expansion, expectations rise that high levels of growth will persist for even longer. Bank managers, investors, and companies can become overconfident and can overinvest (often taking on debt to do so). Historically, shorter business cycles had the opposite effect: indebtedness was lower and more frequent, and recessions had the habit of clearing out imbalances, by which I mean, for instance, uneconomic loans, zombie companies (a company—state owned or private—that needs bailouts in order to survive), and asset bubbles. Business cycles, as the saying goes, don't die of old age but, rather, are usually brought to an end by the consequences of imbalances, most often ignited by rising interest rates.

Not only is the current business cycle very long by historical standards, but it is peculiarly marked by an unprecedented amount of monetary and fiscal stimulus internationally, in return for relatively low growth, meager investment, and slowing productivity, to the extent that nearly six years through this "expansion," academics spoke of "lower for longer" and "secular stagflation."[6] The notion of lower growth for longer periods has, at least in the United States, been pushed to the sidelines by President Trump. His arrival in the White House provoked a rise in sentiment (animal spirits) among small businesses on the prospects that the broad regulatory environment would be more lax and that corporate tax cuts would provide a stimulus to companies and households.

Supporters of President Trump will point to the impact of his early policies on GDP, but in my view such policies are classically short-term. They do not create new growth but, rather, borrow it from the future. This is done at the expense of creating longer-term risks: rising government debt, a historically large fiscal deficit (which means there is no money left to cushion a recession), deteriorating trade relations, and underinvestment in people. This approach has echoes of the classic real estate development model: buy an asset, take on a lot of debt, boost the short-term value and rental stream of the asset, and try to sell it off. That's fine for real estate, but it's not quite as easily applied in the case of countries, especially the United States. The outcome will depend on the ability or inability of the United States and other countries to generate organic economic growth. It is not yet clear that trend growth is picking up meaningfully around the world; in fact, an examination of its component parts suggests the opposite.

No Growth No More

One of the better, more coherent explanations for the troubling lack of organic economic growth comes from Professor Robert Gordon. Gordon's central thesis is that many of the innovations we prize today do not generate increases in productivity, and those that do are less impactful on economic growth than previous waves of innovation (in transportation and urbanization, for instance). Social media are an example. Gordon asks whether people would rather do without older innovations, such as indoor toilets and running water, or their Facebook accounts. His view is that social media offer greater opportunities for interaction and for consumption (on the job and during leisure hours) but don't necessarily boost productivity in the sense of replacing humans with machines. Artificial intelligence may do this, but it is yet too early to tell. He also argues that constraints on growth are coming from consumer, corporate, and government indebtedness, less economically friendly demographics, and the risks posed by climate change. In one paper he eerily states, "There was virtually no growth before 1750, and thus there is no guarantee that growth will continue indefinitely"! Rather, he suggests that the rapid progress made over the past 250 years could well turn out to be a unique episode in human history, and he concludes by predicting a growth level in consumption of only 0.5 percent for decades to come.[7]

Gordon's theory is increasingly plausible in the light of many of the fault lines that now beset markets and economies. Consider "disruption" as a glamorous theme that revolves around the ability of new technologies—or rather, in many cases, technologically enabled processes—to render existing business models obsolete or to enable very significant cost reductions in organizations and supply chains. There are many examples. Blockchain is perhaps the most fashionable, and it is expected to result in cost reductions for financial services companies, for example. Following closely behind is the "rent economy" described very well in Klaus Schwab's *The Fourth Industrial Revolution*. Schwab is the founder of the World Economic Forum (WEF), the host of what is more commonly known as Davos, and he highlights such facts as that Uber, the world's biggest taxi company, doesn't own any cars and that Airbnb, the world's largest "hotel" chain, doesn't own any hotels. In the Airbnb- and Uber-led economy, capital investment is low, incumbent businesses suffer reduced profitability, and cost optimization is pushed to individual producers and consumers.

Of course, this plays havoc with the economic world as viewed by the traditional economist. Business cycle expansions are supposed to be led by growing investment, stickier wages, and robust corporate profitability, but most of these factors have been absent from the global economy for much of the recovery that began in 2009. In addition, disruptors help increase income and wealth inequality, and the benefits of radical disruption go to venture capitalists and a relatively small number of shareholders, while at the same time the pricing model of the likes of Uber keeps their workers' incomes at a low level (with zero social benefits). Investment in workers in the Uber economy is low, so skills do not improve and productivity remains low.

Another aspect of productivity that is worth considering, especially given the increase in the number of academics and corporate scientists in recent years, is that research is either producing fewer new productive ideas or more ideas whose incremental impact is low compared to such earlier innovations as Excel spreadsheets and the computer semiconductor chip. Nicholas Bloom and his colleagues at Stanford University undertook analysis across industries, products, and firms to show that research effort is rising substantially even though research productivity is declining sharply. Citing Moore's Law (based on the observation of Gordon Moore, the cofounder of Intel Corporation, that the number of transistors on a computer chip doubles every year), they hold that "the number of researchers required today to achieve the famous doubling every two years of the density of computer chips is more than 18 times larger than the number required in the early 1970s."[8] They confirm that similar results occur across a range of industries and countries—from semiconductors to soft commodities like wheat, cotton, and soybeans to pharmaceuticals (they examine mortality rates)—and conclude that either research is increasingly less productive (in the sense that more researchers are required to produce innovations) or new, impactful ideas are hard to find. This should be a worry, because in developed economies, where people are turning against immigration, productivity is what will drive growth.

Why Russia Didn't Win?

That productivity is central to the advancement of nations was made clear to me nearly twenty years ago. When I lived in the United States, I once shared an office with a colleague who spent much of his career researching the Russian economy. At that time Russian economic history had little to offer save to act as a case study in economic collapse and crisis management. However, in the 1950s and even in the 1960s America was worried that Russia could surpass it economically. Infrastructure and defense spending combined with substantial agricultural output meant that during those decades Russia registered decent economic growth rates.

However, Russia soon ran into a wall called productivity. Central economic management and lack of flexible labor and capital markets meant that innovation was severely curtailed, and new technologies (at least outside the military and the space industry) and processes were not permitted to flourish. With limited productivity gains, a near absence of competitive funding through capital markets, and scant external trade, Russia's economy stagnated.

The economic decline of Russia is an illustration of the fact that productivity is central to economic advancement and, in some respects, to social advancement. In a very broad sense, economies will grow when labor and investment are applied in clever and productive ways to generate more output with existing resources or even new output (innovation). Economists refer to this as "total factor productivity." Productivity is an essential factor in enabling emerging economies to move from early phases of growth (agriculture and manufacturing, for example) to higher-end ones (such as services and technology). It is also the principal way in which developed economies and societies can sustain high levels of economic growth.

In this context it is a concern that in the five years from 2012 to 2017 productivity growth in both the developed and developing countries dropped to historically low levels (one long-run data source puts today's level of productivity growth in the United States at the lowest since 1880, and much the same is true for Europe).[9] In more detail, in the United States, total factor productivity averaged 1 percent from 1996 to 2006, then slipped to 0.5 percent from 2007 to 2012, and has languished at close to zero since then.[10] Long-term, or perhaps "structural," productivity is more important because it speaks to the capability of a country and its people to boost output. Factors like the quality of governance/political systems and educational attainment are the important drivers. In this respect, with institutions such as the US Federal Reserve and State Department under attack from politicians, and with public education receiving less spending (at the same time as educational attainment rates are falling in the United States), there should be cause for concern.

In addition, the drop in productivity has led to some head scratching, especially in the context of a world that is apparently advancing technologically. One charitable view is that productivity is generally hard to measure and that its effects come with a lag—thus the impact of new approaches to and uses of technology such as social media, 3D printing, and robotics have not been reflected yet in the productivity numbers—and that even the way productivity is calculated needs to change to reflect these new approaches (e.g., to better incorporate the online economy).[11] We might also argue that in order to really boost productivity, we need even more robots!

Yet one might think that in the aftermath of the global financial crisis, with unemployment levels so high, that businesses would already have worked hard to change and streamline processes to boost productivity. But this is not immediately clear in the data, and it suggests that new labor market practices may in fact be affecting productivity.

The UK economy is a good example here, as there has been a collapse in productivity in recent years. This has been associated with new trends in the labor market such as the zero-hours contract (a labor contract where the employer is not obliged to provide any minimum working hours and where, equally, workers have no obligation to accept the hours offered) and the very large number of people who establish themselves as entrepreneurs or as "registered companies," actions that may cause them to lose some of the productivity benefits of organizational infrastructure and learning. The drop in productivity in the United Kingdom has coincided with an apparent absence of wage inflation, even as unemployment falls. One interesting piece of research from the Bank of England's chief economist, Andy Haldane, suggests that the UK labor market today resembles that of the pre–Industrial Revolution seventeenth century (we are not so far away from the Levellers after all).[12] Many workers then had two or three different jobs, technology was not well advanced, and bargaining power was weak.

A more clear-cut reason why productivity is low is that since the global financial crisis, investment has been tepid by historical standards. There are several reasons: low economic growth implies relatively fewer investment opportunities, but it has not deterred companies from more financialized growth. That is, low interest rates have enticed executives at many corporations to focus more on financial engineering (management consultants might call it "financial productivity") in which debt is issued cheaply in order to fund share buybacks and dividend payouts. Higher share buybacks make earnings per share look better, which means greater executive pay.

More broadly, over the last ten years on average, confidence among business leaders has not been high, which has probably led to deferment of investment. We must also bear in mind that many parts of the world economy have experienced investment booms of gigantic proportions (China is the key example), and the later phases of those booms have been less productive in their economic impact. State-owned enterprises, the engines of the early part of China's boom, are now the repository of its toxic consequences: unprofitable businesses, overleveraged construction and property projects, and managerial hubris.

There are two other ways by which we can tie lower productivity to the concept of the levelling. The first is the transition from globalization to multipolarity. Globalization was driven by Western companies investing abroad and leaving a trail of foreign direct investment that crisscrossed the world. This is reversing. Protectionism, security of intellectual property, and rising costs in emerging countries mean that large multinationals increasingly relocate investment to their home countries. In the United States, they are increasingly exhorted to do so by the president.

In many cases, lower cross-border investment or forced relocation can prove to have a diminishing effect on productivity. The debate on corporate investment by US companies in Mexico highlighted this because the complexity of supply chains and differences in labor market dynamics would make it difficult economically and logistically to relocate manufacturing capacity to the United States. A further current constraint is that with the ratio of real wages to corporate profits the most stretched it has been in history—a sure sign that corporate America and its shareholders have been doing very well but labor has not (the wages-to-GDP ratio is close to record lows)—companies may face a productivity battle in that higher labor costs may be the only avenue through which productivity can be increased in a nondisruptive way.

The second Leveller-like explanation for lower productivity lies in anomie and human development. Anomie—a sense of alienation, social disengagement, and disconnection—is the root of more radical political movements such as the Freedom Caucus and the Tea Party Caucus in the United States or the Rassemblement National and La France Insoumise in France.[13] The work of one of the first sociologists, Émile Durkheim, is relevant here, and it is a surprise that he is not spoken of more widely. One of his primary research areas was into the factors that hold societies together, and he explored how societies integrate and form a collective consciousness. One line of inquiry he pursued was the way in which societies that are less well integrated—especially because of a less fraternal work environment—eventually make extreme political choices. This is something we now see across the United States, the United Kingdom, and Italy, for instance. In the workplace, anomie may derive from cost-cutting measures that are taken to make workplaces more productive, and in some cases anomie itself can provoke weaker productivity as workers become disruptive or disengaged. Two reasons for higher anomie and lower productivity are a lack of attention to ongoing worker training and generally poor levels of education. In areas of the US economy where productivity is at lower levels, education attainment levels are stagnant.[14] For example, OECD data show that public spending on worker training in the United States, United Kingdom, Australia, Japan, and Spain is small when compared to the likes of Denmark and France.[15]

Over the Hill

Without sounding too glum, there are other long-term factors that stack up against higher-trend economic growth. An important one is demographics, which from the 1980s until approximately 2010 had a positive effect on growth but which may now act as a drag. Population aging is a particular concern, with the fraction of the US population aged sixty and older expected to rise by 39 percent from 2010 to 2050.[16] Some governments have set up research bodies to better understand the impact of aging on their economies, with the National Research Council's Committee on the Long-Run Macroeconomic Effects of the Aging U.S. Population being notable in the United States. Research findings in this area are stark, pointing to a fall of 1.2 percent in US GDP in the next decade as a result of demographic changes, with a subsequent drop of 0.6 percent expected in the following decade. An aging population is also associated with lower productivity. This demographic, together with lower fertility, also points to a structural drop in long-term interest rates and to a new normal of lower trend growth.[17]

To sum up the economic fault lines ahead, there are, to put it politely, going to be significant challenges—high debt levels, demographic changes, and other economic traps—that stand in the path of future economic growth. Forecasts from the IMF and OECD bolster this assessment.[18] Nor should we confuse the recent cyclical upswing in the business cycle with the long-term trend in growth. In my view, cyclical up- and downswings are temporary; what really matters is long-term trend growth because this is a sign of the economic potential or ability of a country. Moreover, a positive movement in trend economic growth is what matters for wealth creation and our livelihoods.

The trouble is, there is still a great gulf of expectations between where many policy makers and companies expect growth to be and a future where we may experience only very modest growth, as characterized by a world moving away from globalization. In the decade after the recession of the early 1990s, there was a long-lasting positive surprise to economic expectations in that factors like falling interest rates, beneficial demographic conditions, and the rise of emerging economies boosted growth. The danger now is that the world has to deal with a negative switch in expectations.

Having listened to this long tale of lower growth, the economic handbrakes of demographics, and lower productivity, Minister Chidley is thoroughly depressed and wishes she had been made a minister for defense instead. Tackling low growth and its consequences will demand some ingenuity from her.

She has two, perhaps three, options. First, worried that there seems to be very little public acceptance that the future could be less rosy than the past, she asks her mandarin for a quick fix, an economic magic pill. An infrastructure program like Boston's Big Dig might fit the bill. A second option is economic nationalism. With the level of growth likely to be lower than it has in the past twenty years, she might take to megaphone politics, point to growing competing economies and tell her voters that she will take back the growth that is theirs. Third, and the difficult solution practically and politically, she might ask what drives national development and stability in the long term and set about creating a framework to implement those drivers.

We can take each option at a time, starting with infrastructure.[19] In the period since 2011 the policy narrative has been dominated by the role of quantitative easing as a mechanism to support growth and raise inflation. It has succeeded in tranquilizing financial markets and lowering interest rates. But quantitative easing has not worked well in boosting economic potential. To be fair, the aim of quantitative easing has not been to change economic potential, but such has been the amplitude of quantitative easing and the power of central banks that many politicians appear comfortable in allowing central banks to underwrite risks. In the United States, at least, there has been a debate on the possibility of launching large-scale physical infrastructure projects. The poor state of roads, railways, airports, and telecommunication systems in the United States has been the impetus for focusing investment here. Several thorough and in many cases convincing books and studies make the case that infrastructure in the United States, as well as other countries, is in sore need of upgrading.[20] Rosabeth Moss Kanter's *Move: Putting America's Infrastructure Back in the Lead* is worth a read in this regard. As someone who travels in the United States and who has seen the pristine and smart infrastructure in the emerging world (notably China and the Middle East), I agree that American roads, railways, telecommunication systems, and airports need an overhaul.[21] A carefully considered infrastructure program would be a perfect response to the next recession in the United States, though the financial means to support such a program do not now appear to exist, given the aggressive tax cuts of the Trump administration, nor does there exist an overarching well-thought-out plan for American infrastructure.

In addition, funding and timing pose two additional problems. With government debt in the United States now historically very high and with the fiscal deficit uncharacteristically large—imagine someone with a large mortgage and a very big credit card overdraft—there is little financial scope now to undertake a well-thought-out infrastructure program. Indeed, it is a surprise that so many traditional fiscal conservatives in Congress have permitted the deficit to grow like this. Further afield, many other countries also do not have the means to increase government spending, and the few that do, like Germany, do not appear to have the will.

Another complexity with infrastructure projects is in timing. These projects take place with a great time lag (so to have a meaningful impact on growth in 2021, a project would have to have been conceived in 2018). Also, those familiar with Boston's Big Dig will know that infrastructure projects are porous in terms of financial efficiency, and in this regard their governance needs to be stringent.[22] Infrastructure projects are also notoriously prone to politically led decision making, so very often their ultimate impact is less powerful than initially expected. In that light, it is best that planned infrastructure spending be held in reserve for the aftermath of the next recession (in the early 2020s), where in the context of a dip in growth and some debt restructuring, the stimulus from such an investment will be more productive, efficient, and helpful in producing labor market stability. This approach would also allow more time to plan infrastructure projects, which are vastly complex and can invite corruption and incompetence.

In this context, Minister Chidley is best advised to create a blueprint for her infrastructure needs but to wait to execute them. She will at the same time know that physical infrastructure is simply one approach to building a country and that most often the long-run rise and fall of a country depends not on the quality of its roads but on the quality of its people, on the building of institutions around them, on the decisions and laws they make, and on the ways in which they learn to adapt to change.

Raison d'état

A good starting point in understanding the rise and fall of nations is to look at some of the great cities of the world. In this light, I want to highlight a fascinating data set that is based partly on Ian Morris's book *Why the West Rules—for Now* and partly on work by the demographer Simon Kuestenmacher. The data looks at the biggest cities in the world over the past four thousand years. Many of them—such as Babylon, Nimrud (south of Mosul), and Alexandria—were the focal points of great civilizations but, sadly, are now in the news for the wrong reasons. It is surprising how many Chinese cities have been "the biggest" through time, with cities like Nanjing, Xi'an, Hangzhou, and Beijing dominating the period from AD 600 to AD 1800. London briefly took over during the nineteenth century, and the biggest-city baton was then passed to New York. If we adjust for world population and perhaps level of development, Rome has a very good chance of being considered the world's greatest city. At the time of the birth of Christ, Rome had one million inhabitants. Scaling for demographics, Tokyo, to match this, would need to have over seventy million residents today! Rome is also impressive in that it was the world's dominant city for some five hundred years, though by AD 500 it was much diminished as a center of power and population.

The examples of Rome, Alexandria, and Nanjing are very relevant today because, at a time when China is on the rise, the United Kingdom and the United States are going through political crises, and much of Europe is still bothered about its economic frailties, they remind us of the decline and fall of nations, a theme that is central to the idea of the levelling. This in turn should lead us to think of Edward Gibbon's *The History of the Decline and Fall of the Roman Empire*, which is a reference point in economic history in general and in declinism in particular. Gibbon sought to explain why the Roman Empire disintegrated. His thesis is that Rome became complacent, its institutions were weakened, and the leaders in Roman public life lost their sense of civic virtue, or what Niccolò Machiavelli later simply called "virtu"—the good of the republic or common good.

Since Gibbon, other writers have turned declinism into a cottage industry. Germany's Oswald Spengler controversially wrote *The Decline of the West* in 1918, and in recent years in Europe we have had Thilo Sarrazin's book *Deutschland schafft sich ab* (Germany gets rid of itself), followed by books like Eric Zemmour's *Le suicide français* and Michel Houellebecq's *Soumission*. In the United States, the *Nation's* Tom Engelhardt, CNN's Fareed Zakaria, and the *Financial Times's* Edward Luce have all written on the coming decline of the United States. These books and others like them illustrate that the echo of declinism is becoming louder. In turn this points to the fact that we are on the cusp of the rise of some nations (India and China) and the decline of others (the United Kingdom, and some would say the United States) and raises the questions of how faltering countries can best revive themselves and how emerging nations can best manage the next stage in their development.

Why Nations Fail

Two important factors in the success or failure of nations are institutional quality and the need for a sense of civic ethic. Both of these chime through books that track the rise and fall of nations, from Alexis de Tocqueville's *Democracy in America* to Daron Acemoglu and James Robinson's *Why Nations Fail*. In the aftermath of Brexit, the 2016 US elections, and the continued stresses on the eurozone, I imagine that *Why Nations Fail* and Gibbon's book will continue to make very lively, relevant reading for the Katherine Chidleys of the world.

More broadly, these texts introduce two themes into the debate on international relations: the first is the desire of large countries with former glories and empires to become great again (we could call them the "again countries"), and the second, related one is the question, What makes a country successful? They lead toward two competing paths of national development. Some countries will take an elbows-out, nationalistic policy path toward being great again, whereas others will adopt an approach based on the quality of their institutions and structures, preferring to build strong institutions and stable economic growth. Russia is an example of the first; New Zealand, the second.

There is another element that may help unite the notion of the rise and fall of countries and their enduring successes: the extent to which countries move in developmental, economic, and demographic cycles. Several books have explored these themes: for example, Walt Rostow's *The Stages of Economic Growth*, Alvin Toffler's *The Third Wave*, and William Strauss and Neil Howe's *The Fourth Turning*.

One of the places where the rise and fall of nations is visible is in financial markets. Looking at long-term changes in stock market capitalization is one way of examining this. For example, in 1900 the proportion of the world stock market made up by the US market was 15 percent, Germany held 13 percent, Japan held close to none, and the United Kingdom held 25 percent. Today, the United States accounts for 51 percent, Japan has 8 percent, and the United Kingdom and Germany have shrunk to 6 percent and 3 percent, respectively.[23] The implication here is that through financial power, we see how drastically the might of a nation can shrink or grow.

An even more apt financial barometer of the decline and fall of a country is its currency. Intuitively, the decline of a nation, to use Gibbon's term, is usually associated with a weaker currency. Switzerland, which has strong institutions and a very high level of GDP, is the only country whose currency has held its value in the past one hundred years. More recently emerging countries, from Russia to South Africa to Turkey, have seen their currencies drop as powerful political individuals have degraded institutions. (The decision of Turkey's President Erdoğan to put his son-in-law in charge of the economics and finance ministry is one example. Imagine the market reaction if Jared Kushner were to be appointed to chair the Federal Reserve.) In general, political risk and lower institutional quality translate into enfeebled currencies. This should be a warning for the dollar.

A country's currency reflects its place in the world, and the dollar has risen to a very particular place as the linchpin of the financial system. Indeed, one of the most important tenets of the twentieth-century world order and the rise of globalization has been the position of the dollar as the international reserve currency. In the postwar period, the predominance of the dollar prompted France's then minister of finance Valéry Giscard d'Estaing to pronounce the "exorbitant privilege" of the dollar that let the United States both print dollars and require the rest of the world to buy them, to put it very simply. When Giscard made this statement, the dollar was tied to gold, and the response from France and a number of other countries was to exchange their holdings of dollars for gold. This set the stage for the subsequent breaking of the dollar's tie to gold by President Nixon. Since then the dollar has been first among equals in the currency world, and many developing nations have pegged their currencies to it.

Currencies and their fluctuations are tough to figure out, and in my experience forecasting currency moves is one of the toughest analytical tasks in financial markets. One of the more original and interesting takes on the behavior of currencies I have recently read is a paper entitled "Mars or Mercury? The Geopolitics of International Currency Choice" by Professor Barry Eichengreen with two economists at the European Central Bank (ECB).[24]

"Mars or Mercury?" describes two approaches to valuing currencies. First, there is the more conventional "Mercury" approach, which gauges currency strength by analyzing variables like interest rates and currency reserves. The second approach, "Mars," sees a currency as reflecting the standing of a country in the world—the quality of its institutions and its alliances. Using data going back to the First World War, the paper finds that military and geopolitical alliances are a significant factor in explaining currency strength. The rationale is that a country that is geopolitically well placed is engaged with and trusted by its allies through trade and finance.

Eichengreen and his coauthors have set up a framework to capture the impact on the dollar of US diplomatic disengagement with the world. One of the main implications the "Mars or Mercury?" paper finds is that, in a scenario where the United States withdraws from the world and becomes more isolationist, its strategic allies no longer become enthusiastic buyers of US financial assets and long-term interest rates in the United States could rise by up to 1 percent because there would be fewer buyers of American government debt.

Katherine Chidley, if she has the time to use the Bloomberg Terminal in her office,* might also plot the recent moves in the Turkish lira, which also fits the "Mars" hypothesis. She will find its volatility through 2018 sobering, but she might also recognize that the specter of declinism and the vogue for "great againism" are related and that financial markets are eager to express their views on this.

If she is serious about arresting economic decline and getting back on the road to greatness or, better, to "being strong again," she will ask what objectives and scorecards politicians should have in mind. One example that comes to mind is the European Union's Maastricht financial criteria, but eurozone member countries usually ignore them. There are not many politicians today who explicitly set out scorecards, methods, and goals as to what they want to achieve. There is a good reason for this: many politicians give no more precise economic goals than "jobs," "growth," or, to use former British prime minister Harold Wilson's phrase, talk of "the pound in your pocket."

"Growth," "prosperity," and "employment" are the most obvious and common goals a politician can expound, and at a high level they are easy

---

* Many financial market analysts and traders use Bloomberg Terminals to access an array of market data and analytics.

to measure. The quality and durability of growth is an altogether more difficult promise. Political speeches are also often sprinkled with magical promises of prosperity, though here again, achieving stable, sustainable prosperity (in the sense of a durable increase in household net wealth) is hard to attain. If the future is to be characterized by lower growth, then clever politicians will spin their rhetoric around inequality, both within their own countries and among countries. Inequality can be a useful banner under which to shift the benefits of scarce growth from one social grouping to another. More careless politicians might engage in policy populism, which according to Juan Perón, the former Argentine president, has its appeal: "My dear friend: give the people, especially the workers, all that is possible, . . . there is nothing more elastic than the economy, which everyone fears so much because no one understands it."[25]

Another policy option, more in vogue but risky, is to address the idea of "happiness," or rather, of ending "unhappiness." What this translates into is keeping down inflation and unemployment (two contributors to misery). Happiness has become a fashionable political topic in recent years, though in practice few countries aim to foster it. Stable family life is one of the bases of happiness (there is even academic evidence to support this somewhat obvious statement).[26] Another element of economic happiness is that it requires a fraternal and generally equal society (where people tend to have roughly the same level of prosperity as their peers). Karl Marx helped explain this when he stated that "a house may be large or small; as long as the surrounding houses are equally small, it satisfies social demands for a dwelling. But if a palace rises beside the little house, the little house shrinks into a hut."[27] On the basis of fraternity and equality, the Nordic/Alpine countries, are among the happier ones, where social structures and welfare systems are sophisticated. One important happiness-related area where policy makers in general do not dare to tread is mental health, possibly because of its complexity, its taboo status in many countries, and the low political rewards.

Politicians do not typically like to be held to specific policy goals because they are hard to accomplish, requiring at the very least that the business cycle be on your side. Frankly, goals and objectives are far less fun than the cut and thrust of politics. The attraction of political declarations based on the idea of "being great," "being great again," and the "dream" is that they are grand promises, hard to identify, usually fulfilled at someone else's expense, and drawing on nostalgia for justification.

What is also striking is that relatively few politicians elucidate visions that are less glorious but more meaningful than greatness. For example, few politicians today make an active case for the virtue of public goods. In fact, in many countries the opposite is the case: education is steadily privatized, environments are degraded, and health-care systems are crisis ridden. In an unstable world where austerity has become a commonplace policy, one source of stability is high-quality public goods. In this respect it is again surprising that more politicians do not see their virtues and are not more courageous in expounding their value. It may be that the value of public goods cannot be communicated via Twitter and that public goods are associated with the notions of higher taxes and flagrant government spending. This is a pity, because I suspect that many of the people who have voted for extreme political outcomes miss such public goods as high-quality education, livable urban spaces, and low-cost health care.

"What Did We Do Right?"

As she digests this, Katherine Chidley will begin to formulate a sense of how greatness, policy scorecards, and public goods intersect and will set about her aim of creating a workable plan for national development. This notion came to me while writing two previous books on Ireland. In 2006, before the onset of the collapse of Ireland's economy, I wrote a book entitled *Ireland and the Global Question*. It dealt with Ireland's position as a small, open economy that had benefited enormously from globalization and, at the time, from its membership in the eurozone.

My aim was to outline how a country like Ireland might construct buffers against the negative effects of globalization, buffers such as strong institutions run by skilled people, decent public goods, and a sense of strategic thinking. At the time Ireland was enjoying its first (ever) economic boom and was unprepared for the suddenness and severity of the collapse that followed.

As the credit crisis played havoc with the Irish economy, I wondered if Ireland's miracle had been a mirage and whether any of its policies were of value. Professor Rory Miller and I decided to do a postmortem on the Irish model. We put together a book of essays entitled *What Did We Do Right?* for which we asked writers from twelve different countries for their unbiased opinions on what meaningful factors Ireland had deployed that would continue to stand it in good stead.

This led to a distinct line of thought about the factors a country should focus on in order for it to be strong in the sense of not habitually falling victim to the ebb and flow of the world economy and the pressures of socioeconomic imbalances. Strength in this regard is not necessarily made up of military might or large GDP but rather the capacity to stimulate human development, to withstand economic shocks, and to have a stable society, among other values.[28] The idea of country strength, or resilience, reflects a number of factors: an ability to understand and buffer external shocks, a framework through which a country can achieve sustainable economic growth, and an approach to policy that fosters social stability and human development.[29] The idea of country strength is also more than a set of policies; rather, it is a mentality or policy culture that is evident in countries like Singapore and Switzerland that are acutely aware of the potential impact that outside forces (i.e., immigration, currency fluctuations, and world trade) can have on their societies.

One finding that shines through in some of the research projects I have been involved in is that the countries that score well on country strength are also the most globalized.[30] Interestingly, they also score well on many other criteria such as "most innovative nation" or most "prosperous nation."[31] Most of the countries topping these rankings are small, dynamic economies (Singapore, New Zealand, Sweden, Switzerland, Finland, and Norway, to name a few), plus larger developed ones such as the Netherlands, the United Kingdom, and sometimes the United States.

What they have in common are drivers like education, the rule of law, and the deployment of education—their intangible infrastructure. In many respects intangible infrastructure is more important for a country's future than its physical counterpart.

These factors can be political, legal, or socioeconomic. Political factors include the degree of political stability or the strength of the institutional framework. Legal factors include the rule of law, tax policies, and intellectual and physical property rights protection. Examples of socioeconomic factors include research-and-development capabilities, business processes, or employee training and education.

There are arguably five specific pillars of intangible infrastructure: education, health care, finance, business services, and technology.[32] Though developing countries can achieve a record of high growth through physical investment (i.e., physical infrastructure), they need to cultivate intangible infrastructure in order to achieve a high and sustained level of productivity growth and human development. Many developing countries run into the limits of physical infrastructure-led growth without the productivity boosts that come from intangible factors.

Intangible Infrastructure

There is a strong link between the level of GDP per capita a country enjoys and the quality of its intangible infrastructure. Singapore, the Netherlands, and Sweden are good examples here. The Nobel Prize–winning economist Robert Solow studied the role that intangible factors like technology and human capital play in generating economic growth.

For developed countries, Solow suggests that it is largely technological advances (and I would add, a better understanding of how to use technology) and improvements in human capital that determine the level of economic growth.

It is intuitively easy to see how some component parts of intangible infrastructure have a positive impact on society and the economy. For example, education is a key determinant of human capability. The value of education is intrinsic in almost all levels of economic output, and the correlation between high school educational attainment and GDP per capita is particularly strong. We can also track the historical precedents of economies, such as the "Asian Tiger" economies of the 1990s (Singapore, South Korea, Hong Kong, and Taiwan), whose emphasis on investing in education paved the way for their success. Government commitment to education can be shown to have a significant impact on the nature of the growth that economies later display.

With considerations such as life expectancy and related demographic trends, health care is another key factor in determining the average individual's output. Through time and across borders, there are very few exceptions to the rule that better health care fosters an environment of higher economic activity as well as human development. In some economies, such as Russia's, poor health and low life expectancy have been a severe constraint. Reflecting this, Russian president Vladimir Putin's speech after the 2018 election flagged health as an area for future spending. In general though, good public health care is not yet a priority in many emerging markets, and in some countries, such as the United States, it is becoming a rarity. Epidemics in mental health, opioid abuse, and obesity are eating away at society and the quality of human development.

Though the different elements of intangible infrastructure tend to have differing impacts on economies, countries that do one element well also tend to be strong in the other areas. The idea of intangible infrastructure is often a proxy for a mind-set and culture of national development. So, though countries that are in the early stages of developing their intangible infrastructure can focus on the individual metrics, they need time to develop a more holistic mentality that places institutions, the rule of law, and human capability at the center of national development. The fabled Nordic model of development is hard to copy and paste to other countries because, in part, it is based on laws and ways of doing things that have grown up over time.

What is interesting in the light of today's "democratic recession," to use Larry Diamond's term for the fall in the number of democracies worldwide,[33] is that some higher-growth states have thrived by focusing on intangible infrastructure rather than democracy. Singapore is an example. While the economics literature points to a close relationship between democracy and development, the causality of this is increasingly being questioned. Instead, the emerging view is that institutions and intangible factors like the rule of law matter more for economic development than democracy itself.

There is a decent body of evidence to show that institutions, or at least the quality of institutions, drive the distribution of resources in an economy and the way incentives and contracts are set up. High-quality institutions encourage trust and investment in human capital and help lower the frictions of doing business. One way of illustrating this is to take an econometric approach and compare the fit of GDP per capita with World Bank data that scores the rule of law in each country and with political freedom scores (again from the World Bank). The fit between the rule of law data and GDP is tighter, which suggests that the rule of law score is a more important determinant of economic success than political freedom.* The World Bank's rule of law scores from 2017 show considerable variation in the percentile ranks. (To give some examples: New Zealand came at the top with a percentile rank of 98; Belgium and the United States are in the 88th and 91st percentiles, respectively;

---

* According to the World Bank, the rule of law score "reflects perceptions of the extent to which agents have confidence in and abide by the rules of society, and in particular the quality of contract enforcement, property rights, the police, and the courts, as well as the likelihood of crime and violence." World Bank, World Governance Indicators, "Frequently Asked Questions," http://info.worldbank.org/governance/wgi/?xyzallow#faq.

Lithuania is in the 81st; Italy ranks in the 62nd percentile. Among the weak-est countries are China, relatively low at 44th percentile; Nigeria, a meager 18th percentile; and Afghanistan, with a percentile ranking of 4).[34] The idea that "trust" matters is more important in a world where e-commerce is becoming more prevalent, and also in one where financial markets still play a significant economic role.

The framework of intangible infrastructure is a challenge to poli-ticians because it is long-term (and many politicians live in the short term) and because it is based on people and the quality of their lives (not on lower corporate taxes or higher tariffs) and on careful thought (not easy rhetoric). Once populist policies—like a wall between the United States and Mexico, punitive taxes on wealth, or the expulsion of immigrants—have been executed, the challenge is, Then what? Will governments bother to tackle very deep-seated problems like low pro-ductivity, will they address endemic corruption in southern and eastern Europe, and will they take the time to build adequate health-care systems across Asia?

Country Strength

Intangible infrastructure is just one key element in the equation that makes up country strength. The other components in this policy recipe are human development (as measured by the UN Human Development Index), the openness of an economy, the level of its macroeconomic vol-atility, and, finally, with a little overlap with intangible infrastructure, the quality of governance.[35]

In general the idea of country strength strikes a chord with the broad literature on political economic development. The relevance of the no-tion of country strength underpins Francis Fukuyama's theory in *Politi-cal Order and Political Decay*, where he outlines the way in which strong institutions, trust across public life, the rule of law, and an effective state helped underwrite social and economic progress, or more simply, as he puts it, "the road to Denmark."[36]

It comes as no surprise that small, advanced countries tend to do well in terms of strength, but the results are biased in favor of old small countries. Switzerland and the Nordic countries are the usual suspects here, followed by Singapore and Hong Kong. Bigger countries like Australia and the United Kingdom also do well in country strength rankings. What is also interesting are the small countries that do not make the top echelons in terms of country strength. Hungary, Cyprus, Portugal, and Estonia come well below other more developed small European states. Generally speaking, the weaker nations in terms of the variables associated with country strength index tend to be African, both large and small states.

The framework, data, and policy provisions that go to make up the idea of country strength are, I believe, critical to the development of nations. Having said that, they are one side of the economic policy picture. Earlier in the book, I highlighted criticism of economic models and suggested that they should be complemented by a more practical, sleuth-like approach to policy discovery. I think anyone—Katherine Chidley or others—who tries to understand how policy works in practice has to dig into the way a country works at the microlevel. In this respect I have a theory I call the "Grande Bretagne syndrome." During the long financial subordination of Greece at the hands of the "Troika" (the European Union, the IMF, and the ECB), advisers from the likes of the IMF would arrive in Athens, drive straight to the city center, and stay in the impressive Hotel Grande Bretagne (I recommend it), across from which stands the Greek Parliament. For much of the time, the Troika personnel saw little of Greece apart from its center of power and one of its best hotels, and to a degree they missed much of the tragedy of the economic decline across the country. To that end, anyone curious to understand a country should avoid the center of power and get out to see its third- and fourth-sized cities.

In that respect, one of the more telling business trips I have been on in recent years was not to New York or Boston but to Detroit, Michigan, as part of a miniconference on the revitalization of that city.[37] Detroit used to be the richest city in America, though lately it ranks as one of its poorest. There is now a concerted and noble effort to remake the city, led by Mayor Mike Duggan and local entrepreneurs such as Dan Gilbert. Gilbert and some associates have invested in many of the smaller residential buildings in the city center and are trying to convince workers, restaurant owners, and artists to move back into the city in order to revitalize it. Mayor Duggan, as one of the few white mayors in a predominantly black city, has shown an intense focus on the "micro": taking care to visit people in their homes in the evenings to discuss issues relating to the city, fostering a trustful working relationship between white and black communities through his role in managing hospitals, and aiming to solve microproblems such as broken streetlamps.

What struck me were two policy truths. First, Detroit was not going to be made great again by the various policy efforts spawned by Washington, DC, such as corporate tax cuts, protectionism, and quantitative easing. Second, and more important, Detroit was a city deprived of intangible infrastructure, and it was obvious that the elements of intangible infrastructure—such as the prospect of a university in Detroit, better schooling, more attention to both physical and mental health, reskilling of workers displaced by technology, and more apt local institutions—were exactly the factors needed to get the city thriving again. A similar example that reinforces this is the locally focused network of drug courts across the United States, which have an impressive track record of rehabilitating victims of America's opioid crisis.[38]

For Katherine Chidley, the lesson of Detroit is to resist being drawn to the conference rooms of the IMF and the groupthink of policy making and to spend some time with the people who voted for her, listening to the gritty details of the economic problems they face. In recent weeks she has learned a lot. Starting with the role of the business cycle as the basis for basic policy making, she has come to appreciate how fragile the post-financial-crisis recovery has been and, looking ahead, how the future will be conditioned by large imbalances in indebtedness (too high), productivity (too low), and the power of central banks (too much). Her advisers have impressed upon her the tricks of the policy trade: shorter-term ways of boosting growth, such as tax cuts. Some of her colleagues are drawn to the idea of making countries great—effectively getting other nations to take the blame and pain for the end of globalization. Chidley's advantages are her relative youth and her patience—she wants to be in politics for some time. She is drawn to the idea of country strength, which relies on nations' developing a policy mind-set that cultivates economic resilience and that invests in intangible infrastructure. With a recession likely in coming years and with the trend rate of economic growth falling globally, Minister Chidley knows that she has to prioritize this approach.

The country strength framework will equip her with a long-term plan with coherent, detailed policy metrics that will guide her country's development. Country strength should prove an antidote to a world that is running out of steam economically, that is increasingly burdened by imbalances in the form of debt, and that increasingly neglects public goods. As a guide, she has the example of how other (often small, advanced) countries have done it. The country strength framework also incorporates the factors the Levellers emphasized, such as fairness and clarity of law. But before Minister Chidley sets a course for better-quality economic growth, there are a number of imbalances—record levels of indebtedness and the overbearing presence of central banks in markets and economies—that first need to be removed.

SEVEN

A WESTPHALIA FOR FINANCE

*Learning to Live Without the Central Bank
Comfort Blanket*

THE US SECURITIES AND EXCHANGE COMMISSION PRODUCES A LENGTHY guide on how to write financial statements, the preface of which is written by the famous investor Warren Buffett.[1] The essence of his advice is to keep things simple. More specifically, he says that when trying to explain something or write about finance, he pictures his two sisters as the ideal audience: they are clever though not finance specialists. I have taken his advice to heart and often ask my own sisters questions like, Have you heard of bitcoin? or, What is quantitative easing? Readers may pity my sisters. The point I am trying to get across is that even intelligent people (my sisters!) can find finance intimidating and opaque, though it touches their lives in many ways.

A pertinent example is the activity of central banks. What they do is complicated, to say the least, but it affects our mortgages, the savings ability of younger generations, our pensions, and our investments. As a result, when the financial world is reaching extremes, people should take notice. Today, at least two interlinked financial facts are looming over economies, politics, and societies: first, the fact that world debt levels are higher today than before the global financial crisis, and second, the dominant position of central banks, which in their own ways have encroached into the world of politics and arguably diminish the responsibility of elected officials.

To put this in context, let's go back again to the time of the Levellers. A couple of years after they had issued the final Agreement of the People, the philosopher Thomas Hobbes published *Leviathan*, now a well-known text in political philosophy. In this and in his earlier texts *The Elements of Law* and *De cive*, Hobbes takes a pessimistic view of the human race and argues that as a precondition for order to prevail, man must surrender himself to a Leviathan.

The Leviathan as conceived by Hobbes was a greater form of being, thought in the context of the English Civil War to represent both the king and the Parliament.[2] In Hobbes's world, liberty was surrendered for order and a higher degree of sociopolitical certainty. The Levellers had a different view, one that was much more hopeful for humanity and very much the antithesis of Hobbes's view of liberty. (Hobbes spent much of the Leveller period living in Paris, and there is not a great deal of evidence to suggest that he interacted with them or with members of the New Model Army.) The Levellers wanted freedom for all people from dominant political creatures like the Leviathan and from the kind of arbitrary rule they might impose.

Trading Freedom for Order

Looking at the world today, it seems that there is a growing fondness for a Leviathanic approach to governance (freedom is sacrificed for order). Notably, in China it appears from the outside that liberty is curtailed and freedom of expression is rationed so that the greater project of order and national progress can prosper. We can take this view a step further and say that today the version of the world proposed by the Levellers' agreement and that proposed by the *Leviathan* are increasingly competing models of governance. One is the classical republican view that supports strong institutions and democratic and liberal values and espouses a more interlinked and interdependent world order. The other is a world where countries, and perhaps also companies, are run by small groups whose bargain with the people is to exchange liberty for order and a sense of national prestige. The distinction between these two views is not limited to democracy, nor is it limited to the distinction between developed and developing worlds. It can also be applied to finance. Specifically, in the developed economies—the United Kingdom, Japan, the United States, and Europe—Hobbes's vision of the Leviathan seems increasingly manifest in the form of central banks.

Since the global financial crisis, they have become part of a great Faustian bargain in which central banks provide economic and financial stability—at great effort—in return for encroaching deep into the territory of policy making, politics, and financial markets. Central banks dominate all three areas today—though few people realize this.

Going back to the late 1990s, each bout of economic crisis has seen political, economic, and international institutional powers surrendered to central banks, to the extent that in recent years they have been described as the "only game in town."[3] Paul Tucker, an insider in central banking at the Bank of England, makes this point eloquently in his book *Unelected Power: The Quest for Legitimacy in Central Banking and the Regulatory State*. The Leviathan-like bargain central banks appear to have struck is to buy financial and economic stability in exchange for an inordinate level of influence over world affairs. It is important to stress that I am not suggesting that there has been a conspiracy by central bankers to acquire power, but few have tried very hard to unburden themselves of it. But the costs of this bargain are growing. Financially, in the dulling of market sensitivities to economic and financial imbalances, to inequality, and to the numbing of the urgency for politicians to address a litany of critical issues.

"You Must Have Misunderstood Me"

The sense of the mystical power of central banks in the modern era effectively began with Paul Volcker (chairman of the Federal Reserve from 1979 to 1987) and continued during the long tenure of Alan Greenspan from 1987 to 2006.[4] In the 1990s, investors curious to divine the future path of interest rates looked at the size of Greenspan's briefcase.[5] If it was packed with material, then the Fed chief was arming himself to persuade colleagues of the need to raise interest rates. Today, central bankers do much of the predicting for investors, releasing forecasts of the future path of rates (forecasts that have regularly been wrong) and sometimes indulging in brave and bold open communications, memorably in the case of ECB president Mario Draghi's "do whatever it takes" comment during a speech in London in July 2012. At the time, the eurozone economy was struggling, and bond yields for periphery countries (Italy, Spain, Greece, Portugal, and Ireland) were very high. Draghi compared the euro to a bumblebee—which shouldn't be able to fly but does—and then, having accounted for the structural progress made in the development of the euro, he declared, "But there is another message I want to tell you. Within our mandate, the ECB is ready to do whatever it takes to preserve the euro. And believe me, it will be enough."[6]

Greenspan had little time for such clarity. He famously commented, "If I have made myself clear, you must have misunderstood me."[7] This comment was part of a rich heritage of obfuscation by central bankers. Montagu Norman, the secretive governor of the Bank of England in the 1920s and '30s, used to emphasize the code "Never explain, never excuse." Greenspan's generation and that of predecessors like Paul Volcker were inflation crushers and rate raisers (to 20 percent in Volcker's case). He at least believed that investors and economies had to bear the consequences of economic imbalances.

Much of the openness and clarity that characterizes central banks today result from attempts to correct the Greenspan approach. It is generally accepted that the lax regulatory and monetary approach of the Greenspan Federal Reserve led to the swelling of Wall Street and the financialization of the housing sector in the United States, which then helped produce the global financial crisis. One of the ironies of Greenspan's career is that his PhD thesis tackled the link between economic activity and asset prices and examined the danger that rising asset prices pose to the business cycle.

However, in seeking to amend for the sins of the Greenspan era, central banks have arguably been answering too little intervention in the early part of the twenty-first century with too much today. The major central banks now play an outsized role in markets and in many cases have come to dominate them. In the late 1990s, effectively the early part of this period of globalization, a well-known trade economist, Jagdish Bhagwati, called US multinationals the "B-52's of capitalism."[8] This place in the vanguard of world affairs has now been taken by the major central banks, and we might even replace the term "B-52" with something more domineering, such as "empires" or "gods of Finance." Increasingly, central banks have reinforced the fault lines associated with a stretched and strained world, and perhaps without realizing it they have exacerbated many of the causes of the levelling. There is now a strong case to be made that central banks, in overreacting to the economic and financial issues besetting the world, many of them structural or design issues (in the case of the eurozone), are diminishing their own credibility and creating new risks.

Lombard Street

Central banks were not always so powerful. The oldest central banks, the Bank of England (founded in 1694 as the debt-management office of the government) and Sweden's Riksbank (founded in 1668) have great pedigrees, but in general they were not as accommodative in the past as they are now.[9]

The financing of wars, state bankruptcies, and financial crises were more frequent in centuries past, and in many cases the outcomes were starker. For instance, in the second half of the nineteenth century there were several railway bubbles. Indeed, in 1900 railway stocks accounted for over 60 percent of the market capitalization of the US stock market and for 50 percent of the UK stock market. In the nineteenth century, financial panics (such as in 1893) were more frequent than in recent decades, partly because there were few financial system safety nets to prevent them, and in fact many of today's central banks did not exist then.

These frequent crises and the habitual collapse of banks led Walter Bagehot, a journalist (one of the early writers for the *Economist*, which was owned by his father-in-law), to write *Lombard Street*, in which he distilled his observations on the British banking system. One of his recommendations was that in a crisis central banks should lend freely to solvent institutions, provided they would receive high-quality collateral in return and on the condition that this lending would not distort financial incentives. Bagehot's dictum was resurrected during the global financial crisis, though it may well be said that central banks have increasingly ignored his prescriptions in supporting weak banking systems in countries like Italy and Portugal.[10]

The era in which Bagehot lived saw the beginnings of the first wave of globalization, and the later part of this period, in the early 1900s, was marked by financial and economic crises (e.g., in 1907) as well as political ones. The severity of the economic turbulence in the early part of the century begot the need for a central bank in the United States, and by 1913 the Federal Reserve System had been established.

One of the better accounts of how central banks acquired their power comes from Liaquat Ahamed's *Lords of Finance*, which as a book is refreshing for its passion and detail and as a story is notable for the way a small group of individuals coordinated policy and set the foundations of the international financial system as we know it. The heads of the US, British, French, and German central banks in the 1920s constituted the first "committee to save the world."[11] Compared to today's central bankers, those of the 1920s were a somewhat strange and difficult bunch, and one lesson we may draw from the consequences of their actions is that the aftermath of financial crises can have long-running political implications, with Germany of the 1920s and '30s being a case in point.

One policy question that arose in the 1920s is how central bankers should react to bubbles in asset prices: should they act early to halt exuberance, or should they accept that this is neither the responsibility nor within the capability of central banks? Financial market bubbles are usually evident with the benefit of hindsight,[12] though often the behavior of people involved in a financial market bubble is a good indication of its existence. Charles Kindleberger and Robert Aliber's book *Manias, Panics, and Crashes* is perhaps the best text on the topic, though Charles MacKay's *Extraordinary Popular Delusions and the Madness of Crowds*, published in 1841, is a reminder that investors and perhaps policy makers do not learn from history.

Sorcerer's Apprentices

The global financial crisis, centered on the US housing market, had many of the classic characteristics of a bubble. The rise in house prices was leveraged in different ways: in the enormous amounts of derivative contracts that multiplied the risks of a fall in house prices, in the very large amounts of debt taken out by households in relation to stretched housing valuations, and in the business model of banks.

Banks and bankers acted like J. W. Goethe's Sorcerer's Apprentice: their financial innovations produced an explosive cocktail of risk. In this respect, the blame for the financial crisis lies at the feet of the banking and financial services industry. Equally, much of the recent work of central bankers has been directed at undoing and calming the damage done by the financial crisis. We should at the very least bear this in mind when criticizing the extremes to which central bankers have gone in their attempts to revive growth.

Financial market bubbles are an unfortunate and recurring part of central banks' relationship with financial markets and economies. The response to the emerging-market crisis in the late 1990s, a series of emergency interest rate cuts led by the Federal Reserve, helped create the dot-com bubble of the next decade, and, arguably, the policy response to the global financial crisis (over seven hundred interest rate cuts internationally by 2018) is creating extreme risks in economic and market behavior today. Central banks seem to keep wanting to juggle the plates without ever stopping the music and resolving the underlying economic problems we face. Most central banks have yet to raise interest rates; Mario Draghi is representative of many central bankers in that during his time as the head of the European Central Bank, he has only cut interest rates. Even the Federal Reserve, which has increased interest rates, remains a massive holder of government debt and is intellectually and psychologically deeply invested in quantitative easing as an ongoing policy tool.

Quantitative Easing

The debate on central banks and bubbles has evolved from the time of Alan Greenspan. The orthodoxy in central banking now centers on whether and how to use what are called "macroprudential" rules to guide the ebb and flow of financial activity. For instance, instead of raising interest rates to slow the rise of house prices, a central bank can require banks to make mortgage conditions (e.g., loan to property value ratios) more stringent. In China, the authorities are now beginning to face many of these questions. In the context of historically very high house prices, excessive industrial capacity, and generally high levels of debt, Chinese authorities have begun a process of deleveraging: trying to get companies, business people, and companies to pare down debt levels.

Since the financial crisis, central banks have followed two paths in response to the shockwaves unleashed in 2007: a QE-led drive to push interest rates down to and below zero and a regulatory regime that aims to increase the capital that banks hold on their balance sheets and to oversee their activities in much greater detail.[13] In many cases these efforts have helped slowly support economic growth and make banks less risky. But in recent years central banks have overstretched to the extent that they are creating new fault lines. In particular, they are sowing the seeds of a more multipolar financial system where banks are less interlinked than they were before the global financial crisis and where the lion's share of their business takes place within, as opposed to between, regions.

Quantitative easing, the chief element in central banks' response to the financial crisis, has its roots in a 2002 speech by Ben Bernanke, then a member of the Federal Reserve Board and later the successor to Alan Greenspan as its chair. Bernanke's speech may have started as an intellectual musing on what the Fed should do if it were confronted with the enduring combination of low inflation and low growth that followed the collapse of the Japanese house-price bubble in the 1990s. Bernanke listed nine new and dramatic policy measures that could, theoretically, be enacted were the United States to be confronted by a severe financial economic shock. At the time, he probably did not consider that he would end up implementing most of those measures.

One of the first emergency policy steps by the Fed was the announcement in late 2008 that it would buy mortgage-backed securities. From then on, consistent with the Bernanke speech, the Federal Reserve adopted a broad policy of quantitative easing—simply put, of buying government bonds in order to push down long-term interest rates (bond yields or rates move inversely to bond prices, so extra demand for bonds from central banks pushes bond prices up and drives yields down). The first, positive effect of this was to support financial market confidence, providing the conditions whereby US banks issued large amounts of debt to better fund their balance sheets. The intended longer-term effect was that businesses and households, seeing the fall in long-term interest rates, would feel better placed to invest and consume more.

The best analogy I can think of to explain quantitative easing is a medical one. A person who has had a heart attack or a bad accident is often given adrenaline to stimulate the heart. This works well on a one-off basis and helps doctors better manage the patient while a long-term recovery plan is put in place. However, in central banking, every day for the past decade has been an adrenaline day. Central bankers should know that adrenaline doesn't fix broken legs or mend clogged hearts. In this respect, Europe's Mario Draghi has a whole ward full of sick patients—some mad as well as unwell. Giving them monetary drugs will suppress their pain but not make them better. Worse, over time they and those around them will develop an addiction to monetary drugs. So a more disciplined doctor/central banker might prescribe a short burst of monetary morphine, followed by economic restructuring by, for example, permitting bankruptcies, closures of defunct businesses and banks, and skill development and funding for new businesses.

House of Debt

Some central bankers have talked about this line of reasoning, but hardly any have acted this way. So, as QE has continued, its long-run net effect has become steadily less economically impactful.[14] The initial changes in both market returns and growth in response to quantitative easing were strong, but in the period running up to the election of Donald Trump as US president, the immense effort of central banks had produced a lingering, lethargic recovery. Economic growth and inflation had failed to respond to additional waves of QE, so much so that economic commentators spoke of "secular stagnation" and a "new normal" (lower growth being normal). As Atif Mian and Amir Sufi's book *House of Debt* notes, consumers who were encumbered by already-high levels of household debt, lower house prices, and an uncertain economic outlook saved extra cash or used it to pay off debt rather than spend it. Broadly speaking, both of these factors have contributed to a slow and drawn out recovery in the United States. In many instances, the ongoing prosecution of QE created a sense that something was still wrong with the economy (which left a lingering uncertainty in the minds of consumers) and did little to directly lower debt levels.

QE also became fashionable in the United Kingdom, the eurozone, and Japan. One reason may have been that the Fed is regarded as the intellectual leader among central banks, and there is a large degree of groupthink among the major central banks and the academics who feed into them. Another reason for the popularity of QE programs is that one of their pronounced effects, at least in their early stages, is to weaken the currency of the central bank that prosecutes them. In this way, the effect of QE is to help make export-oriented companies more competitive, though often to the detriment of competing companies from other regions.

In this respect, regions beyond the United States had an incentive to also implement their own QE programs. It has led to what a former Brazilian finance minister, Guido Mantega, called "currency wars," the stealth (or in some cases, not very subtle) currency devaluations undertaken by the major economic regions. For example, in the wake of QE programs in the United States and Japan, the euro traded at a stubbornly high level of 1.38 (to the dollar), but once the ECB hinted at and then began QE, it fell to close to parity with the dollar, boosting the competitiveness of German exporters, among other effects. This was good for Germany as the leading export economy in Europe, but it raised suspicions in other currency zones that the ECB was participating in stealth devaluation.

Intended at first as an emergency policy, QE has now become the norm. In the aftermath of Brexit, for instance, the Bank of England reignited its QE program. Sweden's Riksbank gives us perhaps the best example of how QE clouds the judgment of a central banker, and the way QE is prosecuted by the Riksbank is akin to dousing a fire with petrol. Between the years 2016–2017, the Riksbank continued to engage with a QE program, despite GDP growth of close to 5 percent, mounting inflation, and house-price growth of nearly 10 percent.

The Only Game in Town

The impact of QE on markets has been profound, and in sharp contrast to the performance of real-world indicators. From the first announcement of quantitative easing by the US Federal Reserve in 2009 to October 2018, the Standard & Poor's (S&P) 500 Index is up nearly 270 percent, the European high-yield benchmark is up 230 percent, and the Morgan Stanley Capital International (MSCI) Emerging Markets Index is up 150 percent, as compared to only 20 percent aggregate rises in inflation, wages, and house prices across the United States. Understandably, then, financial markets are entirely in thrall to the priming of central banks, and to a large extent "playing" QE has been an enduring investment theme for investors across asset classes. It is no exaggeration to say that central banks have become "the market" in many different respects. First, they simply own large swathes of financial markets, mostly debt (and, in the case of the Bank of Japan, also equity: it owns 3 percent of the total Japanese equity market capitalization and 60 percent of exchange-traded funds in Japan and is ranked as a top-ten shareholder in 833 companies in Japan).

Second, they have turned many markets into one-way, crowded investment positions. It is very difficult for investors to trade against central banks or to try and engage in arbitrage activity in markets. For instance, an investor worried about the economic and political outlook for France might sell or even take a short position in French bonds, but the impact of QE may well render this strategy highly unprofitable. As a result markets are desensitized to fundamental data and to risks in the world economy. The market reaction to Brexit is a very good example. Stock markets initially fell but then rallied as central bank chiefs reiterated their supportive stances for accommodative monetary policy and as the Bank of England cut interest rates to the lowest since it was established in 1694.

More broadly, the ongoing presence of QE produces a confusing investment climate where fundamental factors become less relevant in investment decision making and where investors are induced to follow the activity of central banks. As QE drives down long-term interest rates, there is greater demand for assets with a yield. In many cases, high-dividend-yielding equities and riskier corporate bonds fit that category.

Capital may then be misallocated in that investors who would normally buy government bonds (like Treasuries) for the yield they offer are forced to buy other yielding assets (because QE has pushed down the yield on government bonds, making them less attractive). The problem is that the other yielding assets—risky company debt (high yield), risky country debt (emerging-market debt), and equities—are not as safe as government bonds, so investors may end up holding a riskier asset than intended. Some companies reinforce this, in some cases by issuing debt to pay higher dividends that make their equity securities more attractive, even though the process may make the company more vulnerable in a downturn.

One implication of this is that pension funds and insurance companies, who rely on a supply of yielding assets in order to match them against the stream of liabilities they face, can no longer find yielding assets to buy at reasonable prices. This may in turn accentuate future pension liabilities. Another issue is that the low-interest-rate environment has allowed many zombie companies to tread water, prolonging economic risks and suppressing productivity.[15]

Central banking, as I hope you now can see, is on the one hand, arcane and complex, and on the other, relevant to our daily lives, even though we barely feel its presence.[16] In the past ten years, central banks have reigned over bank systems, the wealth held in pension funds, the sanctity of multilateral organizations such as the eurozone, and the rise and fall of currencies.

The collective response of central banks to the global financial crisis undoubtedly staved off greater chaos in markets and potentially prevented a deeper recession worldwide. A more serious criticism is that central banks have simply delayed the reckoning of deep-seated economic fault lines, have not boosted economic potential, and have created new risks in financial markets and international economies. As their role and importance have grown, they have sapped the power of markets and governments. The now dominant role of central banks makes them a central player in the levelling of the international economic order. In this respect, they are central to several fault lines.

Fault Lines

One fault line is that quantitative easing has dramatically exacerbated wealth inequality, which is at its worst levels in decades. In theory, the aim of QE was to lower long-term interest rates so that households could have access to cheaper capital. However, in the context of a toughening regulatory regime, the effect of the credit crisis on lending standards of banks and the fact that many households and businesses were already overburdened with debt or were risk averse meant that very few households could get access to loans at low interest rates or had the spare capital to buy cheap post-crisis assets.[17]

For example, in September 2016 Italian government bonds traded at a yield of 1.1 percent but Italian mortgage rates were closer to 7 percent. In essence, this meant that only those who already had access to capital could benefit from QE by borrowing at low interest rates to buy cheap assets; ordinary households had to borrow at 7 percent. In some cases, the purchase of real estate by property funds (which were also able to access cheap capital) drove up property prices, putting pressure on affordability.

In many countries wealthier people tend to hold more securities (e.g., equities and corporate bonds), and they have clearly benefited from QE, to the extent that in 2018 equity valuations were close to the most expensive end of their historical range (touching levels only seen in 1929 and 2000); the same was true of corporate bonds. From a relative wealth point of view, this again helps those with existing securities portfolios, though it must be said that investors deserve some compensation for holding risky assets in uncertain times. Underlying this, in May 2017, when ECB president Draghi testified on quantitative easing to the Dutch Parliament, he was presented with a solar-powered tulip (by Pieter Duisenberg, son of the first ECB president, Wim Duisenberg) to underscore to him the parallel between the tulip-mania asset price bubble of the mid-seventeenth century and the price of eurozone financial assets (government bonds).

Furthermore, because valuations for asset classes like equities and corporate bonds are now so high, the future returns they produce will inevitably be limited, thereby limiting the growth in the value of pensions. There is also a growing dilemma for millennials, who will struggle to find assets that generate a decent return around which they can build a pension. It should also be highlighted that households who have traditionally been savers and who may fear investing in financial markets have been financially disadvantaged by the race to lower interest rates.

Most importantly from the point of view of the levelling, there is also an important link between QE, markets, and politics. In some quarters, ranging from academia and journalism to politics, people may believe that financial markets are big casinos (in 2002 the Japanese finance minister, Kiichi Miyazawa, referred to the Japanese market as a gambling den)[18] or mechanisms through which wealthy people manipulate events and fortunes. This is not quite true. Markets play a very important role in signaling. The movements and levels of market prices tell us a great deal about the health of companies and countries and the state of the world we live in.

Markets are important warning mechanisms, especially when it comes to bad economic policy. Famously, Bill Clinton's political adviser James Carville said that if he were to be reincarnated, he would like to return as "the bond market" because it is so powerful.[19] In the past, market strategists, such as Ed Yardeni, have spoken of "bond vigilantes," referring to the fact that the bond market curbed excessive borrowing (and inflation) by governments by penalizing them for reckless borrowing with higher bond yields.[20]

A good example of the role bond markets play in signaling economic health is the information in bond yields across the eurozone countries. Let's pick on Italy again. For a long time the bond yield of Italy traded some way above that of Germany (in the mid-1990s the difference between Italian and German yields was close to 8 percent, signaling that Italy had more inflation than Germany and was a riskier economy). In 2017, for example, Italian bond yields traded at a yield differential to Germany of just above 1.5 percent, which suggested that markets thought Italy was nearly as safe an investment proposition as Germany, but in reality that would be strange for a country with an enormous debt load and little growth. Ask yourself whether a household already laden with debt and whose main bread winner was barely bringing in enough money to cover the mortgage interest payments would get such a generous interest rate from a bank. It is unlikely to happen, though in the case of Italy and other eurozone countries like Portugal, this kind of anomaly is ever present. One might ask whether the market is mispricing the risks of Italian debt or whether it is simply soporifically following the bidding of the ECB. The answer is that investors are not pricing risks as they should but are simply following the lead of the central bank.

European central bankers would argue that artificially low interest rates for Italy are a necessary evil. Their view would be that higher bond yields for Italy would hurt its economy, delay necessary economic and political reforms, and lead to further instability in its banking system. A cynic would argue that bond buying by the ECB is a complex form of a Band-Aid: an improvised attempt to cover up the shortcomings of the euro system. The cynic might point to the lesson offered by the various episodes of the eurozone financial crisis in which Europe's politicians only seemed to act when pushed to do so by market volatility. The logical extension of this is that a market crisis is required in order to advance policy in Europe. This might seem strange and counterproductive to American or Asian ears, but the construction of the European Union has habitually required crises in order to move it forward, because the many nations of the European Union have different aims and priorities, and these only become aligned in the most pressing of circumstances.

Nevertheless, making policy under duress is still the worst way to do so, and an emergency is the worst circumstance under which to implement it. The austerity programs in Greece and Ireland are good examples of this. An alternative would be a marketplace free of the sedative of QE (or even a marketplace where QE was only triggered at certain yield levels so as to prevent chaotic runs on bond markets). Such a market climate would also be one where politicians and policy makers had the moral courage to stick to the rules laid out in the framework governing the euro. In this circumstance, bond markets would more accurately signal the true health of economies and country balance sheets. In turn, this would probably force politicians to enact economic reforms and lead investors, corporations, and to a degree households to act in a more responsible and careful way in terms of the amount of debt they take on.

The Future of Central Banking

In 2018, the Federal Reserve began to step slowly, carefully back from quantitative easing programs, and other major central banks hinted at an era of policy normalization. The next recession or financial crisis will test their mettle. Have they simply throttled back extraordinary monetary policy, ready to rev it up again, or are they willing to step back in principle from the positions of overwhelming power they find themselves in?

There are three avenues down which central bankers can travel. The first is more of the same: to continue to use central bank balance sheets to curb markets and to try to stimulate growth. Under this option there will be plenty of talk of "adding to the toolbox," that is, inventing new measures to try to coax growth out of sluggish economies.[21] The results may simply be more market distortion, a dwindling sense of urgency among politicians as to their task lists, and an undermining of the credibility of central banks as independent public institutions.

If anything, recent pronouncements from central bankers suggest that, in the case of a recession, the consensus view among monetary economists supports more aggressive bouts of monetary stimulus rather than the disengagement of central banks in favor of fiscal-policy-led solutions to low growth.[22] Public discussions by central bankers in the United States and Europe, for example, point toward a mind-set that is now set on zero and negative rates as the default policy stance of major central banks. My worry is that these seemingly aggressive policies will prove ineffective in the face of a serious economic shock, such as a full recession in China, which would sharply curb economic demand globally.

The second avenue is for central bankers to step back and let politicians use fiscal policy more actively. The rationale here is that active fiscal policy in the context of cheap money would stir the embers of the world economy. In certain cases this might work, but it comes too late. Fiscal policy like infrastructure programs tends to work with a lag. For this reason it is often best deployed at the bottom of a recession because it cushions the blow of a downturn and helps provide the basis for a recovery, particularly if money is wisely spent. At the time of this writing, some large economies—the United States and China—are heading toward their next natural, or likely, recession. In this case, their fiscal powder is best kept dry for a couple of years rather than being ignited unproductively now. The other side of fiscal policy, structural reform (such as making labor markets more dynamic), is something for which most politicians have little appetite.

A third option is to stop the range of extraordinary measures being deployed by central banks altogether. A very bold framing of this would be an agreement or world treaty on risk, crafted along the lines of large-scale environmental or nuclear weapons deals. Under such an agreement, the world's major central banks would agree to use extraordinary measures like QE only under preset conditions (great market and economic stresses). It would, of course, be much more appropriate if the political masters of central banks were the ones to sign and seal such an agreement rather than again leaving central bankers with the responsibility. The effect would be that markets would properly price risks and that, in turn, politicians would therefore act to address economic risks and fault lines. If extraordinary monetary policy needed to be launched, it would be more effective. This scenario is my own preference, though I suspect that most central bankers would still opt for the first scenario, in which the central bank acts as a monetary Death Star.

A Treaty to End All Treaties

The most crucial challenge for central bankers over the next decade will be navigating the transition from globalization to a multipolar world in the context of low growth and high debt. The passage from a free-flowing globalized world to a more level one where multiple political economic poles exert growing influence is likely to be noisy and tense. It will be further marked by a natural recession in the United States caused by a mixture of rising rates, credit stresses in student loans (which have now shot past $1.5 trillion) and auto and real estate loans, corporate debt and governance issues, increasingly conservative consumption patterns, the risk of protectionism, and the threat of a global demand shock from a significant economic crisis in China, to list just a few scary scenarios.[23] The ability of the United States and China to digest economic weaknesses and emerge in better shape will shape their competitive relationship for the next twenty years. China in particular faces a bigger risk than the United States because it has not had an official recession since at least 2000 and will probably be confronted with a slowdown in its property sector, and such downturns (i.e., in housing or credit) tend to be more severe than normal cyclical recessions.[24]

In that respect, the rate of China's economic progress may be checked for some time. Against the international landscape, a debt-based recession for China would represent the logical end of the mixture of globalization and debt cycles we have witnessed since 1990. The Anglo-Saxon countries were the first to experience their debt crises in 2008 and are now seeing the political fallout. Then came Europe's turn in 2011, and its political class was slow to respond. For instance, it took five summits of EU heads to decide on measures that would stanch the financial and economic damage of the eurozone crisis. Against this backdrop, a third crisis in the near future centered on China would have a certain logic if not inevitability.

Old Debt in New Economies

A crisis in China's economy would also mean that the three great regions had, with near-biblical significance, been touched by the painful implications of taking on too much risk and too much debt. As Europe and, still, parts of the US economy show, the burden of high debt levels can be severe in its impact on trend growth and on social issues. "Old" debt—that is, debt taken on in a previous business cycle—and the ways in which it is resolved can act as a handbrake on an economy, or, to use a different analogy, old debt is like fat clogging the arteries of the economy and at some stage will need to be operated on.

After the global financial crisis, international debt levels initially dropped (especially in the financial sector), but they have risen again, encouraged by the effects of quantitative easing. World indebtedness (households, companies, governments, and finance companies) stood at over 320 percent of world GDP at the end of 2018, above the 2008 peak of 300 percent. Between 2014 and the end of 2018 we saw government debt rise, bank debt fall, and corporate debt mount.

Household debt in emerging countries has also risen steadily: during the Asian crisis of the late 1990s it reached 75 percent of GDP but is 90 percent today, which is a sign of the consumer and housing boom across many emerging countries. China itself carries a historically large debt burden. Total debt in China now stands at 250 percent of GDP according to the IMF, which notes that a sharp rise in credit, like the one China has enjoyed, is often a precursor to financial and housing crises.[25] The Spaniards and the Irish would, with the benefit of hindsight, agree with this view. As debt has grown in China, its contribution to growth has incrementally slowed in the sense that an extra renminbi of debt taken on today has much less impact on growth than it might have had five years ago.[26]

In developed markets household indebtedness has dropped, just, from its 2009 peak. In certain countries that have seen house prices rally—Australia, Norway, Sweden, Switzerland, Canada, and the Netherlands—household debt has risen to a high level, which is typically a warning sign.[27] In the United States, there are several debt stress points: corporate debt (relative assets) is now higher than in 2007, and at the household level overdue US credit card debt is at a seven-year high of $12 trillion. The Congressional Budget Office's long-term outlook is depressingly bleak.[28] It holds that the United States is on course to reach the highest level of debt relative to GDP in the nation's history by far, whose implications, they very politely state, pose "substantial risks for the nation." In general, in much of the rest of the developed world, especially Europe, debt levels are equally precarious.

Debt has been allowed to build because central banks have kept interest rates low. The trade-off they have made is for short-term stability in exchange for a rise in risk taking as debt mountains have grown. As we move through 2019, the combination of incrementally less quantitative easing and higher inflation could dramatically ignite this great debt burden. Historically, spikes in indebtedness are associated first with a rise in growth, followed by a sharp fall. In general, high levels of debt (from 80 percent debt to GDP upward) are associated with lower levels of GDP growth. For example, countries with debt to GDP in the 50–70 percent bracket tend to have GDP growth rates of 2 percentage points higher than those with debt to GDP in the 110 percent plus bracket. When interest rates are low, the risks associated with bad loans are less obvious, but as rates rise, default rates can climb quickly.

The tide of higher interest rates in the United States has been slowly creeping in since 2018 when the Federal Reserve made a series of rate hikes. With two-year US Treasury yields having pushed close to 3 percent, the pressure on indebted companies, emerging-market countries, and households will grow. Elsewhere across the world, interest rates are still abnormally low. In Germany, five-year interest rates are just popping above zero for the first time since 2014, despite very low German unemployment, which remains a sign that investors do not yet trust the recovery in the eurozone.

In emerging markets, government debt has risen, though only close to 50 percent of GDP, as compared to 90 percent for many large developed countries. The sharpest rise in government indebtedness has come from companies, predominantly in countries in China's orbit (Singapore, Hong Kong, Chile, Thailand, and China itself). It is also worth flagging that China's One Belt, One Road program is creating a trail of debt in the countries through which it passes—Pakistan and Sri Lanka, for example.

China, though its economic management has been miraculous at times, cannot avoid the effects of economic gravity. Its economy is vulnerable to several fault lines: the complex unprofitability and leverage of its state-owned enterprises, extremely high property prices, and the explosive wealth-management products in the financial services sector. The lessons of indebtedness are learned the hard way, but given that slower globalization implies lower growth, it is clear that the large world economies need to reduce debt levels and better manage risk taking.

One discussion to emerge from the eurozone crisis centered on how countries might reduce debt. The main options are growing their economies, allowing inflation to rise, and restructuring the debt (note that as the eurozone crisis deepened, the thinking of bodies like the IMF on debt forgiveness changed and it adopted a more pragmatic, favorable view of debt restructuring, albeit too late for the likes of Greece and Ireland). The solutions that the European Union and IMF had cooked up for the eurozone as a whole—austerity being the lead one—have not worked well in reducing the debt burden. In Europe today, debt levels in key economies—France (99 percent debt to GDP), Spain (99 percent), and Italy (132 percent)—are at multidecade highs and far above what is regarded as sustainable. Ireland has been a relative success, with debt to GDP falling from 119 percent in 2013 to 68 percent by 2018, though the impact of austerity on the country has been severe.

European debt levels are modest only in comparison to Japan's government debt (229 percent). Japan, however, does have a large pool of household savings, which means that there should always be a buyer for its debt. Japanese households might find this an intimidating assumption. It should be mentioned that these figures do not account for household or corporate debt, which in some countries has reached gargantuan levels—notably China, where debt levels are topping those reached in Japan in 1989 (Japanese land prices today are still worth half what they were in 1991), Thailand in 1996, and Spain in 2009, and we know what happened next in those instances. We should, of course, add into this mix the sharp rise in US corporate debt, much of it taken on for the purposes of financial engineering.

In this context, a recession in the near future may well lead to an international debt crisis and a period of dislocation in debt markets. In response, governments may look to the two avenues of monetary and fiscal policy to steady economies. However, we have already seen that monetary policy, even in its most inventive forms, can be ineffective in the context of high debt, low potential growth, and unfriendly demographics because these dull the spark it provides. The best it can do is dull the pain of recession.

One idea that has been circulated among central bankers, especially those fond of quantitative easing, is that in highly indebted countries like Japan, central banks should simply swallow the government debt that they hold on their balance sheets. In central banker and accounting speak, this "monetization" of debt (the financing of government debt by central banks) sounds very attractive: governments print debt, then politicized or intellectually captured central banks swallow it and at most require governments to issue perpetual bonds to cover the accounting transaction on the central bank balance sheet. It is as elegant as a perpetual motion machine.

In reality this cannot work. Suppose that Japan were to do this. Given its recent financial history, households would smell a rat, become more risk averse, and expect that the value of their pensions could be endangered, and, arguably, deflation would take hold again. Then markets, equally suspicious of this monetary magic, would begin to rethink the creditworthiness of the entire Japanese financial system, the yen would collapse, and the yields on Japanese corporate debt would shoot higher, forcing many companies into bankruptcy. If other monetary jurisdictions followed the Japanese example, there would be massive currency volatility and very soon a loss of faith in central banks, with a resulting rush to gold and other proxy currencies (even bitcoin).

In time, further QE-based experiments may bring central banks to a fork in the monetary road in terms of their efforts to support economies. The presence of record amounts of debt in the world economy greatly complicates this. It may well lead to what we call "QE inequality," where the prosecution of QE by diverse central banks will have increasingly variable results. There is a risk that for some central banks, the further deployment of QE will lead to a market backlash and become a policy error in that, for example, currency volatility and economic uncertainty easily offset any impact from asset purchases.

Magically monetizing debt will simply create new financial problems. Fiscal policy might help indebted economies in certain cases, but those that need it most will run into trouble as higher fiscal spending typically means higher borrowing. I might as well also mention structural reforms to labor markets and in general a resetting of incentive structures, but the reality is that in the countries that have the highest debt levels, borrowing represents an easier road than politically difficult reforms. In this context, and barring wild currency depreciations as means of fixing debt burdens, a gloomy scenario is that by 2021 the world economy could be mired in low growth and the three major regions congested with debt. We need to ask whether there are any solutions to this.

Brady Plan and Denial

At some stage economic historians may cast their minds back to debt restructurings of old. Here, the Brady Plan for the Latin American countries comes to mind. The plan, introduced in 1989, was named after Nicholas Brady, the US treasury secretary at the time, who led the effort to restructure the debt of a range of Latin American countries following the Latin American economic crisis of the mid 1980s and the subsequent debt default by many Latin American countries such as Mexico and Argentina. The achievement of the Brady Plan was to break the ties in the original debt chain by making liquid the Latin American debt held by banks. It also provided some forms of guarantees and restructuring options so that the interest rates charged on the new restructured debt could fall and the debt could be widely traded. Without the backing of the US Treasury, international investors would probably not have bought the debt of Latin American countries, making it nearly impossible for them to finance themselves.

The Brady Plan did not happen quickly. It took seven years, from the beginning of the Latin American debt crisis in 1982 to its resolution, which may be indicative of the time it takes for governments to fully recognize the problems that debt presents and to accept the necessity to take difficult policy action to resolve it. David Mulford, the former undersecretary of the US Treasury, has remarked that the Brady Plan was only agreed to once all the participating governments fully recognized the economic truth that lay ahead of them: without a restructuring and the economic medicine that it entailed, their countries would be bankrupt.[29]

All this suggests that a new debt crisis may soon be on the horizon. The facts that the world economy is in the very late stages of a business cycle expansion, that it is lugging around the biggest debt burden in modern times, and that interest rates are beginning to rise point to a precarious start to the next decade. What is troubling is that debt crises can last for some time. The examples of the euro crisis and Latin America's debt restructuring suggest that a debt crisis that starts in, say, 2020 will really only end up being addressed after a lag, once things get really, really bad. That could be in 2024. Serendipitously, that would be the centenary of the 1924 International Debt Conference that produced the Dawes Plan to lessen the burden on Germany of the economic consequences of the First World War. Prior to 1924, the German economy had slowed, inflation had picked up, and its currency (the reichsmark) had collapsed. A new parallel currency, the rentenmark, was introduced.

It was backed by land, which effectively provided a store of value. After nearly nine months of negotiations—and following collateral damage to the French franc—a deal was struck. The Dawes Plan reduced the burden of reparations on Germany, funneled US-backed loans to Germany, and produced a temporary uplift in its economy. The Dawes Plan helped stabilize Germany, though arguably it tied the nation more closely to the fortunes of America, as the 1929 crash loomed on the horizon.

My forecast, and proposal, is that by 2024 the world will have had another recession, with high debt levels in China and corporate America as the kindling for this economic bonfire. Low productivity, political unrest, and exhausted government budgets will be some important factors that will make the escape velocity from the recession very slow. Central banks may try wave after wave of quantitative easing, but they will have little effect, save to heighten currency volatility. For some time, the developed world will blame the recession on China and then on the fat cats of corporate America. Soon, the realization will dawn that, with the third debt crisis in twelve years (after America in 2007 and Europe in 2011) upon the world, a massive and thorough debt restructuring is necessary.

In the event of a deep economic crisis, international governments and central banks may decide that an international debt conference is in order. It is hard to think that many governments would take part in such a conference voluntarily; such a conference would only come after rounds of unsuccessful quantitative easing, wild currency volatility, and market stress and with the world facing the prospect of a long global recession. Once conceived, an international conference on debt and economic risk taking may be part of the laying down of the initial rules of the game for a multipolar world, and, not unlike the system put in place in the Peace of Westphalia of 1648 that followed the Thirty Years' War, the new system may be one where nation-states begin to bear greater responsibility, in this case for their financial health.

Such a conference, though not unprecedented in recent history (think of the 1924 and 1953 debt conferences that allowed Germany debt relief), would be highly unusual, marking a debt restructuring of global proportions and bringing together the governments of the major economies. Ordinarily a body like the IMF would have a role here, but given the trend away from globalization and toward a multipolar world, I am going to speculate later in the book that some of the twentieth-century economic policy institutions we take for granted—the IMF, the World Bank, and WTO—may not exist by 2024. An international debt conference would mark an end of the road to the debt cycles spawned from the globalization process and would also mark an attempt to establish some of the financial rules of the new, multipolar world order.

I can see the conference taking place in Raffles Hotel in Singapore: the hotel's old-world charm might chime with 1924, and it is luxurious enough for bankers, ministers, and advisers to spend weeks there. Conveniently, it is located in a well-run country that is yet within reach of China. The debt conference would have an overriding aim of encouraging risk bearing rather than risk sharing of debt, in much the same way that the Peace of Westphalia encouraged individual states and statelets to bear political and identity risk. The conference would have two parts: an international debt-reduction agreement and a risk treaty that would encompass central banks and financial markets.

The debt agreement would have several components: to curb the debt issuance of eurozone countries; to provide a framework for the apportionment of regional, financial, and corporate debt in China; and to insulate the international financial system from the consequences of a debt implosion in Japan. Other issues will arise, such as the high burden of corporate debt in the United States, though one would expect that market forces would resolve this.

In other countries, the unwinding of debt is complicated by other factors. Consider Japan, where there is an intricate system of cross-holdings: trying to resolve the ultimate ownership of assets and liabilities is not at all clear. In China one of the great obstacles to a debt restructuring is the cultural need for the Chinese not to lose face. What this means is that, given the way the European Union and IMF treated the likes of Ireland, Greece, and Portugal, a debt restructuring may be construed as humiliating China, and as others drawing moral lessons from China's debt taking. If this were the case, it would greatly reduce the potential success of such a restructuring. Given these various complexities, such a debt conference would probably be a long one, and the bar at Raffles would probably be a busy place.

Solving Italy

The conveners of the debt conference will have a complex task, to put it lightly. This much is clear if we consider Italy and China as case studies. Let's start with Italy. It has one of the biggest bond markets in the world, and a Greek-style debt crisis in Italy would easily destabilize debt markets in the United States. With government debt in the United States rising to record levels, Italy is a cautionary tale.

Typically, in Europe when an economic crisis loomed, someone raised a hand to repeat the dictum by Jean Monnet (one of the founding fathers of the European Union) that "Europe needs a crisis to move forward." It is, however, worth noting a different point of view, from Monnet's father, a merchant from Cognac. This wily Charentais (Cognac is in the Charente department in France) is on record as saying, "Every new idea is a bad idea." Both Monnets might like the old idea of a debt restructuring conference, though applied in a new way.

With Cognac in mind, let's stay in Europe and look more closely at its southern members: Spain, Greece, Portugal, and Italy. This group of countries is unique among OECD member states in that their economies did not grow at all in the decade from 2007 to 2017. Considering them on their own, bond markets would avoid their debt, but the reassuring presence of the ECB—and its bond buying—means that investors are happier to buy Spanish debt today at lower yields (and therefore a lower premium for the risk that Spain presents) than at any other point in history, even the time of the Armada. The same is true for Italy. With over 130 percent debt to GDP and structurally low growth, Italy's long-term interest rates should probably be closer to 5 or 6 percent to reflect higher default risk (more like emerging-market than developed-world debt: household debt in Italy is relatively low but regional and local debt is high and underperforming).

The European Union has rules in place to warn, scold, and fine countries when they breach the so-called Stability and Growth Pact criteria. Weak leadership means these warnings have failed before (in the cases of Greece and France) and continue to fail. The best way of ensuring that countries stick to the rules is to introduce a form of market discipline and to place the burden of excess debt accumulation on individual states rather than on the eurozone itself. The aim should be to ensure that countries take responsibility for excesses in policy.

The task of paring down existing debt levels for the large eurozone countries will be complicated and politically vexatious.[30] It is likely to be made more difficult by the fact that by 2024 a lot of eurozone government debt will still be held by the ECB. Restructuring debt held by the ECB will be politically difficult, as it means that there will be a fractious debate as to who owns the losses associated with that restructuring. One hopes that by 2024 the European Union and the ECB will have put in place a formal mechanism by which a eurozone member country can exit the euro system (or be thrown out) and that this will not be costless, which might invite countries to default and leave. This might help to make the restructuring process more clear.

One solution, especially in the case of Italy, is to tie government debt to specific state assets. For example, the Italian government would take a bundle of government bonds that mature in 2032 with a face value of 20 billion euros and back these by 16 billion euros' worth of state assets (i.e., real estate, toll roads, and railways).

The idea here is that, depending on specific legal provisions, the interest payments and capital value of the government bonds would be backed, or collateralized, by the specific assets. In the case of Italy, a specific slice of debt might be backed by the revenues from the motorway from Milan to Venice, for instance, or by the equity in a state-owned enterprise. Then, if there was a default on Italian debt—which is what many people in the bond market habitually worry about—the ownership of the assets tied to the debt, or revenues from them, would go to the holders of the bonds.

The role of the debt conference would be to specify what assets could realistically be used to back the debt and the conditionality that might attach to such an arrangement. This would be politically very difficult, but financially it would redirect credit risk to individual country balance sheets and away from the euro system. Such a move would recognize the fact that there is only a limited amount of pan-European debt that can be issued or, as is currently the case, warehoused in the financial citadel that is the ECB.

This would mean that in terms of future debt issuance, the eurozone could rewrite its rules. Individual eurozone states could be given the right to issue between 60 and 70 percent's worth of their GDP, depending on the economic circumstances. This debt would have the backing of the eurozone's institutions in that it would be regarded as "euro debt." The result would mean lower bond yield differences between eurozone states, a reapportioning of risk back to national governments, and, it is to be hoped, a significant drop-off in existential risk for the euro system.

Then, any additional debt that a eurozone country feels it needs to raise after this would, as with modern bank loans, be backed by the revenues from specific projects or assets. This would help introduce some fiscal and financial discipline to government spending because politicians and debt management agencies would think more carefully about what debt is issued for. Markets would have a much better sense that, in the event of a debt crisis, specific assets would exist to support the debt. The aim here is to restore discipline to government finances, without imposing austerity, and to tie the raising of debt to specific assets. This should make for less corruption, lower defaults, and more-efficient government spending. In countries like Italy, it would severely discipline the spending and indebtedness of regional and city authorities.

An additional advantage is that it should encourage stimulative, development-oriented borrowing (e.g., for new ports). Other innovations can be introduced here—for example, a class of "euro city" bonds could be launched so that specific European cities could tap debt markets for development-led projects. Again, this would take some of the burden away from the European and national-government balance sheets and would have the benefit of tying specific assets and projects to debt issuance. In countries like Italy, this could help regional development: its government could decide to allow northern cities to issue city debt (which would probably trade at a low interest rate) and then tax the northern cities (or reduce federal spending on them) as a means of transferring development capital to the south.

In an age when further financial integration of the eurozone looks, to be euphemistic, challenging, the value in this approach is that, rather than spreading risk across the half-baked eurozone system, it ties debt issuance as closely as possible to its origins and therefore places the credit burden as closely as possible on the borrower.

Is China Spain?

In China a different approach may prevail, though similar risks are present. To a significant extent China is a closed financial system. Western banks and investors have relatively little direct exposure to Chinese investments (foreigners own only 2 percent of Chinese stocks), the renminbi makes up a very small proportion of international currency trade, and the Chinese banking system is not well integrated into the global financial system. Restrictions on capital outflows from China, by both the Chinese and US governments, have further closed China to the international financial system.

To this end, China might well be left to its own devices during and in the aftermath of a debt crisis. There are, however, other motivations for considering China part of an international debt conference, most notably its ability to cause a global economic shock and its potential role in the future deepening of global financial markets. Once it has de-leveraged, China will probably do with its financial markets what it has done with its physical infrastructure since the turn of the twenty-first century, and in time it will become a very significant player in debt and equity markets.

In addition to being the second-largest economy in the world, China is the locus of what we can call the "emerging-market complex," which now stretches from Russia to Peru and which more recently is winding its way along the Silk Road. China is the source of marginal demand for property in Australia, copper in Chile, and milk products in New Zealand. A prolonged Chinese recession would leave its mark across the rest of the world. It could cause China to sharply devalue its currency, which would undermine the economies of other emerging markets be-cause China's willingness to allow its currency to drift higher during the development of globalization has helped many Asian and other emerg-ing economies whose currencies were comparatively weaker.

China has lots of debt on the balance sheets of banks, regional au-thorities, and companies, and this has fueled an investment boom. In terms of the mass of investment relative to GDP, China today stands at 43 percent, which is higher than the peaks seen in Japan (36 per-cent in the 1970s) and South Korea (38 percent in 1991). In the years after investment peaked in Japan and South Korea, those countries had property and debt crises. Examining real estate–related indebted-ness in China today, we see that only three countries have accumulated private-sector debt (mostly for property speculation) at a greater rate than China's: Spain (2000–2010), Thailand (1987–1997), and Ireland (1999–2009). Each of these three countries subsequently had severe banking and economic crises. China has so far escaped a debt reckoning, but no country has had such extended credit growth and not had a cri-sis. China has so far avoided this by deft and at times aggressive tactical moves such as cutting capacity in heavy industries, attempting to balance growth and environmental demands in big cities, and shepherding the transition from a manufacturing to a services economy.

However, defying the consequences of indebtedness is very difficult. A raft of research by the IMF makes clear that China does not, by Western standards, have the processes, rules, or frameworks in place for a large-scale treatment of its debt overhang.[31] In one paper, the IMF staff poses the question, with regard to credit booms, "Is China Different?" And they answer with a stark no.[32] In this context, China's next recession will be a proper test of multipolarity in that it will show whether China deals with its credit crisis in a Chinese way or in a more orthodox Western way.

Doing so in a specifically Chinese way would make sense from the point of view of where China is in terms of its social and political evolution. Debt restructuring would take on some of the aspects of Confucianism (in that it would be done in a way that doesn't upset social and cultural norms) and would be driven by the internal political realities of the Chinese Communist Party.

Under this approach, China's debt mountain and the blame to be apportioned for its rise would be resolved in China's way. What I mean by this is that the emphasis would probably be on minimizing the political consequences of the credit shock and, consistent with this, on minimizing unemployment. Such an approach would be unlike that used in the United States after the global financial crisis and in Europe in the aftermath of the eurozone crisis, both of which left socioeconomic carnage in their wakes. To a certain extent the Chinese authorities have been taking actions that appear consistent with a realization of the dangers of a credit crunch and have been becoming steadily more adept at acting and communicating than some Western policy makers in the run-up to the global financial crisis.

This increasingly vigilant attitude is in contrast to the attentiveness of UK politicians like Alistair Darling, who as the UK's chancellor of the exchequer found out about the global financial crisis when passing the newsstand of a Majorca supermarket. His report of the discovery—"I was sent down to the local supermarket to get the rolls and the papers. My friend noticed they had an FT [*Financial Times*], so I bought it to

see what was going on"—is scarcely believable given the tradition of the
Chancellorship and the Treasury, though it was perhaps a sign of things
to come in terms of the quality of the British policy response to Brexit.
Darling cut short his holiday to return to Britain to attend to the collapse of Northern Rock bank.

China is thankfully well ahead of a Majorca moment and may have
already distilled a number of lessons from recent financial crises in the
United States and Europe: resolve the situation of bad banks quickly,
do not emerge from a debt crisis with an enlarged debt burden on
the state, let individuals bear the costs of financial mistakes (this goes
for businesspeople and bankers; more bankers were barred from the
financial services industry in China in 2008 than in all of the developed world), and where at all possible allow investors to bear financial
burdens of falling assets. Perhaps the most important lesson is not to
disenfranchise the man or woman in the street, lest he or she decide to
take to the streets.

China's response to a credit crisis could take the form of cutting rates
and, arguably, of letting its currency steadily depreciate. It has started to
open up access to its debt markets, which some cynics see as a move to
export credit risk out of China. At a more strategic level, the Chinese
authorities could reset its emerging social order by forcing wealthy business owners to accept the full burden of bankruptcies. In some cases,
debt restructuring could lead to debt-for-equity exchanges. Some of this
equity could be granted to employees to incentivize business (though
mindful of the lessons from Russia's experiment with this approach in
the 1990s, where stakes in state companies were given to its citizens,
then fell in value and were scooped up by the businessmen who now
form Russia's oligarch class) and, ultimately, social stability. A related
idea would be for the government to offer companies some specific tax
relief on interest payments provided that employment levels were kept
above a threshold. This would help avoid heavy unemployment that
might result from corporate restructuring and that would simply make
an economic downturn more severe.

One important area of focus in China may be regional economic policy. In the last decade in particular, trends in economic development have exacerbated the differences in wealth and quality of employment among China's regions (from coast to inland, and also between the Tier 1 and Tier 3 cities). A clever approach would be to take advantage of a recession to replant new industries in poorer regions, such as Guizhou, and to take a much tougher approach on debt and property defaults in wealthier areas. Failure to take these actions could mark the beginning of new, regional sociopolitical divides in China, of which property prices are an indicator. Since 2010, for example, data from the IMF show house prices in Tier 1 cities (e.g., Beijing) rising by 200 percent, which is double the rate of increase in lower-tier cities such as Dalian.

Yalta II

Some of the policy options outlined here have the makings of a neat domestic economic solution for China, so why include it in an international debt conference? There are three reasons. The first is simply to pare down the inventory of debt internationally and to begin to reignite global economic growth. The second, from a Western point of view, is to have some degree of influence over China's development. A debt conference and the risk conference that might accompany it would be an important milestone in setting the rules of the multipolar game and would in some respects resemble a cross between the Peace of Westphalia and the Yalta Conference in 1945 among the heads of state of the victorious Allies of the Second World War.

Applying Western bankruptcy rules, corporate governance standards, and debt-resolution processes to China's corporate sector would help integrate China further into international debt markets and would form a basis for more liquid markets in some of the newer securities that would emerge from a post-credit-crisis world, securities such as junk bonds and securitized debt in China. Alternatively, a more Chinacentric approach could form the basis for an entirely different form of capital market formation, one not unlike Rheinish capitalism in Europe. "Rheinish capitalism" refers to the European approach to corporate finance, which relies more heavily on the financing of business by banks than by debt and equity markets, on dual board structures, and on a lesser emphasis on mergers and acquisitions.[33] In China, and more broadly in Asia, a homegrown approach to finance would probably take some time to crystallize, and its success would depend on the severity of a Chinese credit crunch.

A third reason to involve China in a debt conference is geostrategic. China may wish to participate in a debt conference as a means of further opening itself up to international markets and of influencing debt restructuring in other economies across Asia. Equally, mindful of how the Washington Consensus (a liberal, promarket policy approach to countries that is associated with the IMF of the 1990s) has led many economies astray, China may prefer not to have the imprint of Western policy on its economy. For its part, the United States may have the strategic aim of bolstering the relevance of US-centric institutions such as the IMF, the dollar (the yuan-dollar relationship may become strained should China look to break its explicit link to the dollarized system), and dollar-centric capital markets. Alternatively, the United States for its part may conversely feel that it is strategically better off leaving China burdened with debt than helping it restructure and clean up its financial system.

A quid pro quo for China's participation in a debt conference would be participation by Japan. Not unlike China, Japan is a closed, or less-open, financial system in that the lion's share of Japan's government debt is held by domestic investors and the Bank of Japan. The structure of Japan's economy and the problems it has suffered since the late 1990s— deflation, zombie companies, and sluggish growth—are reminders of the consequences of debt and banking crises.

However, compared to China, Japan is more interlinked with the international system in terms of its banks' exposure overseas and international investors' exposure to Japan. Economically, it is still the third-largest economy in the world, and its currency has enormous potential to provoke wider volatility. Like China, Japan to a degree has its own way of doing things in that it has a distinctive model of corporate governance, finance, and ownership.[34]

To all appearances, Japan is a debt time bomb because it has the highest combined (private, corporate, and government) debt to GDP ratio in the world. Much of this debt can be recycled between households and the government, but in the context of another prolonged recession, Japan's debt poses an existential threat to the country. Optimists and theorists, as has already been mentioned, believe that Japan's debt can be made to magically disappear if the Bank of Japan decides to monetize the government debt. This would simply unleash other risks, with unpredictable consequences for the yen, consumer behavior, and Japan's corporations.[35] A Japanese debt restructuring, however, may finally provoke changes to the cross-holding system across corporations and might potentially see the introduction of a more international corporate governance system.

This is one of the key fault lines in the distinction between a truly globalized world and a multipolar one. In a multipolar world, different corporate governance systems would prevail and grow, allowing weaker, more permissive systems to spread like weeds. The ultimate outcome would be to raise the cost of capital in a world where capital can flow freely, to leave investors (in some cases) at the mercy of the arbitrariness of governments, dominant shareholders, and corporate management.

In the context of financial markets, corporate governance does not matter much, most of the time. Companies with poor governance characteristics can outperform those with good governance for extended periods of time. However, in the context of an economic downturn, where debt levels are high, companies with strong governance characteristics tend to perform better. When they do arrive, episodes of bad governance can be very costly.

If more companies and regulators internationally were to adopt rigorous global governance standards, it would create a layer of global corporate actors with global governance standards and in this sense would challenge the notion that the corporate world also needs to be divided on a multipolar basis.[36] My expectation that this can happen is low. Recent experiments with broad corporate governance reforms have failed. In Japan, for example, one of the tenets of "Abenomics"—after Japanese prime minister Shinzō Abe—was the intention to make Japanese companies less complicated and somewhat more Western (e.g., by returning capital to shareholders), the ultimate aim being to improve the return on equity of Japanese companies. This has not materialized, and the follow-through in corporate governance change has been weak. Equally, in the United States, there is no formal corporate governance code, which is why more aggressive governance mechanisms—takeovers and publicly pugnacious shareholder activism, for example—tend to be more prevalent. At the same time, regulators and attorneys general have not been as severe on white-collar crime as some might like.[37]

Governance Bubble

In a number of respects, the United States is building a governance bubble: executive pay levels are very high and are often out of kilter with many metrics of performance (nearly two-thirds of top US companies benchmark executive pay against earnings per share, which is a very malleable metric), debt levels are rising to record highs, and in general shareholders are exhibiting a disturbing degree of docility. The last time the United States was troubled by a corporate governance crisis was in the first years of the twenty-first century, when WorldCom and Enron Corporation became prominent examples of poor governance. In both cases, suspect accounting and high debt led to high-profile bankruptcies. The title of a book about Enron, *The Smartest Guys in the Room*, gives a sense of the hubris involved.[38] At the time of writing, corporate debt ratios and levels and executive pay and its relation to performance metrics are more stretched than they were in the run-up to the Enron scandal in

2001, and the overall pattern suggests that there is a growing, systemic governance problem in the United States.

There are two ways to resolve this. One is the traditional approach of letting markets discover and price corporate governance issues. The other is to try to frame the governance problems and ensure they do not happen again. In the United States specifically, this would entail a much tighter linking of executive pay to long-term increases in the value of a corporation (and possibly to the welfare of stakeholder workers, the environment, and suppliers, though this approach is not popular in the United States) and the organic growth of an enterprise. Another requirement would be for debt and equity holders to take a more active approach to governance.

Furthermore, the introduction of a governance code like the Cadbury framework in the United Kingdom (based on a 1992 report by Sir Adrian Cadbury that set out a number of measures designed to raise the standard of corporate governance)[39] would be revolutionary for Wall Street and Silicon Valley (many technology companies have very weak governance provisions in areas like voting rights). Clearer, cleaner earnings- and tax-reporting standards would also help. Much of these criteria can also be applied, in a slightly different way, to the private equity industry, which for a long time has been a silent governance offender. The question remains, however, of whether internationally respected corporate governance criteria can be transmitted across the major economic blocs, and whether American corporations will tackle their governance risks before a crisis of governance.

Risky Business

As the importance of good corporate governance and the risks of high levels of indebtedness become clear, the future appears gloomier. Currently high levels of debt suggest that the ongoing international problem of indebtedness has not been cured but has simply been put off for another day. This, in turn, clogs up economies and financial systems and in many countries leads to distributional consequences (i.e., wealth inequality). Over the past twenty years, the policy community has failed to come to grips with indebtedness. We could easily make the case that since the 1998 Asian and emerging-market crises, policy responses to various crises have postponed a reckoning—that is, debt bubbles have not been allowed to clear in the way they did in the nineteenth century. Instead, the approach has been to prop up bad debt, bad banks, and bad investments in the hope that reflation would wash away the underlying risks. This view is an expression not of financial bloodlust but, rather, of a desire for those taking and building risks to accept the consequences when things go wrong.

There have been a few exceptions to this risk dodging. One I recall was the collapse of the Long Term Capital Management (LTCM) hedge fund. In the mid 1990s, LTCM was one of the world's largest hedge funds, run by a team of high-profile bond traders and famous academics. It had a range of highly leveraged positions in fixed-income markets. In the face of market volatility, it was forced to unwind, in turn crashing financial markets and provoking the rescue of the fund by a consortium of investment banks. I recall witnessing a presentation on the collapse of the fund from one of its principals, whose voice broke as he recounted its demise. More generally though, the architects of many episodes of financial volatility have gone unpunished or have been relatively untouched by the consequences of their actions. Few bankers involved in the more egregious episodes of risk taking that led up to the global financial crisis have gone to jail. Consumers and households in Ireland, Greece, and the United States will also bear testimony to an absence of a sense of justice following the financial crisis. This is in contrast to more historic crises (à la the nineteenth century) in which the end effects of risk taking were often brutal. At a very broad level, one might say that there is a contemporary and repeated tendency for there to be a mismatch between risk takers and risk bearers. In other words, in recent history, those taking risks have not borne the downside consequences of their actions.

This has come about partly because policy makers have sought to spread risk across the financial system, partly through a desire to save the world. The trouble with saving the world is that very often it saves those who have the means to be saved (and who may not deserve to be saved), leaving others floundering. In the white heat of the global financial crisis, much of this was readily apparent to policy makers, and some serious policy initiatives were implemented (such as the Dodd-Frank Wall Street Reform and Consumer Protection Act), though as the postcrisis fear fades, legislation designed to reduce risk taking is being whittled away.

Risk taking cannot be eliminated, and it should not be, for some very healthy economic reasons. But in the spirit of the Levellers' declaration in the 1649 agreement that "laws ought to be equal, so they must be good, and not evidently destructive to the safety and well-being of the people,"[40] we would be much better off if the consequences of risk taking were better aligned with or matched to those taking them.

If my earlier sense of the need for a debt conference is correct, then such a conference could well be accompanied by a Treaty on Risk, which, in the spirit of the nuclear arms reduction treaties or other more traditional treaties in the international relations arena, might be undertaken between the large regions. The aim of the treaty would be to ensure greater sensitivity to risk taking and better alignment of the consequences of risk with those who instigate them.

There already exist risk policy guidelines for countries; notably, the OECD has already produced a risk governance framework, though it seems that many countries do not regard them as in any way binding on policy.[41] Though fields like corporate governance offer means of potentially reducing risks, or at least of better elucidating them, corporate governance is so rooted in national cultural norms that achieving homogeneity across nations will be difficult. In this respect it may be better to concentrate on areas where nations and regions face common problems and to propose agreed frameworks to help curb them.

The central pillar of such a Treaty on Risk would be an agreement to limit the use of extraordinary monetary policy in all but extreme market and economic situations. By restricting the use of quantitative easing in all but emergency circumstances (which could be defined according to threshold levels of inflation, growth, and market or financial system stress), governments and central banks would prevent quantitative easing being deployed in ways that dull markets' sensitivities and that thereby encourage reckless leveraging and financial engineering by corporate actors. This treaty would also attune political leaders to the fact that the monetary comfort blanket could not be deployed against every threat and that they would thus have to adopt a more proactive approach to avoiding and curing economic crises.

A final point worth making here concerns the degree to which individuals bear the consequences of the financial risks that they create. My own sense is that relatively few people in the financial services industry bear the consequences of their decisions. Corporate actors and their shareholders are punished more often than are individuals, and in many cases, the end consumers of savings and mortgage products bear a very high cost.

Here, the story of Robert Morris is instructive. He was one of the Founding Fathers of the United States and was known as the "financier of the Revolution," having conceived the idea of the Nova Constellatio, a monetary unit that would facilitate the change of Spanish, Portuguese, and British currencies into an American one. It can be seen as a precursor of the dollar (and even the euro). One of its innovations was that the currency would use decimal accounting, something that is generally accepted today. He also turned down George Washington's offer of the position of first treasury secretary in favor of Alexander Hamilton. His fortunes took a turn for the worse when he lost his capital in a land speculation (the Panic of 1796–1797) and spent three years in a debtor's prison, until the Bankruptcy Act of 1800 was passed.

His case is sometimes taken to support the argument that risk taking should not be too harshly punished and that failure in business should not be stigmatized. Today, in the United States, bankruptcy procedures can be more ruthless, though more rapid and less stigmatizing, than comparable procedures in Europe. The underlying aim of such laws should be to achieve two purposes: to enable the relatively speedy recycling of assets encumbered by debt and to do so in a way that is just in terms of the risks taken in accumulating that debt. In this respect, Morris's story might echo through the International Debt Conference of 2024, where the aims will be to unclog the world financial system of the burden of debt that has accumulated through the age of globalization and to do so in a way that will ensure that in the future those who take on too much debt will directly bear the consequences and, very importantly, that the burden of risk taking is felt by the architects of speculative and debt-laden projects rather than by the projects' end consumers.

EIGHT

A MULTIPOLAR WORLD

As the World's GDP Moves Eastward

IN 2018, I HAD THE OPPORTUNITY TO VISIT ONE WORLD TRADE CENTER, the skyscraper in Lower Manhattan that has replaced the two towers of the World Trade Center destroyed on September 11, 2001. The new building showed a splendid riposte to the evil visited on New York that day. As the tallest building in the Western Hemisphere, it affords a spectacular view of New York City and the environs of the Hudson River.

There was a time when the majority of the skyscrapers in the world grew out of the granite of Manhattan. They were a mark of progress and confidence. Today, an attractive and intuitive way of seeing how the world has evolved from a unipolar, US-focused one to a more multipolar one is to look at the location of the world's hundred tallest buildings. The construction of skyscrapers (two hundred meters or more in height) is a nice way of measuring hubris and economic machismo (think of Trump Tower). Between 1930 and 1970, at least 90 percent of the world's tallest buildings could be found in the United States, with a few standing in South America and Europe. In the 1980s and 1990s, the United States continued to dominate the tallest-tower lists, but by the early twenty-first century there was a radical change, with Middle Eastern and Asian skyscrapers rising up.

Today about 50 percent of the world's tallest buildings are in Asia, another 30 percent are in the Middle East, a meager 16 percent are in the United States, and a handful are in Europe. In 2015 three-quarters of all skyscraper completions were located in Asia (China and Indonesia principally), followed by the United Arab Emirates (UAE) and Russia. Following the trail of skyscrapers illustrates the way growth, urbanization, and the notion of progress have spread beyond the United States to other parts of the world. On a related note, as of 2018, the United States only had three (Hartsfield-Jackson International Airport in Atlanta, Georgia; Los Angeles International Airport; and O'Hare International Airport in Chicago) of the eleven-busiest airports in the world, a number of which (Beijing Capital International Airport, Dubai International Airport, and Shanghai Pudong International Airport) were fledgling airports twenty years ago. This pattern of infrastructure also illustrates how the center of gravity of the world economy has shifted eastward, to the extent that some writers now describe a process of "Easternisation." Danny Quah, a Singaporean academic has a wonderful chart that shows how the center of gravity of the world's GDP has moved eastward over the past twenty years.[1]

This shift in the center of gravity of the world is an essential part of the levelling: the levelling out of economic power between the regions of the world. It also helps put in context the trade tension between the United States and China, which is simply an expression of the realization by America's political, military, and commercial elite that China has caught up. What will alarm many, especially in the United States, is that the levelling is not about the rise or fall in the GDP of one country compared to another; rather, it is about a change in the system, the way of doing things internationally, or, as many put it, the world order. Changes to systems tend to produce unpredictable and volatile consequences. Earlier chapters in this book have outlined them. To reiterate: inequality, indebtedness, and political volatility are now at multidecade highs.

Trade tensions and the envelopment of entire economic systems by their central banks are leading to a more regional approach to economics and politics. America's disengagement from world affairs, a more confident European Union, Brexit, and China's One Belt, One Road program are all reverberations of the end of one way of doing things and the passage to another. Most worryingly, democracy is no longer a magnetic policy goal for many countries, and lesser and weaker forms of democracy are now considered acceptable around the world.

Those in the West may view the levelling with trepidation, but that is not necessarily the case in emerging nations, where the idea of a more balanced, multipolar world is recognized and welcomed. Many of those nations will have little patience for the tendency of Western institutions and governments to lecture and condescend to them.

The uncertainty that the passage of the levelling brings, even at this early stage, will make many in the West yearn to roll back the clock so that they can continue to enjoy the fluid prosperity of globalization. Many politicians and institutions are in denial that globalization has come to an end, and fewer still ask what will replace it.

Sustaining globalization in its current form would require several nearly miraculous policy steps. There would be an onus on proglobalization political leaders to develop a tangible narrative on globalization's benefits, followed by actions that would better distribute its positive effects. A new, imaginative trade round would need to be launched, possibly encompassing the implications of Brexit, the desire of the United States to recast nearly all its trade relations, and the cementing of more stable trade relations between Japan and China. Yet when one considers the political effort and goodwill required to enact such measures, globalization fades away into the distance. There is already entrenched skepticism over its benefits, and the reality is that demographics, indebtedness, and to a large degree productivity weaknesses are likely to persist and hold down the trend rate of growth.[2]

Some of the policy steps to reinvigorate globalization and limit its perceived negative side effects could be controversial and populistic. For

instance, we may hear calls for "taxes on technology" or levies on mo-
nopolies, which would be attention-grabbing means of turning public
opinion but which may only replace right-wing populism with that from
the left. Another policy strand associated with limiting the overreaches
of globalization is the reining in of the very large technology and social
media companies. Today, tech is as big as banking was before the global
financial crisis, and, with a little irony, bigger (in terms of revenues and
earnings) than tech was in 1999. There is growing evidence to show that
the large technology companies are dominating the industries in which
they operate. A paper from the staff at the Richmond Federal Reserve
highlighted the fact that the concentration of a small number of large
companies is in some cases as high as it was during the Gilded Age.[3]
This has allowed the dominant companies to enjoy higher margins,
higher stock returns, and more-profitable merger deals. The authors flag
lax regulatory oversight (as well as technological barriers to entry) as one
reason for the rise of dominant firms.

In this light, one proposal that we may hear more of is that, echoing
the 1933 Glass-Steagall Act that separated the activities of commercial
and investment banks (some banks and the sectors they had invested
in—oil, railways, and steel companies—were nearly as dominant as the
large technology companies are today), there would be a Glass Steagall–
themed act that would break up corporate giants such as Amazon,
Google, and perhaps even Tencent Holdings, China's media-enabled
e-commerce player. This could involve separating cloud-computing
businesses from e-commerce ones, with data-intensive activities split to
preserve privacy. Widely used search engines may be classified as public
goods and required to have a truth filter that, for example, would priori-
tizes information from verified data sources. As an example, a search for
"climate change" would prioritize data and research from NASA, governments, and the United Nations. As interesting as this proposition is,
large tech companies in both the United States and China are strategic
assets for their governments and are unlikely to be treated in an overly
harsh manner.

Good-bye to Globalization

It may well be better that those who have grown fond of globalization get over it, accept its passing, and begin to adjust to a new reality. Many will resist and, like the thirty-five foreign-policy experts who published an advertisement in the *New York Times* on July 26, 2018, under the banner "Why We Should Preserve International Institutions and Order," will feel that the existing world order and its institutions should be maintained. I disagree. Globalization, at least in the form that people have come to enjoy it, is defunct. From here, the passage away from globalization can take two new forms. One dangerous scenario is that we witness the outright end of globalization in much the same manner as the first period of globalization collapsed in 1913, as I outlined earlier. This scenario is a favorite of commentators because it allows them to write about bloody end-of-the-world calamities. This is, thankfully, a low-probability outcome, and with apologies to the many armchair admirals in the commentariat who, for instance, talk willfully of a conflict in the South China Sea, I suggest that a full-scale sea battle between China and the United States is unlikely.

Instead, the evolution of a new world order—a fully multipolar world composed of three (perhaps four, depending on how India develops) large regions that are distinct in the workings of their economies, laws, cultures, and security networks—is manifestly underway. My sense is that until 2018, multipolarity was a more theoretical concept—more something to write about than to witness.[4] This is changing quickly: trade tensions, advances in technologies (such as quantum computing), and the regulation of technology are just some of the fissures around which the world is splitting into distinct regions. Multipolarity is gaining traction and will have two broad axes. First, the poles in the multipolar world have to be large in terms of economic, financial, and geopolitical power. Second, the essence of multipolarity is not simply that the poles are large and powerful but also that they develop distinct, culturally consistent ways of doing things. Multipolarity, where regions do things distinctly and differently, is also very different from multilateralism, where they do them together.

China, in particular, is interesting in the context of the switch from globalization to multipolarity, not least because at the 2017 World Economic Forum the Chinese president claimed the mantle of globalization for China. China benefited greatly from globalization and its accoutrements (e.g., WTO membership), and it played a vital role in the supply-chain dynamic that drove globalization.[5] However, trade flows into China increasingly betray a move away from a globalized world and toward a more regionally focused one. For instance, IMF data show that in 2018, compared with 2011, Cambodia, Vietnam, Laos, and Malaysia traded more with China and relatively less with the United States. These countries, together with Bangladesh and Pakistan, have allowed themselves to be enticed by trade- and investment-based relationships with China and are now in its orbit.

However, China is itself not globalized: it is increasingly hard for Western companies to do business there on equal terms with Chinese companies, and the flow of both money and ideas—out of and into China, respectively—is heavily curtailed. Flow of people is another indicator. Flows within China are dynamic and are perhaps more managed than before, but flows of foreigners into China are miniscule by comparison to other countries, and China has only recently established an agency (the State Immigration Administration created at the 2018 Party Congress) to cultivate inward flows. So as China has become a major pole, it has become less globalized and arguably is contributing to the trend toward deglobalization.

On a broader scale, without picking on individual countries, we can measure the extent to which the world is becoming multipolar by examining aggregate trends in trade, GDP, foreign direct investment, government budget size, and population. All of these are much less concentrated, or more dispersed, than they used to be, and increasingly they are collecting around several poles. For example, in the five years from

2012 to 2017, total foreign direct investment into Australia from China increased at a rate of 21 percent per annum, compared to 6 percent from the United States to Australia, suggesting that Asian investment in Australia is picking up.[6]

Several trends show that population flows are becoming more regional. Migration is becoming more region specific or region internal. For example, in 2015 there were 244 million migrants between countries, but at around the same time there were 763 million migrants within countries, according to the World Economic Forum. India is a case in point: from 1991 to 2011 the number of internal migrants more than doubled. In 60 percent of cases, global migration consists of people moving to neighboring countries. As an example, a large proportion of Indian migrants move to regional neighbors, such as the United Arab Emirates, Kuwait, and Saudi Arabia.[7]

An excellent resource here comes from the data scientist Max Galka, who graphically tracks the flow of immigrants across the world.[8] He produces long-term charts showing the waves of immigration into the United States over the past two centuries. His data show that America is founded on a bedrock of German, Irish, Italian, and eastern European immigrants and that lately (since the late 1980s) the biggest flow of immigrants has come from Mexico. The most desired migration destinations worldwide are the United States, Germany, Canada, the United Kingdom, France, Australia, and Saudi Arabia (according to the 2017 World Economic Forum Migration Impact on Cities report). However, data from the World Bank show that the growth in international migrants (excepting refugee flows) into the United States, the United Kingdom, and the eurozone is at its lowest in fifteen years. This may reflect political events—Brexit, for example—and a generally less welcoming climate toward migrants. Today, most of the significant migrant flows are driven by emergencies such as the conflict in Syria, which is driving immigrant flows to Turkey, Jordan, and Lebanon. Venezuela to Colombia is another new, major crisis-driven corridor, with over one million Venezuelan refugees now living in Colombia.[9]

The one area where the world is still globalized, or unipolar, is finance, which we can see in a number of ways: the tenor of global equity and bond markets is still set by Wall Street; American investment banks beat Asian and European banks in trading and advisory leagues; and, most importantly, the usage of the dollar is nearly universal (about half of all transactions globally involve the dollar, with the euro and yen coming far behind and the renminbi accounting for only 2 percent of foreign exchange transactions) according to the Bank for International Settlements.[10]

Even if multipolarity is based on the growing dispersion and regionalization of economic power, it is also expressed in other ways, notably military power, political and cyberfreedoms, technological sophistication, financial sector growth, and a greater sense of cultural prerogative and confidence. These are not as easily measured as economic multipolarity, but some clear strands are emerging. To try to synthesize what a pole entails, we can point toward several initial factors: size of a country's GDP, size of its population, the existence of an imperial legacy, the extent of its regional economic role, its military size and sophistication (e.g., absolute spending, number of fighter jets and ships), its place on the UN Human Development Index relative to its region, and its participation (or not) in a regional grouping (such as NATO or the European Union).

Under this schema the European Union, the United States, China, and potentially India are poles, but Japan and Russia would not qualify as distinct poles. Russia, for instance, scores well on certain aspects of multipolarity (e.g., militarily), but in its current state it may never become a true pole in the sense employed here. It has spent heavily on its military, now actively exports military technology, and has demonstrated its ability to launch large-scale interventions at speed. Russia's president, Vladimir Putin, is also becoming a role model for some politicians in other countries who are attracted to the notion of a more medieval and muscular form of leadership, and his notion of managed democracy also has followers around the world.[11] However, for a country to be truly multipolar, its characteristics need to be institutionalized rather than simply reflected in the abilities of a single leader. Russia, with a structurally weak economy and financial sector and low human development scores, may not be as powerful in a post-Putin era, whenever that is.

Hard and Soft Power

Still, Russia is a good example of how a country leverages hard power (measured in terms of fighting readiness and tactical ability, as set out in military analyses by Jane's Information Group and think-tank assessments).[12] It and a select number of other countries have reserves of hard power, such as nuclear, space, and cyberwar capabilities.[13] From a diplomatic point of view, Russia is also an example of the way certain countries can look at the same set of facts and, disturbingly from the point of view of international peace, reach different conclusions. The Western narrative on Russian diplomacy is that it is a reckless and aggressive provocateur. Russia sees things differently. It sees the incorporation of eastern European states into the European Union, NATO-led military adventures into Iraq and Libya, the encroachment of Western missile systems onto Russia's borders, and Western support for revolutions in Serbia and Ukraine as provocations. Given this worldview, it has bolstered all aspects of its military and has struck out to push threats away from its borders and gain international diplomatic leverage.

A complement to the employment of hard power is to use cultural institutions to build what Harvard professor Joseph Nye (former dean of the Kennedy School of Government and former chair of the National Intelligence Council) calls "soft power." In very simple terms, Nye defines soft power as the ability to co-opt rather than coerce (hard power).[14] Europe is perhaps the leader here. One simple illustration of this is a survey of attitudes to "made in" labels. According to the study, products with German, Swiss, EU, or UK "made in" labels are most admired, and those with Chinese, Bangladeshi, or Vietnamese labels are the least admired.[15] From a cultural point of view, the British Council, BBC World Service,

Alliance Française, and Goethe Institute are some specific examples of how old Western countries sustain and grow soft power. (China has the Confucius Institute.) The BBC, for example, is seen by many as the benchmark in news broadcasting, and from a soft-power point of view it devotes considerable resources to broadcasting news and radio programs in forty languages (World Service). In general, there is now recognition that a country that takes itself seriously as a geo-economic pole must have a network of neighbor states with which it has cultural ties.

Most countries don't have the military, cultural, or economic power to match the large poles, and many countries are caught between poles. Australia, for instance, is a close political and military ally of the West but falls within the economic orbit of Chinacentric Asia. Equally, we might quibble that India has the ingredients to be a distinct and powerful pole but does not have an overall sense of its capabilities and how to marshal them. In this regard it is a geopolitical adolescent.

India is interesting in this regard. It has an economy that is gaining velocity, a potentially enormous consumer sector should its wealth base grow and become better distributed, and a substantial agricultural sector. It is a democracy, with diverse regions and cultural cross-currents, and is also a nuclear and space power. India's army is not as skilled and experienced as that of, say, Russia. Unusually, for a large country, India has a relatively large amount of soft power. Large countries tend to have had empires, to have been involved in wars, or generally to have pushed their weight around in world affairs. India, by comparison, has been relatively gentle and enjoys some goodwill as a result. India has trade and cultural ties to London, Dubai, and Hong Kong and is one of the few countries whose internal and external people flows are fluid and representative of an interconnected world. What India has not yet done is to harness and use its power and assert itself as a distinctive pole.

Looking elsewhere around the world, Latin America should, given its population and geographic size, constitute some form of pole. But in the areas of foreign policy, military power, financial sector mass, and ability to innovate, it falls behind other regions. Furthermore, to a large extent, with the rise in the Hispanic demographic in the United States, the détente between the United States and Cuba, and the primacy of the dollar, Latin America remains part of the satellite region of the US pole. Sadly, it has been overlooked by Washington. The prime example of this neglect is Venezuela. The country is failing and in the grip of an underreported humanitarian crisis. Economically, this crisis may lead China to take a deeper role in Venezuela and in its oil production. Diplomatically, the lack of a comprehensive reaction from Washington brings to mind an article entitled "The Forgotten Relationship" that Jorge Castaneda published some years ago in *Foreign Affairs* in which he bemoaned the deteriorating relationship between Latin America and the United States.[16]

Latin America can be criticized in the multipolar context in many respects. One of these is that it lacks a sense of command and control across the region, an ability to act cohesively and coherently. A modus operandi and an ability to speedily execute decisions and transmit their effects is, however, evident in other regions. The US president, White House, Pentagon, and other institutional trappings of the United States provide a single foreign-policy voice, as do the day-to-day workings of the French and British systems.

By comparison, the European Union lacks a central, European foreign-policy persona (it has an official foreign minister, the high representative of the Union for foreign affairs and security policy, but the individual in the position is rarely as powerful and influential as, say, Mario Draghi), who must always compete with the foreign ministers of other states. Imagine, during a crisis, twenty-seven foreign ministers huddled around a speakerphone, with the official EU foreign minister trying to get a word in sideways. In areas like trade and competition policy, the European Union has a much clearer and more unified stance, but for it to fully develop as a pole it needs to have a more singular voice in foreign policy.

Size—be it economic or strategic—is one of the two determinants of what constitutes a pole; the other is the distinctiveness of that pole's approach to economic, cultural, and political life. This distinctiveness is colored by the aims of each region or pole and by the extent to which what might be called "hinterland states" would agree and acquiesce.

Primus inter pares

In considering the strategic aims of each pole, let us start with the United States. One might suspect that its goal is the preservation of its role as primus inter pares financially and militarily and also in terms of its grip on trade and international institutions. Europe aims for stability, both of the European Union politically and of the eurozone financially, and from there, a deepening of the European project in terms of its institutions and framework. China's view of itself in the future, or the Chinese Dream, is colored by past generations of economic and cultural greatness.[17] It wants to elevate itself to a position of economic power (perhaps regional dominance) and of policy power in Asia with its own regionally relevant rule-based order so that it is, at the very least, not subject to the domination of Western countries and institutions.

Assessing the "ethos," or distinctiveness, of each pole is more difficult. For example, if one were to try to get a sense of the nature and quality of institutions and democracy in China, the best publicly available metrics come from sources like the World Bank's worldwide governance indicators.[18] China does not rank well here, but that does not exclude the possibility that China's institutions and policy apparatus serve its aims very well. Judging China or Russia through Western eyes goes against the very idea of growing distinctiveness.

Bearing this in mind, we could select five factors through which a view of the distinctiveness of each pole might emerge: governance, democracy, civic control, economy, and power and its deployment. Europe is perhaps most distinctive in the area of democracy, in its low level of civic control (e.g., on freedom of expression), and in culture (the flow of tourists to Europe is perhaps proof of this). The European Union is notably distinctive in that it has its own currency, even though the euro system is not yet complete from an institutional point of view. One might also say that individually many European countries have strong institutions and that at least the European Union has a distinctive though perhaps inefficient approach to governance and policy making.

In terms of power and its deployment, Europe is culturally very distinct, but it is not at all effective in the way it deploys either its diplomatic power or its military power, though one might argue that the European Union's rather passive approach is a form of distinction.

The United States, having led the contemporary wave of globalization, is distinctive in its own right. Its way of doing things has pervaded international institutions and policy mind-sets (the Washington Consensus). In each of the five factors it has a distinctive position, and in many of them a dominant one, with Europe edging the United States out in terms of the quality of its democratic processes. One challenge to the United States now comes in the deployment of its soft power, which was much more easily done in the context of postcommunist Europe and the early phase of rising emerging economies. With other countries and regions now adopting more authentic and assertive identities, the smooth flow of American soft power becomes more difficult.

China, by comparison to the United States and Europe, has a political system that few in the West would recognize as a democracy, but its distinctive approach to curbing personal freedoms and its top-down political control serve the aim of advancing China as an entity. To this end, a positive interpretation of China's model is that it is following a "prince-like" republican approach as described by Machiavelli, where policy is directed toward the common good, which in this context is interpreted as the furthering of China's (and the Communist Party's) prestige. A less kind view would point out that China's citizens are subject to tyranny from above.

In terms of other variables: China's use of military power is yet untested, its soft power is not well developed, and many non-Chinese see China's economy-led expansion as a reflection of China's sense of its own greatness. One area where China does forcefully express its power is in trade relations, where it uses its size and influence in a manifest way on its Asian neighbors (stretching to Australia). The challenge for China is to use soft power to win over neighbors and to stealthily create regional integration so that it oversees the South China Sea while confounding those who believe in what Harvard professor Graham Allison has named the "Thucydides's Trap."[19] Thucydides was an Athenian general who turned historian after an unsuccessful battle. In his famous *History of the Peloponnesian War*, he recounts the fifth-century-BC wars between Athens and Sparta. More recently, appreciation of Thucydides has grown following publication of a book by Allison in which he coined the phrase "Thucydides Trap" to refer to the inevitability of a war between an established power (the United States) and a rising one (China).

For each pole to be truly distinctive, it must have its own way of doing things in the legal and political senses. The United States and Europe are the obvious examples here. One interesting legal trend in China is the way Chinese laws and legal rulings are (opaquely) springing up to challenge the commercial prowess of the West. China also shows an ability to independently innovate in the arenas of military technology, telecoms, and information technology, all determinants of being a pole.[20] China is now a world leader in solar, smartphone, and telecom technologies. It has introduced a suite of cyberlaws that effectively cordon off a distinct internet space for China—a space in which it has the power to request decryption support from internet companies and in which social media products are liable to a security review—and that require that data on Chinese customers be stored in China. This trend helps make the point that as multipolarity takes over from fully fledged globalization, national-champion companies will form part of the essential capabilities of poles, and in a sense these galleons of multipolarity will replace more globally oriented companies like Apple.

Orwell Was Right

By thinking through the characteristics or determinants of a geo-economic pole, we can begin to flesh out the base of the main axes of power. We can also bring in some literary color through a very appealing framework found in one of the most important books of the twentieth century, George Orwell's *1984*. Orwell divided the world into three regions—Oceania, Eastasia, and Eurasia—on the basis of economic power and forms of government. For a world where reality has trumped fiction, this may not be a bad schema at all, as it fits nicely around the major poles that are now beginning to form.

Although it requires some shoehorning, we could well fit the major countries of the world into the following categories: Oceania (the United States and possibly the United Kingdom), Eurasia (the European Union plus Turkey, eastern Europe, and Israel), and Eastasia (Chinacentric Asia). Though today's world does not map cleanly onto Orwell's classification, the three broad regions he sets out give a good guide to how a multipolar world might evolve. Some countries, such as the United Kingdom, Japan, and Australia, could just as easily fit in two categories. Taking our inspiration from Orwell, we can sketch Oceania, Eurasia, and Eastasia in more detail.

Oceania

In the multipolar world, Oceania, or the Anglo-Saxon countries (principally the United States, the United Kingdom, Canada, and Australia) will continue to do what they do best: fighting and finance, backed by a mixture of classical republican institutions and democracy.[21]

From the point of view of the levelling, the United States and the United Kingdom have an important heritage to live up to: both have been the origin of periods of globalization and each has helped foster the rise of democracy in the past three hundred years. In particular, by the nineteenth century America was regarded by Europeans, much as Alexis de Tocqueville did, as the model Europe should follow.

Globalization was born out of two Anglo-Saxon empires: the British trade- and land-based empire of the nineteenth century and the American hegemony of the twentieth and early twenty-first centuries. Though the British Empire was undemocratic in its impact on other countries and though it sought to transfer value from the rest of the world to its core, it did at least set up transport routes, the cultural, legal, and linguistic structures that globalization still travels by today. As a result, most of the facets of globalization have a strong Anglo-Saxon flavor, especially if we think of globalization as a legal, political, economic, and perhaps cultural network.

The original free-market philosophy that spawned globalization was propagated by thinkers like David Ricardo and Adam Smith and was spread by US and British policy makers. The notion that free markets are the most efficient mode of economic activity is one of the intellectual pillars of the proglobalization camp. This spirit lives on in academia, in that many of the world's leading economists have trained or worked in the large universities of the US East Coast, which supply many of the staff members of organizations like the World Bank and IMF. (Joe Stiglitz is scathing of the mind-set of the IMF senior management.)[22]

Also, many international financial institutions—such as the Bundesbank (Germany's central bank), a significant chunk of the Japanese financial system, and economic restructuring programs in Latin America, to name just a few—can claim Americans as their architects. The dollar remains the world's reserve currency, the US Federal Reserve is considered the most powerful central bank in the world, and, importantly, the investment banks that drive activity in the global financial system are American. The financial crisis has done little to dent this position, and most international equity markets follow the pulse of Wall Street rather than follow the beat of Frankfurt or Shanghai.

Eastasia

An alternative to the Anglo-Saxon approach is taking root in Asia, where since the 1990s the Asian Tiger economies—Singapore, Hong Kong, Taiwan, and South Korea—have outperformed the rest of the world economy and are now all highly globalized. China is their economic epicenter. Singapore and Hong Kong, whose economic growth in the past thirty years has easily outstripped that of competing small states like Ireland and New Zealand, have become entrepôt economies, importing and then exporting huge quantities of goods and services. They have been followed in this regard by other Asian countries, whose approach to development is distinctive enough to be labeled the "Sinatra" doctrine (i.e., "Do it my way").

Broadly speaking, what China and many other Asian nations have in common is the active "Colbertian" direction to economic policy. Jean-Baptiste Colbert was minister of finance in France for much of the late seventeenth century and was known for using the state as a promotor of economic activity. In this light, Colbertism denotes an active state involvement in economic policy. To stretch the comparison with France a little more, one might say that a better comparison with China today is the Second French Empire under Napoleon III (1852 to 1870). It was a period of limited democracy, curbed parliamentary and press freedoms, and active surveillance of France's more vocal citizens, but also a time of infrastructure building, innovation, and gentrification. Yet toward the end of the Second French Empire, the emperor's legitimacy was withering, and he fell into a trap that snares many rulers: using war to bolster their standing. His mistake was to cast an eye toward Prussia, which was being shaped into a formidable military power by the combined talents of Otto von Bismarck and Helmuthe von Moltke. A victory for Napoleon III would have installed him as the de facto ruler of Europe. His wife, Empress Eugénie, is even said to have underlined the importance of the conquest of Prussia, saying, "If there is no war, my son will never be emperor."[23] Napoleon III's reign ended badly, in hubris, war, defeat, and rebellion. After the Battle of Sedan in the Franco-Prussian War in 1870, he capitulated, and in a few years, he found himself, with Eugénie, in declining health in Chislehurst, England, where he later passed away.

The point of recounting all of this is that politics and markets share a common trait: the propensity toward overconfidence, underestimation of risk, and swift turn in fortunes. Though the globalizing Asian countries do not follow the economic and political prescriptions of the received Anglo-Saxon model, what they do have in common are well developed systems or architectures of government, in addition to intricate social and cultural norms. For instance, China's deep-seated culture and the political structures built up during communism have allowed its authorities to promote progrowth economic strategies while at the same time maintaining a high degree of control over both economy and society.

These superstructures, as Marx referred to them, have given Asian countries the ability to engage globalization in a controlled manner. In this respect, understanding China in particular is a question not simply of absorbing the values and priorities of its culture but also of interrogating the aims of its government. For many Westerners, Beijing, to redeploy Churchill's famous characterization of Russia, is a political "riddle wrapped in a mystery, inside an enigma."[24]

Yet in trying to understand China, many commentators are guilty of looking at China through Western eyes, which implies on the one hand that China has not quite yet arrived and on the other that a globalized rather than proper multipolar worldview still colors the judgment of many in the West, who continue to underestimate China. On the scale of the very long sweep of socioeconomic history, the transformation of China, and in particular its economy, in a relatively short period of time is a great accomplishment.

To a large degree, China has achieved what American and European governments took much longer to do. For instance, in 2000 Chinese households had the same amount of wealth that Americans had in 1905 (about USD 6 trillion), but by 2023, according to IMF forecasts, China's households will have the same amount of wealth that America had in 2000 (USD 60 trillion).[25]

In more recent years, there has been a sense that China has what one might call a "learning" administration—that is, one that has observed how the United States and Europe have mired themselves in financial crises, how they have dealt with it, and what lessons can be drawn from financial crises in the other poles. Quick adjustments to stock market regulation and currency management in China have highlighted how quickly Beijing has been to learn market communication. Policy makers in China have doubtless been absorbing lessons from what developed world central banks have done over the past ten years in respect of the extraordinary measures taken to combat debt crises. In particular, if China has learned from Europe's crisis, it will know, first, that it must not end a debt and banking crisis with large amounts of debt on the government balance sheet, and, second, that it must not allow the burden of economic pain to fall on the ordinary man and woman lest that provoke social unrest.

Looking ahead, there are two components to the political impetus in China. The first, overriding one is the goal of advancing China and increasing its prestige, or its dream, to be consistent. This may sound obvious, but it is a common, driving factor across China's political class and is internalized across the country. China had this dream well before Trump's promise to "Make America Great Again" and even as far back as Reagan's proclamation of "Morning in America," but it is only now that the West is becoming more aware of it.

The focus of debate among Western commentators is the extent to which China wishes to reinforce its prestige. European countries, and then the United States by virtue of its economic and military power, have in recent centuries spread their influence, and in many cases empires, far and wide, even to the shores of China (in the Opium Wars, for example). Westerners may worry that it is now China's turn, and its every step will be scrutinized in this light. Will it, for example, take a more active role in international politics with respect to Africa with its emphasis on "Chinese solutions"? In its rhetoric, and increasingly in policy, there is a growing tendency on the part of Chinese foreign-policy leaders to assert that the US-based international system and way of doing things are no longer working.[26] China's deepening commercial involvement in African countries, such as the Congo, calls to mind the book *The Scramble for Africa* by Thomas Pakenham (an Anglo-Irish historian, formally known as Lord Longford) in which he details the partition and despoiling of Africa in the nineteenth century by European powers such as England, Italy, France, and Belgium.[27] A subtle variant on Chinese promotion of its prestige internationally is apparent in Chinese cinema, which is already forging ahead here with films like *Operation Red Sea* (2018) and *Wolf Warrior 2* (2017) depicting the bravery of Chinese overseas interventions. An important diplomatic litmus test will be whether these fictional interventions are played out in real life, as Chinese troops may in future perform national security operations outside China (in broader Asia, Africa, and possibly Latin America). China may sensibly stay out of areas like the Middle East.

China may well refrain from territorial expansion, but it may continue to use its economic size to exert itself over other countries in Asia and to impose its own standards on other countries in areas such as internet freedom, security, and food security. The One Belt, One Road plan ingeniously extends China's influence across Asia, through the Middle East, and up through eastern Europe (China has established a trade and investment project, "16 + 1," with sixteen eastern European states, including the Baltic states, the Czech Republic, Hungary, Romania, Serbia, and others) without explicitly compromising the sovereignty of the many countries this project will traverse.[28]

Ducking the Dreadnought

Like many large countries before it, China has also shown a tendency to dial pressure up on regional trade partners and then dialing it back down once agreement is in sight. One looming test for China is how it reacts to the hostile treatment of Chinese communities in populous Muslim countries like Indonesia. It is this kind of problem—rather than South China Sea naval battles conjuring up the likes of *Dreadnought* or USS *New Jersey*—that will be one of the key tests of Chinese foreign policy.

The second part of the Chinese puzzle relates to the inner machinations of the Communist Party. Since Xi Jinping became president of

China and general secretary of the Communist Party, party members have been more disciplined with regard to divulging the party's inner workings and internal intrigues (such as concerning the sudden political demise of Bo Xilai, a charismatic Chinese politician who was considered a strong candidate for the top Politburo Standing Committee until, intriguingly, he and his wife were jailed for the murder of a British businessman). In some respects, the party may be riven by many of the same policy issues that dog political groups in Europe, but we just can't see or hear the debates within the Communist Party.

Still, from the outside it is just possible to discern several factions within the party, younger members versus old, career politicians versus military brass, Premier Xi's supporters versus those of previous regimes, and to a certain extent, emerging policy divides appear to cluster around urban versus rural constituencies, anticorruption groups versus those with a more laissez-faire attitude, those who favor the cultivation of religion in China versus those who prefer to shut it out to the greater gain of the party, and more environmentally conscious cadres versus those less concerned about climate change.[29]

Technology may also become a live issue, as China is now a leader in robotics and artificial intelligence. Though China's proficiency in computing power is catching up with that of the United States, especially in quantum computing, its real advantage in the area of artificial intelligence is the vast pools of data it can gather on its citizens and economy and its ability to use this in a practical sense. In order to make the kind of productivity gains that would sustain its economic growth, it will probably have to use more technology in industry and services, to the detriment of human capital. Don't be surprised to see the rise of a Luddite wing in the Communist Party. In general, technology will become a problematic political issue for emerging economies that have hitherto been focused on labor-intensive industries and that now feel an impetus to improve productivity through technology.

On other related issues, such as trade, the Communist Party might take the innovative and unusual step of encouraging (or creating) party mavericks to speak up on topics of international importance. Someone who sounds off on trade and against the West in a loud and eccentric way (to the staged and public disapproval of the party leadership) might be a useful megaphone to deploy in trade relations. Such a character would give the party leaders a degree of plausible deniability—for example, in official relations with the West while the maverick was being deployed to stoke up boycotts of Western goods.

At a higher level, China's national good and that of the party are currently synonymous, but it is likely that tension will grow between them in the event of a debt crises. This is because the national good will be used as the guiding principle in apportioning the losses of such a crisis, but many supporters of the party may not be happy with that principle, given that many of them have business interests and would stand to lose out to the national good as financial pain is apportioned.

There is also the intriguing possibility that the Chinese Communist Party today resembles the sociopolitical setting that the Levellers faced, and it is not at all unlikely that a Leveller-type group will emerge (to be quashed by the Grandees). Suppose, say, that in 2021 China is mired in a debt crisis, its unemployment has soared to 10 percent, the rise of robotics in its factories has raised the natural rate of unemployment, a dip in property prices has imparted a significant shock to savings, there is little social welfare, and environmental issues continue to plague the many large Chinese cities. Ordinary Chinese citizens are beset by the same issues the Levellers confronted: harsh treatment for indebtedness, arbitrary application of the law, abuse of the environment, and domination by a concentrated political elite.

The rise of such a movement in China, or at least in some of its poorer regions, would, first, mark the sociopolitical evolution of China, and, second, represent such a threat to the established order that the Chinese authorities would invest a great deal in subverting it. Indeed, the Chinese authorities are investing an unmatched amount of capital in surveillance technology and artificial-intelligence-based behavioral analysis. According to some estimates, China spends nearly 20 percent more on domestic than external security, with a focus on Tibet, the Xinjiang Uygur Autonomous Region, and Beijing.[30] It is possible that, as happened with the Putney Debates, Chinese authorities would stage a listening before taking responsive economic and social policy actions, as well as political action to shut down a Leveller-type movement (unlike in the seventeenth century, social media might make a shutdown like this more difficult).

Another related possibility that may help smooth the passage through a crisis is that the Chinese authorities, having watched the political fallout from the global financial crisis and the eurozone crisis, would take great care that the costs of an economic downturn would be borne by the wealthy and that some form of emergency social welfare framework would be put in place for the duration of the downturn.

Eurasia

Though Europe may provide the lessons for what China should not do, it nonetheless has its own distinct way of doing things. Its brand of capitalism is less aggressive than the Anglo-Saxon model, and it is far more democratic a region than Asia. However, the European Union is a project that has run into the limits of its two-dimensional geometry. Since 1999, it has grown deeper (through the introduction of the euro, for example) and larger. It is now twenty-seven states, one fewer since Brexit but still far larger than it was in 2006. Its future now depends on being able to either intelligently track back on these two dimensions (institutional depth and enlargement) or find a new dimension on which to perch itself. Its next great challenge will be on immigration. The backlash against immigration across the EU countries, together with security risks, may entail a more fine-tuned interpretation of its freedom-of-movement principle, at least as far as immigration from outside the European Union is concerned. In the future, the relationship of the European Union with countries like Turkey and Nigeria will be tested by the question of immigration. These two increasingly populous countries (the World Bank expects that by 2045 Nigeria's population will be greater than that of the United States) are beset with economic, political, and institutional frailties, and both are already established as very large sources of immigration into the European Union.[31] Should this immigration pick up materially, it will in turn set the scene for a popular backlash against those countries and a deterioration in their relations with the European Union.

The question of immigration, like the bumblebee-construction of the euro (recall Draghi's comment), betrays a sense that the principles, laws, and policies that govern the European Union are fine in theory but fall apart as soon as something goes wrong. There is a design problem in the European Union's structure, and also one of vision: it often appears that the aims of the European Union are opaque, even to its leaders.

Indeed, my own experience is that Asians, Americans, and those living in the Middle East regard Europe with disturbed curiosity. From an investment point of view, Americans, or American-based investors at least, have regarded Europe not as an investable region in its own right but as a special situation, an asset one might at best trade but not own. The fact that Asians cannot understand why Europe has a leadership (the European Commission, which is the executive of the European Union) but its Parliament effectively plays second fiddle to some national parliaments should underline to Europeans the inelegant labyrinth of their democracy. It is worth saying that if Asia were to put together an "Asian Union," its early years might well be as shaky as those of the eurozone (and the early years of the United States system, also). The eurozone crisis and its subsequent tremors have done much to harm the credibility of the European Union and lessen confidence in the way it is run, and to a large extent this has profoundly colored the opinion of non-Europeans regarding the European Union. To a large extent, the euro crisis and its episodes resembled the circles of hell in Dante's *Inferno*.

As a result, it is now a ritual among commentators and economists to profess the view that "Europe will fail" and demand that it "reform."[32] This approach misses several points. The first is that economic prowess is, thankfully, not the overriding goal of Europe; it is conjoined with aims of stability and social development. The second is that Europe is held together by a very Catholic (in the sense of a deeply ingrained blind faith) form of political creed that in moments of crisis has acted as a sort of political energy to bind the European Union together. The third is that there is still much recognition by Europeans that in its current form the European Union is preferable to a very long history of conflict.

The European Union has four officially stated aims: to promote EU citizenship, to support economic and social progress, to underpin justice and security, and to define and defend Europe's place in the world. The last of these aims is arguably the weakest, and the others could be summed up as promoting an enlightened form of social democracy (whose benefits I feel are wholly underappreciated and underestimated). The European Union is, however, silent on how it can better govern the relationships between its states, how it manages crises and responds to trend changes in areas such as migration and foreign policy, and how it positions itself relative to China and the United States. In reality, one could boil Europe's aims down to two goals: The first is the more expedient option of staying together, in the sense of maintaining harmony between its member states and within its electorates. The other is the more distinct aim of fostering social democracy, which is faltering in the light of the rise of extreme political parties across Europe and of recalcitrant eastern European governments amid the pressures of immigration, terrorism, and fiscal constraints.

The European Union may find that, in an emerging multipolar world, having a clear identity ought to become more pressing. If the United States were to leave Europe to fend for itself and if China were to become a more challenging trade partner, then that would create the pressures, or impetus, for the European Union to better define itself. Thanks to the more isolationist stance of the Trump White House, there are already plenty of signs that the European Union is becoming more singular. There are now regular calls for the European Union to become self-sufficient in terms of developing its own battery technology, artificial intelligence, and military capabilities (i.e., an EU Army). Some

European politicians also demand that the European Union create its own payments system, to break free from the US-based Society for Worldwide Interbank Financial Telecommunication (SWIFT) system.[33]

The road to a more defined and independently powerful European Union will need to overcome several obstacles. One major issue is optimizing foreign policy in a realistic institutional form. Europe's foreign minister has more often than not been a relatively powerless, second-rate politician, a role embodied in its worst form by Catherine Ashton (a minor, low-key British politician whose tenure as European foreign affairs representative was widely criticized). The power dynamics of the European Union mean that in foreign-policy commissioners, for instance, are chosen less for their ability and stature and more for their inability to counter the interests of the larger states. What, for example, would the French foreign ministry do in the face of an EU-level Madeleine Albright or Henry Kissinger? Or what might the German finance ministry think of a powerful EU treasury secretary?

A coherent and meaningful EU foreign ministry, together with colleagues in areas such as trade (which is one area where the European Union has focus and power), would intermediate the European Union's relations with large poles such as China and the United States and might also serve as a fulcrum for EU policy on common defense and cybersecurity. The installation of a more powerful foreign minister would be an important step toward deepening the ability of the European Union to act on the international stage. This more meaningful role might also take on some of the lessons on crisis management learned by the economics and finance side of the European Commission. It would be a shame if other parts of the European Commission did not learn from the economic management process of the eurozone.

The deepening of some parts of the European Commission should not at the same time be an excuse for making it bigger. Politically, election results and opinion polls consistently point to EU citizens' desire not to take on more members. In this respect, the impetus for further enlargement comes, it seems, solely from Brussels. The European Union is now at a critical size where the introduction of new members (e.g., the Balkan states) may encourage others to leave, or at least to begin to make their own policy breakaway groups. If it is not careful, the European Union may gain Serbia but lose Sweden in the process, which in my view is not a good bargain. Europe will also face the long-term consequences of waves of immigration, principally from the African continent as its population grows. In addition, the leverage that Turkey has over Germany (owing to the very large Turkish immigrant population in Germany) will play a role in the European Union's immigration policy and will probably exacerbate tensions between EU nations such as Austria and Germany.

I suggest that, in the aftermath of Brexit, the European Union should institute a formal process whereby the aims and tenets of the European Union are reexamined in the light of Brexit and growing political volatility across the European Union. This may provoke some change to EU principles and policies and may even drive existing countries to adopt more stringent criteria for countries to get into and stay in both the European Union and the eurozone. It may come to pass that member states of both the European Union and the eurozone can be expelled from those unions for grave breaches of political and economic values. Such mechanisms are a necessary part of the governance of the eurozone and would make very clear to new EU members that accession comes with responsibilities.

Now the Trilemma

One of the problems the European Union has is that it is trying to be many things at the same time: a democracy, a functioning group of nation-states, and an economically powerful coalition (via the euro). In a multipolar world, other large regions may face the same difficulty. Indeed, the breakdown of globalization and the emergence of a multipolar world may be the logical consequence of what Dani Rodrik calls "the trilemma of globalization."[34] Rodrik is a professor of international economy at Harvard and one of the academic experts on globalization. His trilemma underscores the near impossibility of individual states' managing to achieve deep economic integration with the world and regional economies while preserving national sovereignty and also managing to uphold a democratic form of politics.

This balancing act is central to the theme of the levelling, where we find regions and some nations becoming less integrated with each other economically as some of their leaders emphasize sovereignty over democracy and liberty. Some of the remedies put forward in this book so far—such as reducing imbalances (stopping QE and holding a debt conference) and recognizing country strength—are intended to ease if not resolve this trilemma.

Specifically, Rodrik's trilemma has been proven correct in the sense that Brexit, the election of Donald Trump, and political agitation in parts of Europe represent, through democratic political processes, the preference for national sovereignty over economic integration. Multipolarity is a response in that at the regional level, poles begin to craft their own distinctive forms of sovereignty, economic integration, and democracy, as opposed to continuing to shoehorn themselves into a one-size-fits-all global version.

The path toward multipolarity will not be smooth. One tension is that since the Industrial Revolution the world has had an anchor point in terms of the locus and spread of globalization (Britain in the nineteenth century and the United States in the twentieth century). The fact that there are now at least three points of reference introduces a new and possibly uncertain dynamic to world affairs.

The potential is high for friction, misunderstanding, and conflict among the increasingly different ways of doing things across the major poles. Essentially, multipolarity means that instead of speaking a common language, the major poles speak different policy languages. Trade-based tension is an obvious possibility here. Another form of tension is the crisis of identity created for countries that are not wholly within one of the poles—again, Japan, Australia, and the United Kingdom are the prime examples—and the crisis of ambition for countries, such as Russia, that want to be poles but lack the wherewithal to do so convincingly.

At a more grassroots level, the implications of the end of globalization as we know it and the path to multipolarity will become a greater part of the political debate. At the margin, the flow of people, ideas, and capital may be less global and more regional and in time could be reinforced by a growing sense of regionalization across the main poles. In a negative way, a more multipolar world may be the watershed that signals the peak of democracy and potentially the beginning of contests within regions for competing views of democracy, institutional strength, statecraft, and control.

Levelling versus Leviathan

The beginning of the transition to a multipolar world is germane to the levelling and will play out in at least two respects. First, the levelling out of many political and economic variables (from voter participation to indebtedness to low real-wage growth) marks a watershed in the end of globalization and the onset of a new world order. Second, power among nations and regions is being levelled out and the multipolar world into which we are moving is characterized by regions doing things in their own distinctive ways.

The most distinctive approach to nations' doing things their own way will be their approach to what the Levellers might call the "rights of freeborn men," or the idea of the open society mentioned in chapter 3. The code of the Levellers presents a very clear political formula that Europeans and Americans will recognize for its values, though decreasingly in its practice. The challenge to this code will come from the rising acceptance of less democratic ways of ordering society in both developed and emerging countries. A related clash will be the desire of a growing proportion of electorates to have a more open society as economies also open up.

It is possible that as the world evolves along the lines of Leveller-type and Leviathan-type societies, in some countries, such as Russia, a Leviathan-like approach of order in exchange for reduced democracy and rights will be the accepted way of life. In other countries, most interestingly China as its economy loses momentum and then evolves, there may be a growing tension between groups holding the Leviathan view, supported inevitably by Grandees, and opposing Leveller-like groups who favor equality of opportunity and a multiparty system. The role and views of women, especially in China, and of minority groups like the gay community will be pivotal here.

The emergence of a new world order, based on large regions and colored by Leveller and Leviathan modes of governance, echoes several periods in history. Again, the time of the Levellers (and Hobbes's *Leviathan*) is apt and worth revisiting, though beyond the shores of Britain this time. Though the Putney Debates and the role the Levellers played in them are very important events in the history of democracy, they were tame compared to the wars that raged in Europe at the time. Notably, as the Levellers' second agreement was struck, the Thirty Years' War was drawing to a close. The Thirty Years' War was fought across Germany among Denmark, Spain, France, and Holland, to name but a few of the antagonists. These wars devastated parts of Europe; for instance, in Germany, violence and disease wiped out a third of the urban population and nearly two-thirds of the rural population. The Thirty Years' War was perhaps the most damaging conflict Europe has endured outside the world wars. In 1648, however, the Thirty Years' War and the Eighty Years' War were brought to an end by a series of treaties collectively referred to as the Peace of Westphalia.

The Peace of Westphalia, masterminded by the French cardinal Jules Mazarin, constituted a vast logistical exercise, with nearly two hundred states and statelets attending. The treaties that make up the Peace still mark the landscape of international relations and are seen as setting down the principles for the recognition of the nation-state as we understand it. The Peace recognized the right of the leader (prince) of each state and statelet to anoint an official religion and the right of those whose (Christian) religion did not conform to the official state religion to enjoy the right to practice their religion. Importantly, another provision was that the sovereignty of each state(let) was to be recognized. The implication was that future conflicts would be fought much less on the basis of religion and that individual states and statelets would act in a more strategic way, forming alliances, seeking overseas trade, and innovating in the areas of transport and military technology.

There's not a lot of evidence to suggest that the Peace of Westphalia resonated with the Levellers or the Putney Debates regarding the 1649 Agreement of the People, though the world that the Peace created would soon shape the destiny of England. However, I feel that there is a rhyme with today's world, where political change (led by "Levellers") is taking place at a time when the world of international relations (as at the gathering in Westphalia) is also changing.

Westphalia cut free forces and structures that would dominate the balance of power in world affairs for nearly three hundred years. It is also worth noting that at around the time of Westphalia, the dominant world power, the Ming dynasty in China, was fading. Weak trade, climate change, disease, and inequality were some of the factors to upend it. The next major structural change in international affairs came in the aftermath of the Second World War with the emergence of two superpowers and the creation of such international bodies as the United Nations (1945).

Following the fall of communism, globalization began and changed international affairs in several ways. First, globalization aided the spread of democracy; second, it has bound countries together through trade and through economic and financial links; and third, it has created a common culture of consumerism across nations and regions. Globalization has acted like glue across countries and institutions in its impact on international relations, and to a large extent this glue has been "made in America."

As a result of globalization, there has been a much better distribution of the world's economic output, led by what were once regarded as overpopulated third-world countries such as India and China. Globalization is now coming to an end, to be a replaced by a multipolar world, a critical strain upon which is the tension between Leveller and Leviathan approaches to social governance. However, the policy consensus remains wedded to globalization, and there are few signs that thinkers in the foreign-policy space are ready to break with established models of looking at the world.[35] We are now on the verge of another fissure and a paradigm shift in international affairs, and there is therefore a need to find ways of illustrating what the new world order might look like.

NINE

A NEW WORLD ORDER

Levellers or Leviathans?

G EOPOLITICS, INCREASINGLY DRIVEN BY THE LEVELLING OUT OF ECONOMIC and geopolitical power and wealth among nations, is central to our story. Two trends will drive the evolution of geopolitics over the next twenty years, as the levelling takes hold. The first is that three Orwellian regions will come to dominate the multipolar landscape: Oceania (the United States and possibly the United Kingdom), Eurasia (the European Union plus Turkey, eastern Europe, and Israel), and Eastasia (Chinacentric Asia). The second is that these poles will increasingly differ ideologically, not to the extent of being communist or capitalist but on where they stand as Leveller or Leviathan nations politically.

These trends will trigger a number of new departures in international affairs, some of which I will sketch here and then elaborate in the rest of the chapter. Middle-sized nations will struggle to find their place in the world; Brexit and its aftermath will be a widely watched experiment; small, advanced nations will club together; and the international institutions of the twentieth century will wither and will be replaced by new institutions.

The trade dispute in 2018 between the United States and China is an apt illustration of the last—with the WTO standing idly by in the background, whereas in the 1990s it was much more prominent. The institutions designed for the twentieth century will increasingly run into the limits of their own relevance. Many of the problems they were designed to solve, from acute underdevelopment across the emerging world to the funding of countries, have largely been resolved, and in many cases, new, more complex problems have grown up to replace them.

The emergence of a large-pole-driven world will also be to the detriment of medium-sized nations. Thus, another issue is what medium-sized nations do about their status as satellite, orphan, or vassal states (to use a favorite term of Brexiteers). Britain, Russia, and maybe India are examples here. Britain, denuded by Brexit, might fall back on its roots as the linchpin of the rule of law to become a global center for law, commerce, and corporate governance. It could become the location of choice for multinationals, legal-dispute resolution, and global standardization in payments and digital currencies, for example (Switzerland has stolen a march here). Similarly, Russia could be more influential if it had a more solid economy and was trusted with the investment capital of other nations.

Unlike Britain and Russia, India's economic potential is growing. It now faces the dilemma of matching its economic potential with hard power as it spends more aggressively on defense. A very interesting development here is that, together with the United States, Australia, and Japan, India is a member of the Quadrilateral Security Dialogue alliance (the Quad) of Western-oriented Asian nations. It is based on "shared values and principles" and has the aim of securing a free and open Indo-Pacific region. It was initiated a decade ago but was parked owing to objections by China. China's rise has now caused a revival of the Quad. Commercial and military ties among the Quad countries are growing. India, an increasingly aggressive military spender, is one of the most significant markets for American defense equipment, and it is employing Japanese financing and technology in the construction of high-speed-train networks. Set against the Quad (and NATO) is the

Shanghai Cooperation Organization (SCO), founded in 2001, whose principal members are Russia and China (Pakistan is also an active member, and India is also a member but is understandably less active). The Quad and the SCO are significant to the levelling in that they are the two rival teams on the geopolitical fault line, located between the two large poles of the Americas and Asia. Each team (or perhaps gang) will increasingly carry out joint military exercises and will purchase their military equipment largely from their allies.

From the Quad to the Hanseatic League 2.0 to the SCO

At the same time, this changing world has the potential to liberate other countries. One such group consists of small, advanced countries (i.e., Austria, Belgium, Singapore, Sweden, Switzerland, Ireland, Hong Kong, Norway, Denmark, Finland, New Zealand, Israel, and the Netherlands) with a number of distinctive features. Small, advanced economies also have very open economies and are effectively the canaries in the coal mine of the world economy in the sense that they pick up new developments, such as fluctuations in world trade, before these issues are experienced in larger economies. They also all tend to suffer the same problems. For example, in the wake of the quantitative easing programs of the Bank of Japan and the European Central Bank, the currencies of countries like Norway and New Zealand became more volatile. Geopolitically, this group of countries has a growing incentive to come together as a group (there is already a budding Hanseatic League 2.0 of small northern European countries, made up of the Nordic and Baltic states together with Ireland and the Netherlands, whose initial activities have focused on a more stringent approach to EU fiscal policy) and may soon be regarded as the moral authority in world affairs.[1]

So the SCO, the Quad, and the Hanseatic League 2.0 may well grow to be some of the important reference points in twenty-first-century geopolitics, and in my view they will help form the skeleton of the new world order.

In this respect, the great experiment of this emerging order is what happens to Britain in the post-Brexit era. British politicians have coined the phrase "Global Britain" to represent their vision of Britain in the future, but very few of them have added color to what remains a blank canvas. The evolution of Global Britain is worth watching beyond Britain's shores, especially in the United States, for a number of reasons. First, Brexit is the first major event of the levelling. Second, together with the United States, Global Britain is central to the narrative of the levelling. Not only are those two nations the focus of many of the trends described in this book, but, in the eyes of many, they are also countries coming to terms with decline from greatness and confronted with the challenge of renewing themselves. The current predicament of the United Kingdom should act as a warning for the United States, because the United Kingdom is treading a path that the United States and other nations (such as Italy) may follow. We need to carefully watch whether and how the United Kingdom reinvents itself. Global Britain will be a marker of how well countries can reinvent themselves in a changed geopolitical setting and of how well they can reinvigorate their economies. Not only is Britain a close ally of the United States, but it also shares many of the same socioeconomic issues and political fault lines. If, say, the Tory Party splits, I feel that that makes it easier to envisage the same happening to the Republican Party.

Hotspur

The previous chapter relied on George Orwell's *1984* to explain the three large poles that may dominate a multipolar world. Another Orwell text is also useful in explaining recent events in the United Kingdom. In an essay entitled "Boy's Weeklies," Orwell encapsulates the stereotypes of foreigners prevalent in comic books like *Magnet* and *Hotspur*, surmising the French and Italians as "excitable," Scandinavians as "kind-hearted," and most other nationalities as "treacherous."[2] The picture he paints in 1940 is of an Anglocentric world where upstanding English men need to be on their guard once they pass beyond the shores of the United Kingdom and into the distasteful, inferior world outside Britain. Reading it, I was reminded of an apocryphal British newspaper headline that read, "Fog in the Channel, Continent Cut Off."

This view of the world beyond the channel is outdated, but it does chime with the schoolboy tone of much of the debate on Brexit and underlines a sense of British exceptionalism that many other Europeans, Asians, and even Americans might feel has not dissipated. Indeed, much of the discussion of Brexit has set the tone for political events internationally; it has seemed stereotyped, with scaremongering and bullying as the main channels of communication. Both sides in the Brexit debate made the mistake of treating the public to a low form of badgering. Politics has been diminished, but there is yet little apparent response to the desire of voters for new, coherent, and arguably constructive political solutions. The sense of Orwell's essay is still pertinent today and suggests that the British never considered themselves to be European, which is perhaps why they felt it relatively easy to consider leaving the European Union.

In the scheme of things, Brexit was a significant breakpoint in history for a number of reasons. It represents a rupture, an unexpected backlash by a people, and the first major event that crystallizes the feeling that something is changing. It is also the first break that a country has made with the established order and the first clear signal of dissonance between the people and the Grandees.

Brexit serves as an important indicator of the way relationships among power, wealth, and democracy are being subjected to a stress test. Brexit, by threatening to rupture the relationships among England, Scotland, Northern Ireland, and Ireland, takes us back in history, all the way back toward the Levellers to 1706 and 1707 and the Acts of Union between Scotland and England. At the same time, the debate that was led by the Levellers was very different from that which has taken place over Brexit. The discourse of the Levellers was, as far as we know, hopeful, constructive, and detailed in its prescriptions, whereas Brexit has been nasty, negative, and chaotic.

The pungently negative Brexit debate also has a revealing and very worrying element. It has opened up a crater-sized policy vacuum within the great apparatus of the British state, whose leaders were neither able nor, apparently, willing to fashion a credible Brexit negotiating plan and are struggling ever harder to produce a meaningful and credible vision of Britain's place in the world after Brexit. To paraphrase Churchill's quotation on Bolshevism: "Brexit is not a policy; it is a disease. It is not a creed; it is a pestilence."[3]

Decline and Fall

Brexit will delight the "decline and fall" crowd. Brexit gives the professional declinist a live experiment of a nation going it alone, going against the multipolar current, and, arguably, going against the gravity of productivity, demographics, and indebtedness. In chapter 7, I noted that long-term moves in the price of currencies reflect the rise and fall of countries. And the currency market has already delivered a verdict on Brexit.

When the dollar made its debut as the currency of the United States in 1794, it cost $4.75 to buy £1. This ratio stayed generally stable for the next one hundred years (though it dipped down toward $3 for £1 during the Napoleonic Wars and then rose as high as $10 for £1 during the American Civil War). Yet the relationship changed materially after the Second World War; by the 1950s, it only took about $2.50 to buy £1. Post the Brexit referendum, the dollar-to-pound exchange rate dropped to a low of $1.18 for £1.[4]

Making a success of Brexit would be much easier if globalization as we have known it for the last thirty years were to persist and if the global economy were to continue to strengthen in the near future. However, because globalization is over and a multipolar system, of which Britain is not a major player, is now evolving, Britain will find that, after Brexit, it will enter a more complex world-trade environment and will be under pressure to surrender its privileged place in many world institutions (in the UN Security Council, for instance). Nor is it likely that the global economic recovery will continue for much longer; the world will probably be in recession by the time Britain finally sails away from Europe.

Compared to the three large poles, Britain is now dropping into the second division, a geopolitical reality that has been publicly underlined by the likes of Sir John Sawers, who, as the former head of the Britain's Secret Intelligence Services, knows a thing or two about what is happening behind the scenes in world affairs.[5] He has warned that Britain's role in international diplomacy will be severely diminished in the post-Brexit era. There is a very large gap between expectations and reality here. Many British politicians still talk as if we are back in the 1940s (some even hark back to empire) rather than heading to the 2020s. This gap will bear heavily on UK politics. It will become the basis for a new divide in British politics between those people whose vision of Britain is sentimental and those people—arguably younger members of Parliament—who have a sense for the role Britain can play in a modern, multipolar world.

Their task ahead will be tough and reminds me of a story from an earlier period in British politics. In 1964 Jim Callaghan took over as UK chancellor of the exchequer from Reginald Maudling, who had left the nation's finances in a precarious state. Upon arriving at his desk, Callaghan found a note from Maudling that read, "Good luck old cock. Sorry to leave it in such a mess." With Brexit now underway, perhaps Downing Street should now write such a note to the next generation of Britons and especially to Ireland and Scotland given the economic and political uncertainty that Brexit may visit upon them.

The crafting of what Global Britain looks like will be the next great political challenge. It will take time for Britain to carve out a new, distinct role. The chief way for it to make a success of Brexit is to engage in arbitrage among the large poles in a multipolar world. What this means in practice is that Britain should establish itself as a trading center and standard leader for goods and services that the three regions share (corporate governance, for example, is one such area). Equally, it can establish itself as a supplier, independent from the major poles, of goods and services (e.g., internet security, artificial intelligence applications, media technology, and content-generation ability) that are too costly for less-well-resourced nations to develop on their own.

In this way, Britain can establish itself as a jurisdiction where individuals and corporations can avail themselves of independent, high-quality services across the industries of accounting, law, banking, and, to an extent, education. Individuals and corporations in countries across the world would go to the United Kingdom to settle accounts, disputes, and their bills in a way that would adhere to a global standard. This is a very optimistic account of one aspect of the United Kingdom's place in the world economy. The journey to such a place will be strewn with obstacles. Consider the disruptive effects of Brexit on Scotland, Ireland, and Northern Ireland; the incentives of the European Union and its member states to pursue a difficult and testing Brexit process into the transition period; the risk that Britain will lose its place at the top table of international institutions (e.g., the UN Security Council); the leakage of financial capital away from London to other European capitals; and the difficulty of striking bilateral trade deals with the likes of India and China.

On the positive side, the United Kingdom has its role as a significant security power to use as a bargaining chip, and it is possible that any future political economy crisis in Europe or the eurozone will end up making Brexit look like a move of strategic genius. On the same side, it may now be pushed to take an approach straight out of the small-country manual. To some extent, the United Kingdom may end up looking to position itself as a more pugnacious version of Switzerland, or to take a position in Europe analogous to Japan's in Asia: geographically in Europe but standing off politically and culturally.

To focus the post-Brexit response on what the UK government terms "Global Britain" may, however, miss the lessons of Brexit, which speak of hostility to immigration, a loss of identity, and a sense that the UK regions are underdeveloped both economically and in terms of social and intangible infrastructure when compared to London.[6] Rather, much of the hard policy work will need to be done domestically in the post-Brexit period, and attention will need to be focused on the necessity for the British state to craft new economic and industrial structures.

The long-term lesson here is that the UK economy needs to be better balanced and more robust in a world where globalization is slowing. Intangible infrastructure is the key. In hard terms, this will require considerable innovation: a sophisticated regional approach to corporate taxation, tax credits, and company financing. In addition, there will need to be a wholesale renewal of physical infrastructure in the regions beyond London on a scale that would be on a par with the work of Isambard Brunel, the great engineer whose creations—railways, steamships (SS *Great Britain*), viaducts, bridges, and tunnels—changed the landscape of nineteenth-century Britain.

Similarly, there would probably have to be a rethinking of the UK school system so that funding and expertise are made available to foster the growth of more and better schools in the regions of the United Kingdom outside London. A UK-regions-based tax system—a tax system in which rates would be different in different regions—might be one way to achieve this, with large companies in particular being enticed by lower corporate taxes (or lower social changes and more attractive investment write-offs) in less-well-developed regions of the United Kingdom. This will partially help make the capital a relatively less attractive place to live. The post-Brexit period will be more fruitful if the government focuses on public goods in the United Kingdom and on sectors of the economy where the United Kingdom is distinctive and fashions a less aggressive foreign policy.

The United Kingdom may have little choice here, partly because of the impetus that Brexit will give to the Scottish independence movement and to the socioeconomic and political changes it may trigger in Northern Ireland. For these regions, and for Ireland, Brexit is a historic event that may set off new economic and political journeys.[7] Like the characters in the 1939 film *The Wizard of Oz*, each country is searching for a different quality or solving a distinct challenge. England needs to navigate the potential shock of the Brexit process and then must fill out the vision of "Global Britain." Scotland has to build a new economic base and the institutions needed to support it. Northern Ireland must wean itself away from a state-supported economy and a sclerotic political system. Ireland, for whom Brexit holds clear threats and opportunities, needs to learn to overcome persistent extreme socioeconomic imbalances.

At a broader international level, all of this is relevant in many ways. First, the world is watching Brexit for signs that it marks a new beginning for Britain and potentially the end of the European Union, or vice versa. Second, small countries around the world, from Singapore to Dubai, not to mention emerging markets and reviving cities, will be examining the way policy makers in Scotland and Ireland deal with the multiple challenges posed by Brexit. Third, for eighty million Americans, at least, the nexus of Ireland, Scotland, and England is part of their cultural identity, and this debate has broader emotional resonance.

After Brexit, Scotland will be the next test case, in that it may hold another referendum on independence sometime in the 2020s. Though many who held that Brexit would benefit the British economy also said that Scottish independence would be an economic disaster, this does not need to be the case. The post-Brexit era will present a range of opportunities as well as the need for a competitive discipline. Scotland, for instance, has not yet had a chance to build the policy capability to make the most of its brand as a country and of its access to markets. Indeed, until recent decades, the absence of very distinctive Scotland-facing policies from London has been a real constraint on Scotland; most notable has been the absence of a policy response to the (global) process of deindustrialization that Scotland experienced starting in the 1980s. Today, its economic model will need to be the small-country one described earlier in this chapter.

In Scotland, the first referendum on independence was fought largely on the basis of the potential for independence to bring economic gains or losses. Indeed, it must have been one of the first independence debates to have been fought by spreadsheet. It was marked by a noisy and often misleading debate on what currency Scotland might have: the pound, the euro, or a new Scottish currency that would start life pegged to the pound. Another way of framing this argument is to say that too much of the 2014 referendum debate was focused on high-level macropolicy—on currency and public finance—and not enough was focused on the future investments that needed to be made so that an independent Scotland could act to position itself for success in the global economy. Scotland will need to make investments in establishing institutions and building capability—for example, a Monetary Authority and an Office for Budget Responsibility (OBR)–style institution on the fiscal policy side. A key lesson from the international small-economy experience is that there is a need to develop economic strengths in the economy; for Scotland, these strengths range from finance to tourism, renewable energy, and life sciences.

Moving west of Scotland, scanning the world map in terms of attainment on intangible infrastructure and related metrics, such as the human development indicators, reveals that Northern Ireland stands out as a poor performer. Brexit threatens Northern Ireland in that it may force a repositioning of Northern Ireland with respect to the Republic of Ireland and to the European Union. The peace in Northern Ireland is still fragile, and there needs to be a recognition in London and Dublin that Northern Ireland needs a second wind in terms of its socioeconomic development. Northern Ireland should not be parked as a political issue but should be cultivated economically and socially.

One suggestion is that a small portion of Britain's Brexit exit fee to the European Union be set aside to underwrite a Marshall Plan–type fund for Northern Ireland, which would follow the small-country model. A few examples of what this might tangibly focus on include the kind of skill-based apprentice schemes found in Austria and Switzerland, rezoning of housing from deeply politically entrenched areas using the social-impact-investing model found in Belgium, investment in cultural projects that are common to all communities (such as is done in Scandinavia and Switzerland), and the establishment of poles of excellence in certain professions, such as legal financial services. Such a fund might draw on the expertise and governance capabilities of other small states. This might help by removing some of the baggage from policy decisions (for example, the advice of Swiss technocrats might be easier to take than views from London or Dublin), and the employment of detailed rolling five-year plans might help speed up what is at times a sclerotic policy process.

South of the border, Ireland is a prominent member of the small country success club. Having had its first major boom and bust through the first decade of the twenty-first century, its economy has recovered, posting the best growth rates of any European economy from 2011 to 2018. To an extent, and unsurprisingly given its economic links to the United States, in many parts of Ireland the recovery does not feel like a full and broad one, and many Americans may sympathize with this. There are two broad policy issues facing Ireland.

First, as with many other small economies, Ireland does best when it faces the outside world: its best institutions (diplomacy and the Industrial Development Authority [IDA], for instance) are outward facing, but many domestic institutions are under severe strain. To distill the meaning of crises in the police, health care, and housing: many of the administrative institutions in Ireland are slow and badly suited for the twenty-first century.

Instead of trying to tackle each symptom of this structural problem on a piecemeal basis, the Irish state should reexamine its approach to governance and public service. Such an examination should not exclude examples of what works in larger countries, but, arguably, factors in Ireland such as homogeneity of population, geopolitical standing, and proximity of policy makers to the public mean that Singapore (rather than China) and the Netherlands (rather than Germany) offer more plausible lessons for Ireland in the area of public administration. This examination should result in a new method and approach to public administration: one that is more flexible than compartmentalized, one that quickly deploys pilot projects rather than spending years rolling out huge, unwieldy initiatives, and one that reasserts the value of education and health care as public goods. Some of Ireland's sports teams and cultural institutions are models here. Then, also, Ireland needs to develop more acumen in the governance and management of state-related enterprises, needs to approach them from a position of principle (i.e., that education and health are public goods), and needs to better oversee the state's role as an economic actor and procurer of services.

The second issue is that Ireland still regularly suffers from imbalances in its economy, the most obvious one today being that house prices and rental charges are higher than during its bubble period, and that there is a resulting housing crisis. Ireland's overheated property market is one area where it can learn from other small countries. In the past it has found it too easy to copy the policy model of the United Kingdom and has ignored the lessons of other small open countries (notably, the Scandinavian banking crisis of the 1990s came to the notice of Irish policy makers only after the collapse of the Celtic Tiger). Brexit will, naturally, change this.

As regards housing, Ireland as a country still needs to decide that "houses are for living in, not for speculation," to quote a recent remark from China's president.[8] It must then act accordingly from a fiscal and regulatory point of view. A further challenge is to build up the domestic economic sector. Sweden and Switzerland (and to a much more specifically technological degree, Israel) are good examples of countries that have created the cultural, financial, and human capital conditions allowing medium-sized enterprises to thrive. If Ireland can do this, it will have less need to be concerned about a global race to the bottom in corporation taxes.

Overall, Brexit is unleashing a range of powerful dynamics and opportunities across the United Kingdom and Ireland. One reality is that the small-economy model will become more relevant in that part of the world. Another is that Britain's interaction with the Commonwealth will change in the same way that England's relationship with Scotland and Ireland will change. Brexit itself and a changing dynamic between developed and developing countries will curb the geopolitical relevance of the Commonwealth for its members, many of whom recognize it as a colonial construct.

End of Condescension

For Americans, the levelling at a geopolitical level largely will take the form of the US-Chinese rivalry, but there are other, more acute examples, one of which—the relationship between Britain and the Commonwealth countries—is instructive about the changing dimensions in world affairs.

Demographics mean that countries like Nigeria and India will probably outgrow the Commonwealth; their populations and economies will increase such that they no longer feel the Commonwealth is relevant to them. Their growth and their increasingly poor fit for networks like the Commonwealth—colonial in origin and relatively meaningless institutionally—may well spark a change of tone in international relations. In particular, the bigger emerging powers may, and should, have much less patience for being condescended to in diplomacy, not merely by the United Kingdom but also by larger powers such as the United States.

One figure who comes to mind here is Robert Hart, an Irishman and one of the more influential foreign figures in Chinese history over the past two hundred years. He was born and grew up in County Armagh and was educated in Dublin and Belfast. After leaving Queen's University, he joined the Consular Service and was posted to China. His career flourished, owing to the good relations he established with the Chinese. Hart's role soon involved the establishment of a network of customs offices across China, and in 1863 he was appointed inspector general of China's Imperial Maritime Custom Service. He was a modernizer, and among his achievements were the upscaling of Chinese ports and river transport systems as well as a streamlined tariff-collection process, which soon produced 20 percent of China's government revenues. He prompted the Chinese government to open embassies abroad and encouraged Chinese officials to learn foreign languages. His other notable contribution during his fifty-year career in China was to counsel his staff to deal with the Chinese in a manner that avoided offense and ill feeling. The Chinese, for their part, referred to him as "our Hart."

This story is highly relevant today for the way in which it highlights the importance and complexity of trade systems and infrastructure and also for the manner in which Hart engaged in and insisted on a respectful conduct of business with the Chinese. It is fair to say that in the course of the last century or more, older or richer Western countries have not always treated emerging countries in a respectful way. This has sowed the seeds of resentment in some quarters in the emerging world, not least in India. India is interesting in this context of colonial condescension, given that the structure of its institutions, its multilayered society and education system, and the development of its independence have been fashioned through its relationship with the United Kingdom.[9]

Today India, compared to China, is at the relatively early stage of its development as an economic power, lacking the breadth in wealth and income distribution of China, and, importantly, lacking the very forceful way in which policy can be implemented in China. India is beginning to discover the potential of its soft power, and it still lacks experience and expertise in hard, military power (notwithstanding its nuclear and space programs). In time, the contrast and friction between India and China may grow, especially if Chinese presence in ports in Sri Lanka and Pakistan grows (spending on Chinese military equipment by Pakistan now dwarfs that spent on US military goods), if China's One Belt, One Road plan encroaches on India, and if the two countries grow apart ideologically.

For the moment, the United Kingdom might well be a more telling reference point for India. As the United Kingdom deals with Brexit's threat to its geopolitical power and economic size, India will prove an interesting counterexample to the United Kingdom. Its economy should continue to grow speedily under its own steam, and the country will discover that its size and growing influence (consider, for example, the role of the Indian diaspora in the Gulf States) will bring the opportunity and responsibility to assert itself more in world affairs. In time, Indian politicians may look to cement this institutionally by taking the United Kingdom's permanent seat on the UN Security Council (if that body continues to have relevance).

In the meantime, India will be interesting for the bubbling array of economic forces—not all of them well marshaled yet from a policy point of view—that will drive its economy. Reforms are beginning to affect the structure of its economy. In November 2016, for instance, the government withdrew from circulation five-hundred- and thousand-rupee notes, the country's two largest denominations. The objective was to curb the black economy. The aim is to formalize transactions and to drive savings into the banking system. That the introduction of a relatively simple policy measure like this can have such a profound impact on the Indian economy speaks to the possible level of growth that can eventually be attained from reform, even if the path toward it is slightly chaotic.

India is replete with fascinating microtrends, such as the impact of social media and the digitization of social security. The Aadhaar system—or Unique Identification Authority of India (UIDAI)—is now the world's largest biometric identity program; India's residents are given a twelve-digit identification number based on demographic and biometric data. Other important trends include the spread of telecommunications-related payment systems, the nation's growing rural economies, the challenge of urbanizing the country in a sustainable way, and the promise of properly developing a financial and wealth infrastructure that can enable a more fluid distribution of capital across companies and that will improve the profile of wealth distribution.

Success of Small States

Much of this chapter, and indeed the book, has focused on the fortunes of large countries, which is understandable given that clashes among them will reverberate around the world and that their economic weight is considerable. In contrast, though many smaller countries may find a world of big beasts harder to deal with, one group of small, advanced nations may gain and seek greater prominence.

In chapter 6 we discussed the country strength economic model, which is inspired by the Nordic model of countries like Sweden and Denmark, which themselves are pioneers of what we have described as having strong intangible infrastructure. They are part of an increasingly coherent group of small, advanced economies that may emerge both as a political economic species and as an informal grouping, especially if the great powers or great poles prefer to exercise power in a regressive manner.

For many years, the geopolitical fate of these small, advanced economies has been determined by their geography and, in particular, by their relationships with their larger neighbors (i.e., Singapore with China, Ireland with England, Finland with Russia, and so on).[10] Indeed, geography is still a determining factor in a country's fortunes, and there is substantial research to support this, from Paul Krugman's book *Geography and Trade* to recent books like *Prisoners of Geography* by Tim Marshall. However, size may also become a defining variable.

Small, developed states have distinguished themselves in that they have overcome geographic constraints in building successful and resilient socioeconomic models. They are the policy models that the likes of Katherine Chidley will follow closely. They have done so in somewhat different ways: Israel has focused on technology and innovation, Switzerland on high-value-added products, and Ireland on fiscal policy. But their secrets of success have several common factors: policy agility and speed of implementation, a focus on intangible infrastructure factors such as education and human development, and an economic openness that has permitted them to ride on the coattails of globalization. Small, developed states are now the most globalized of nations and also rank well on more balanced measures of national well-being, such as human development scores and levels of inequality. For instance, the Bloomberg Innovation Index counts ten of the small, advanced countries (Sweden, Singapore, Switzerland, Finland, Denmark, Israel, Austria, Ireland, Belgium, and Norway) in the top fifteen of its ranking.

These nations are also among the most equitable countries in the world, together with being the most advanced in terms of human development. Most are at the pinnacle of democracy. The Economist Intelligence Unit's Democracy Index report looks at five criteria—political culture, political participation, the functioning of government, electoral process, and civil liberties—and classifies just nineteen countries as "full democracies."[11] The top five countries in 2017 were Norway, Iceland, Sweden, New Zealand, and Denmark; the bottom ones were North Korea, Chad, Syria, the Democratic Republic of Congo, and the Central African Republic. Of the nineteen countries classified as "full democracies," fourteen are small countries, with eight of them in the top ten.

These facts point in two or perhaps three directions.

The first is that, as I've said, these "canaries in the coal mine" are the first to respond to trends that materialize in larger economies, and their experience thus has something to say to larger countries. It should also be stated that small states are policy innovators and in many instances react to and solve problems ahead of larger states.

The second direction is that, given their shared problems, small states may increasingly feel the need to gather together to discuss topics where there is a specific small-state angle and to share expertise on solutions. Some examples of this are fiscal policy in the eurozone, the role of research and development in industrial policy, and the nexus between multinationals and nation-states. The evolution of the Hanseatic League 2.0 in the eurozone is a very good illustration of this. This league is grouped around the finance ministers of nine small eurozone states—Ireland, the Netherlands, the Nordic states (except Iceland), and the Baltic states—who have come together to express their views on the importance of fiscal independence for small states in the eurozone. The group is now a powerful political presence within the broader group of European finance ministers and may grow to express views on other policy strands.

In this light, the "notion of a voice for small states" increasingly makes sense to governments and policy makers in some of the countries mentioned above, though many of them express a preference for less formal discussions lest such conversations trouble existing relationships (either with big-country neighbors or with bodies like the European Union).[12]

However, if a new reality of distinct political channels between the large poles emerges, then it will increasingly make sense for small, developed countries to come together in a more formal group. A more global small-country grouping could be called the "g20" (with a lowercase g) as opposed to the G20. A g20 is perhaps more likely to be on the cutting edge of the economic pulse and policy innovation than the larger countries and on the whole is likely to be more impartial on many issues, such as environmental damage, corruption, and military intervention.

In this respect, such a g20 group would have three common factors that are not found across all the world's larger countries. First, small states are very globalized: eight of the top ten most globalized states are small (population up to ten million), whereas China ranks 132nd in globalization out of 174 countries, India comes in 137th, and the United States is in 57th place. With globalization changing, small states' experiences will be instructive for all other countries. Second, small states are a model to follow in terms of the quality of their institutions. Third, most of them have well-established, healthy democracies.

So it is not inconceivable that in a world fixated on classifications—such as "emerging economies" or "frontier markets"—a new geopolitical grouping will emerge in the form of a select group of small, developed countries whose defining characteristics are that they are open economies and open societies.

One might ask what contribution a ragtag group of small countries—whose collective population is lower than that of Russia or
Indonesia—can make to international relations in a world dominated
by large poles. There are several. One is that, among the accolades won
by the likes of Sweden and Singapore, is the recognition that they are
neutral and impartial and leaders in the area of transparency and fighting corruption. Thus, one contribution from the small, developed countries may be to draft a practical code of transparency and corruption,
which would set a higher bar compared to similar codes from the United
Nations and the OECD. Another innovation is that small, developed
countries are leaders in the area of technologies that can be deployed
to bolster transparency, such as cybersecurity, payment systems, and accounting and finance systems.

Consider the impact of a two-pronged approach whereby procure-
ment and payments by state, regional, and local authorities are made in a
secure tabulated electronic form, with the same being done for political
party funding and political expenses. Such an approach is in operation
in some small countries, and a common standard among them, with
common technologies and systems approaches, could form a gold standard on transparency and corruption, a standard that other countries
could adopt voluntarily.

The Future of International Institutions

The rise of new alliances and the potential division of the world order
into, say, a biosphere built around large poles, ambitious and anxious
midsized nations, and a coalition of democratic, developed small states
may prefigure the way international relations develop in other ways. In
many parts of the world, the role and influence of international institutions such as the World Bank, the IMF, and the WTO is fading quickly.
The OECD has at least managed to reposition itself as the brains trust
of the G20. Growing wealth in Asia means that the World Bank is now
concentrating on Africa, the eurozone crisis has diminished the IMF,

and trade disputes (such as tariffs on steel) have exposed the WTO's lack of clout.

The economies of the Middle East are another example. Much of the development in the Middle East has been financed locally, led by key families and entrepreneurs, with some American expertise. In the past, the United Nations had a physical and moral presence in the region, but the aftermath of the Arab Spring and the UN's nearly total failure in the Syrian refugee crisis contribute to the view that it is a twentieth-century rather than a twenty-first-century institution. The lesson here is that for many regions of the world, and potentially for the large poles, twentieth-century institutions like the UN, the World Bank, and the WTO are defunct. The large poles may well prefer to settle disputes among themselves rather than, for instance, having recourse to what will be an increasingly divided UN Security Council.

As a multipolar world materializes to replace today's more US-centric one, the collection of institutions that have served the evolution of the world order in the twentieth century may well be rendered obsolete. The fact that many of those institutions (the World Bank is a leading example) are bureaucratic, founded on consensus building, and, according to many accounts, resistant to change is a recipe for their being superseded. Indeed, before he joined the World Bank, former president Dr. Jim Yong Kim contributed to the book *Dying for Growth*, in which he scathingly attacked the Bank.[13]

Several emerging trends may contribute to the obsolescence of bodies like the World Bank and the United Nations. The most obvious is that many of the problems they were established to tackle—such as poverty, development-project funding, and economic development—have improved to a degree that they are much more localized, and in many cases individual governments are more focused on them. The second is that, in a multipolar world, the poles may be more prone to resolve matters among themselves—trade is one such area; another is geopolitical conflict, where, for example, issues like the diplomatic strategy toward North Korea are more likely to be resolved between two poles, the United States and China.

Relatedly, the failure of the United Nations in the midst of the horror and complexity of the conflict across Syria in the post–Arab Spring era has not enhanced its credibility. A further issue in geopolitics is the emergence of unconventional warfare, where perpetrators are harder to identify and where rules of engagement are not yet well developed; cyberwarfare and cybercrime are examples of unconventional warfare, and so is the ambiguous tactical approach of the Russian military in Ukraine and parts of Serbia. In addition, new constellations of nations may emerge—such as the Shanghai Cooperation Organization (SCO)—that may defy the United Nations, or simply paralyze its voting structure.

To borrow the earlier analogy between political parties and companies, if the United Nations, World Bank, IMF, and WTO were companies, they may well have failed, been taken over, or been broken up at this stage. We should not extend this analogy too far because these institutions have been valuable international public goods and in many instances have contributed a great deal to world affairs. However, they are a poor fit to today's changed world and need to be reordered and reshaped to better serve it.

The World Bank should be drastically reduced in size and relocated to Africa, which is the one part of the world that still needs an institution like it. Being closer to the economies and societies it is supposed to serve, rather than being cosseted in Washington, will make the work of the World Bank more impactful. Having helped microfinance grow, it should support the emergence of impact investing (where investments have a social as well as a financial objective) across developed and emerging countries.

The WTO should also cease to exist, given its poor performance, near irrelevance in the face of emerging trade wars, and the tendency of large poles to hammer out agreements among themselves. Ironically, and with a little imagination, London may replace many of these international institutions as a place of dispute resolution and as a legal base.

Similarly, the IMF needs to be overhauled, both in its structure and in its expertise. Many of its functions, such as research, economic surveillance, and capital raising, are better performed by the private sector and, increasingly, by central banks. The eurozone crisis has seen the IMF contort itself in terms of the policies it considers appropriate for different types of indebted countries.[14] To an extent, much of its role as a lender has been superseded by large central banks, development institutions, and private capital. Furthermore, the potential advent of an EU Treasury may further negate the need for the European Union to partner with the IMF on financial rescues. The next potential global financial accident spot, China, will probably not call on the IMF to resolve its debt overhang in a conventional manner; rather, it is likely to deal with a financial accident in its own way.

Bring Back Bancor

There may be scope for the IMF to maintain its relevance as a specialized debt-oversight institution. In that area, at least, one aspect of the IMF's policy arsenal might still be useful. At the time of the initial Bretton Woods Conference in 1944 at the very charming Mount Washington Hotel in Bretton Woods, New Hampshire, the economist John Maynard Keynes suggested the creation of a supranational currency to be called "Bancor." His idea was that Bancor would, especially in times of recession, create a world reference currency that would help regulate imbalances in trade among nations and would therefore stimulate commerce. In the end, the Bretton Woods Conference opted to reference, or peg, currency values to the value of gold, though this effectively laid the grounds for the emergence of the dollar as the first among currency equals.

Bancor might have a use today as an idea that could permit the IMF's Special Drawing Rights (SDR) facility—effectively a supranational currency (ironically, in today's terms it is like a cryptocoin, with a coordinating institution)—to allow both developed and less developed countries to issue what one might call IMF or SDR bonds.[15] They would do so in the immediate aftermath of a financial crisis, which would hasten their financial and economic recovery. These bonds would be issued as the supranational currency of Bancor, they could potentially have preferential terms and conditions, and, importantly, they would be overseen by the IMF as a form of rating agency, or approval body, for these bonds. An important innovation could be added providing that, in the aftermath of an economic crisis, this type of bond could be issued with coupon payments tied to GDP and inflation levels, so that the holders of the bonds as well as the issuing countries would have an interest in its recovery.

Existing world institutions could be recast in two more ambitious ways. First, given that one of the aims of the levelling is to focus policy more on people (e.g., on health and education), there is a greater need for a more robust and coherent international policy on human development or intangible infrastructure. This policy effort would involve codifying a framework on intangible infrastructure, undertaking deeper research on the topic, and developing more-detailed global standards and measurements. Most importantly, it implies the development of practical means and policies by which countries in different parts of the world, with different standards of development, can improve human development and intangible infrastructure. To make such an organization work, parts of the United Nations—such as the UN Development Program (UNDP), some element of the WHO, departments of the World Bank, and the OECD—should be brought together in a new body, in a new location, and perhaps in a country that exemplifies this policy approach. Denmark is an example of such a country: it scores well in terms of such intangible infrastructure variables as social cohesion, education, wealth equality, and quality of institutions.

Another complication for the IMF and WTO as they lose credibility is that the nature of conflict between nations is becoming more focused on finance. In particular, central banks may encroach more into geopolitics. I have already argued (chapter 7) that central banks are too powerful and that far too much policy lifting has been left to them. Their overlordly roles in markets and economies should be pared back. Yet this is not a given, and in a multipolar world some players may have a different view.

One dimension that may complicate the need for less central bank intervention and diminish their independence is the quest by the large poles for financial dominance over each other. Central banks could become a vital instrument in such pursuits. Echoing Carl von Clausewitz's view that "war is the continuation of politics by other means," in a multipolar world central banks could become the monetary battleships of the large regions, with currency wars shadowing trade wars.[16] Indeed, the epidemic of countries sanctioning each other in 2018 (Saudi Arabia sanctioning Canada and the United States sanctioning Turkey, Russia, and China, for instance) suggests that finance is a key part of the geopolitical arsenal.

Against this backdrop, governments may be tempted to allow central banks to take on a more strategic or geostrategic role than the "mere" economic function they play today. For the United States and Europe, this compulsion may well grow. Financial globalization is the only area of globalization where the United States is truly dominant, and using financial architecture to entrench its dominance is a compelling strategy. In one scenario, the government might urge the Fed and the US Treasury to do several things.

The first is to deepen market and institutional ties to countries that use the dollar or that fall within the US orbit: most of Latin America, Saudi Arabia, and the Gulf states. As it stands, these countries are already, in economist speak, "price-takers" of the moves in Fed policy and US financial assets. That is, these countries must accept US interest-rate and dollar moves as given and try to maneuver around them and, if they are clever, ensure that their economies are not vulnerable to sharp moves in the dollar. In time the Treasury and the Fed may look to help dollar-relevant countries deepen their markets, build policy frameworks that make them less vulnerable to moves in US policy, and potentially bring large banks in regions such as Latin America more closely into the Fed system. Second, especially if China has a debt-induced recession in the next few years, the US financial authorities may look for ways to limit the broadening of China's financial markets so that its cost of funding is higher than it might be in a very open global financial system.

Internationally, the ECB is in second place to the Federal Reserve but is still a colossus compared to other central banks. In Europe, it has the unique distinction of being a successful, powerful European institution. The first step for the ECB is to drive banking and financial market uniformity across Europe. The easiest way to do this is to support the creation of several regional champion banks through a wave of consolidation and bank closures. The harmonization of regulation in areas like the recognition of bad debts and nonperforming loans would be a helpful start here.

In the case of the Fed and the ECB, tensions between poles may mean that they are drawn into situations of geopolitical tension. In the same way that cyberwars are now being fought silently and invisibly, the two large central banks may be called upon as sources of nondeadly but nonetheless consequential power. For instance, might a cyber- or even military incursion by Russia on Estonia be met with the selling of, say, the ruble, or the selling of Russian government and company bonds by the ECB? This is a somewhat extreme suggestion but not altogether out of the realm of possibility.

Climate Urgency

Many twentieth-century institutions (e.g., the United Nations, the World Bank) were set up to solve at least two problems: the coordination of policy and views across countries and the development of technical expertise. One field that needs more rather than less coordination and expertise is climate policy. Climate change and the increasingly obvious damage being done to the planet is something I would have liked to feature more in this book. When people ask me to state what the biggest risk to the world is (they usually use the phrase "black swan"), I usually reply that it is climate change. The slow buildup of evidence for global warming, the risks it poses to the world, the denial, and the lack of real policy change remind me all too much of the lead-up to the global financial crisis. Consistent with this template, I do not expect drastic action by the larger industrialized countries to address damage to the earth's atmosphere until the human cost of climate change becomes stark. However, I have not devoted more space to climate change because I feel that I lack the specialized knowledge to speak with any authority on this subject, at least from the point of view of the science of climate change.

Yet tackling climate change is more about politics, the way policy makers make decisions, and collective action than it is about pure science. This is somewhat depressing in the light of the disintegration of the international order and the divisive trade dispute that marked 2018. The economic toll of the trade dispute is relatively small in the grand scheme of things, but the cost of climate change can be enormous. It can potentially, for the first time in centuries, render whole cities uninhabitable (if sea levels rise), destroy vast tracts of agricultural land (as is already happening across Africa and the United States), alter the wealth of nations permanently, and exacerbate diseases (such as cancer and malnutrition) within countries.

The approach to climate change lies in the same process as that behind world trade negotiations and, potentially, as that described in chapter 7 for international debt restructuring. Individual nations will have to recognize the toll that climate change will take on their economies and societies and militate for broader political pressure. Sadly, in the case of climate change, it seems that people only become attuned to it once they witness its effects and fear of its implications becomes intense. In the United States, despite rigorous research by a dozen federal bodies to the effect that this period is now the warmest in the history of modern civilization owing principally to greenhouse gases, many Americans are skeptical that climate change is man-made.[17] For instance, only 30 percent of Republican voters believe that climate change is driven by human activity, yet academic research has shown that among Republican voters, there is a significant degree of difference of opinion on climate change.[18] For example, Republicans living in coastal areas—in California and Florida, for instance, two states where climate change is increasingly evident—have a much higher than average (compared to other Republicans) sense that climate change is ongoing. Having noted this, it still doesn't make sense to wait until the earth is entirely parched to convince people of the need for action on climate change. From a political and institutional point of view, there are a number of options.

A more conventional one is a world authority with teeth so that it can enforce action on climate change. The existing climate-change governance framework is largely made up of the UN Framework Convention on Climate Change (UNFCCC) and the Intergovernmental Panel on Climate Change (IPCC), though in recent years, the IPCC has struggled to gain credibility and power. Another element here, the Paris Agreement signed in April 2016, is neither binding nor enforceable, and the United States withdrew from it in June 2017. My tentative suggestion is to create a World Climate Authority. I use "authority" rather than "forum" or "council" because such an important body should not be a debating or research group but a body with power to curb climate change and solve the lack of collective action that undercuts efforts to halt global warming.

A World Climate Authority would be charged with monitoring the earth's climate, pinpointing the factors that cause warming, and overseeing a system of fines, incentives, and rationing that would act to reduce environmentally detrimental activities. It would have to have some framework for enforcement in place so that governments and regions could act if their neighbors did not adhere to the guidelines agreed as part of the establishment of the authority. Sadly, for such a body to come into force would require a large scale environmental disaster.

Given the poor recent track record of world bodies—from the UN Security Council to the World Bank to the WTO—skeptics might argue that such an approach is not credible. A better solution would be to change the emphasis of governance to a more meaningful level. One proposal is to simply relocate the decision making on climate policy from governments to cities, which would be appropriate because cities generate much (between 71 and 76 percent) of the pollution that creates climate change. (One source of pollution not the result of cities is cows, which generate a lot of methane, usually through belching. Each of the 1.5 billion cows in the world creates nearly as much greenhouse gas as a car.)[19] In addition, cities tend to suffer many of the effects of climate change—flooding and extreme temperatures being cases in point. Cities are, without generalizing, more progressive in their attitude to climate change than many corresponding governments are. The reaction of large-city mayors across the United States to President Trump's decision to withdraw from the Paris Agreement highlighted this. In the future, governance at the level of the city may become more common. One of the strands of research I have pursued with David Skilling in our work on small countries is the growing tendency toward governance at a more concentrated regional or city-specific level. Climate policy may lead this trend.

The climate framework struck at the level of the city would set out a climate taxation template, which would be structured to prevent companies from engaging in arbitrage activities in tax differences across cities and would provide a legal basis for cities to adopt taxes and charges (in different countries, cities may have varying levels of ability to levy taxes and charges). Revenues from these taxes and charges would be spent on environmentally relevant technologies such as flood barriers, better water piping, and green public transport infrastructure. At a time of rising urbanization in Africa and Asia, the city-based climate framework would also facilitate greater learning and cross-fertilization of views on city management and on the concept of greener, smarter cities.

Focusing on cities as political and policy entities has several advantages. In large countries, cities have a strong sense of identity, are increasingly progressive environmentally, and have a policy and communications proximity that aids the spread of information and policy. The governments of most medium to large cities, as opposed to national governments, are in a position to control or dominate their hinterland and the surrounding infrastructure and would plan the development in the way they saw fit to reduce pollution.

This approach could have several positive effects: notably, cities being given direction and the know-how to tie local tax, spending, and city planning more closely to the quality of the environment. It would work best in cases where there is an active city-based democracy—an elected mayor and city assembly—which for large cities may increasingly become the case. The former mayor of New York, Michael Bloomberg, has, together with environmentalist Carl Pope, underlined these points in a compelling book (*Climate of Hope*) on the role of cities in the battle for climate change.[20] A related proposal might be to have common campaigns across cities threatened by the same environmental dangers, such as rising sea levels provoked by global warming.

Cyberlaws

Better climate and environmental policy coordination is an important global, public good of the future. Another is the policing of the internet, specifically in the areas of cyberwar and cybercrime. In the same way that cities can play a distinct policy role in climate policy, the large technology companies—Facebook, Google, and Tencent, for example—are vital parts of the policy process in the domain of the internet. Their centrality to the concept of the levelling, as strategic assets for large states and regions, will condition the way governments and regulators address them.

Europe has few, if any, technology giants, and therefore Europe regulates Big Tech. In the United States, the technology companies make up 25 percent of the stock market and an equally large proportion of corporate earnings, and they have garnered the key innovation clusters in the technology space. They are cultural and strategic tentacles of the United States overseas. In many cases, their innovations (such as the screens on iPhones) stem from collaborations with the US military. These are some of the reasons why the US government will continue to have a close relationship with the technology sector rather than an arm's-length one. A close relationship between government and the tech sector is even more likely in China, not least because of the vast pools of data the Chinese technology companies hold. Chinese consumers, compared to any others in the large economies, are the most active on social media. In addition, they can perform many services from one account (e.g., using the multipurpose app WeChat Pay). As a result, there is a vast store of data on the behavior of China's citizen shoppers, and this trove of data is one of the reasons why China has made significant advances in artificial intelligence and socioeconomically applied algorithms. So China's technology companies have an infrastructure that is of great use to its government. Given this backdrop, there are perhaps three areas where new rules of the internet game can evolve.

The first is in the sanctity of personal data. Here, the European Union's General Data Protection Regulation (GDPR) initiative is a first step. In the future, however, more data on our lives and behavior will be generated by different industries. Health care is one. Many people might not be overly concerned if their Yahoo account was hacked but would be upset to find that their medical data had fallen into the wrong hands or was being used against them, by insurance companies, for instance. This suggests the need for tougher regulation of personal data, and it also points the way toward new technologies such as blockchain (i.e., distributed ledger technology) being deployed to protect data, and of the need to think about how fifth-generation telecommunications networks are protected. With blockchain, data is much more secure, and data owners can explicitly give permission for the use of their data (e.g., to doctors or pharmacists in the case of medicine). The potential use of blockchain—where not only can someone's data be better protected, but a person's identity can also be more easily verified—opens up the possibility that internet users could carry a form of verified online identification certificate. On the one hand, this would make online activity such as shopping more fluid, and it may also curb antisocial behavior on the internet. An ideal guideline for the use of social media is that people should behave the same way online as they do in public. Verified social media–based identification is one way to encourage this, as antisocial behavior could then be tracked. In turn, this could produce a two-tiered internet: one core tier would be made up of "identity verified" consumers and social media participants, and consequently social media on that tier would be somewhat more thoughtful, less dangerous, and more truthful. Then a second, outer tier would consist of unverified users, who could transact at a higher cost, hide their identities, and engage in a social media free-for-all.

The second area where better governance can structure the internet is cyberwarfare. There is already a policy discussion ongoing on the need for a digital Geneva Convention, and Microsoft, for example, has already published a policy paper on this in relation to the hacking of personal data.[21] The governance of the military aspects of cyberwarfare is even less clear. While there may exist "understandings" between large nations as to what constitutes a cyberaggression, there is not yet a Geneva Convention surrounding cyberwarfare. In the geopolitical domain, such a convention would define what kinds of attack constituted aggression or acts of war and would also define what the range of possible responses would be—from escalation, to referral to a world body like the UN Security Council, to a counter-cyberattack, to a response based on military or financial sanctions. For instance, could a country launch a military attack in response to a cyberattack? In this respect, there would have to be clear rules that set out in detail the burden of proof of the origin of such an attack, channels of communication between the large cyberpowers if a cyberprobe went awry, and a set of measures and procedures by which rogue cybergroups could be sanctioned. From a geopolitical point of view, the likely and necessary axis around which such a cyber treaty could be based is the strained relationship between Russia and the United States. Such a move would be an important step diplomatically for both countries.

The enormous difficulty of verifying the origin of a cyberattack may necessitate the need for cyberforensics, or a sort of international cyberpolice. This force could have several tasks: it would gather evidence on the origin of cyberattacks and cybercrimes by rogue and criminal cyberoperators, and it would work with government agencies, cybersecurity, and information technology (IT) firms to limit the ability of listed terrorist groups to use the internet for their own advantage. The admissibility of such cyberevidence, and its actionability in terms of the sanctions that might follow, could form the basis of a treaty on cybersecurity. Such a treaty would also encompass the way people behave on the internet, and large internet companies from Google to Tencent would form part of this agreement and its implementation. There could be various elements; one would be the identification and criminal prosecution of those found culpable of internet-based abuse or crime, another would be the use of better procedures and technologies to avoid hacking. Large internet or social media firms would be employed to combat online abuse and fraud, based on international guidelines. Under such a treaty, signature countries would agree to use evidence on cybercrime in prosecuting people within their physical jurisdictions for cybercrimes.

Such a treaty would draw the large internet and datacentric companies into the realm of international public goods, institutions, and geopolitics. Many of them already play outsized technological, economic, and strategic roles. In many cases, the size and reach of the large technology companies (from Amazon to Google to Alibaba Group) have dominant, monopoly-like market power. They stretch this in other ways, dominating innovation, research and development, the acquisition of small technology companies, and the related venture-capital market to such an extent that some people complain of corporate inequality.

A growing number of academics and policy makers now call for the large tech giants to be regulated or even broken up, given the power they hold over consumers and consumers' data. In a strict economic and moral sense, such calls are well placed, but they ignore the reality of the multipolar world, where one of the ways in which the large poles are becoming both distinctive and powerful is through the internet and data. In my view, it is far more likely that the big tech companies will not be broken up but will be co-opted as strategic partners of large states. If this occurs, Europe—which, as noted earlier, has no internet and social media giants of its own—may suffer, and it may respond with tougher regulation of non-European internet, IT, and social media platforms.

The paring back of old institutions and the building out of new ones is one of the vital tasks of the twenty-first century. To be perhaps overly critical, many politicians today seem wedded to the status quo, and there are few obvious institution builders. In that regard, we might again head back in time and seek the inspiration of someone who has done it all before, Alexander Hamilton.

TEN

THE HAMILTON PROJECT
What Would Hamilton Do?

THE CHANGE IN AMERICA'S PLACE IN THE WORLD PLAYS A SIGNIFICANT ROLE in the process of the levelling. The ebbing of America's influence, profound questions over its economic model, the apparent decay in its society, and turmoil in its public life are forces that are driving the prospect of a weaker rather than a greater America. This is especially sad to contemplate, given the genius of its Founding Fathers.

Two of my favorite historical figures are Benjamin Franklin and Alexander Hamilton. They shared a creativity and an energy, and both were crucial figures in the foundation of the United States as we know it. Franklin is attractive for the range of his talents and interests, and Hamilton is worthy as a builder of institutions. Today, interest in Hamilton has undergone a revival, thanks in part to the musical bearing his name, even if it does not do full justice to his achievements.[1] Ron Chernow's biography of Hamilton does, and I recommend it as a comprehensive and worthy treatment.

In my mind Hamilton stands out as someone who planned, established, and built many of the important institutions of the United States.

He had a hand in the creation of its currency framework; in the foundation of the Treasury, a prototype central bank (the Bank of the United States), the Coast Guard, and West Point; and in the structuring of the army. He was also a mastermind of American foreign policy and was one of the lead authors of the *Federalist Papers*, the collection of essays that sought to clarify, strengthen, and promote the US Constitution.

Few men or women have had as enduring an impact on their nation. Indeed, without being uncharitable, it is hard to imagine a group of contemporary political leaders drafting a set of essays comparable to the *Federalist Papers* that would elaborate the structures and paths to lead their countries forward. This is another reason why a modern Agreement of the People will have to be written by new, politically active people rather than by contemporary politicians.

Hamilton is also interesting because, like the Levellers, he was interested in both democracy and the idea of the republic (i.e., institutions and laws) and was keenly aware that they served different purposes. The ideas of democracy and a classical republic are often taken to be the same thing, though they are very different. Republics do not have to be democratic, though the best ones are.

Take modern-day Greece as an example. When Greece was incorrectly permitted to join the eurozone, it was waived through the admission criteria partly on the sentimental basis that one couldn't refuse entry to the birthplace of democracy (this viewpoint is credited to François Mitterrand). Subsequently, though Greece was a eurozone member, its institutions and those who populated them were found wanting, being corrupt and unable to execute policy or to respond to market and economic stresses. This shows that though democracy should be a requirement for EU membership, it is not a basis for eurozone membership (EU membership does not automatically imply membership of the eurozone). Institutional quality and economic strength should be the bases for this, and in the case of Greece, the frailty of its institutions continues to undermine its democracy, in that poor policy making or policy implementation saps trust in the democratic process.

Hamilton's achievements encompassed both the fostering of American democracy and the mastering of the architecture of its republic. The nucleus of his achievements was as a craftsman and implementer of what we have called intangible infrastructure, to such an extent and level of excellence that there are few historical figures who might match him (Napoleon, perhaps).

In this chapter, I take "Hamilton" as shorthand for the establishment of the institutions, laws, and skill sets needed for countries and regions to be able to thrive, in the sense of enjoying durable economic growth, high human development, and a stable public life. In the case of the great powers, one might also add the goal of the completion of the institutional armory that would allow each pole to hold its own in a multipolar world.

We, therefore, deal here with the reality that the three great regions of the world—the US-led Americas, Europe, and China—are to a large degree incomplete in different respects: Europe needs more force in geopolitics, the United States needs a better-balanced society, and China is still adolescent financially, militarily, and socially. To this end, these great powers may change significantly in the next ten years, and the ways in which their societies change, the extent of their investment in intangible infrastructure, and the way they conduct themselves diplomatically will be the central themes in international relations for future decades. It will be a defining part of the levelling, and in my view, the extent to which countries adopt the mind-set of Alexander Hamilton will condition their place in the world.

Hamilton, were he alive today, would rub his hands at the rebuilding and recrafting that needs to be done. He would scan the great regions (poles) of the world and the shabby shells of twentieth-century institutions like the WTO, and he would wonder where to cut, prune, and replant. We could imagine him making a shopping list of the things that need to be done so that each pole will reach its full potential. This approach might also reflect Hamilton's gift, which is now a very Western or "Washington" one, of telling people and countries how they should run their affairs.

Europe

Were he to stumble on the European Union today, Hamilton might have a sense of having seen it all before. In the late eighteenth century, he was instrumental in helping stitch together the "jarring, jealous and perverse petty states" of what is now the United States.[2] His use of federal power, funding, and military resources in facing down the Whiskey Rebellion of 1791–1794 makes the more recent tribulations of the eurozone look tame. As someone with an instinct toward federalism, he might relish the prospect of sticking Europe together. He might pursue two broad avenues, one constitutional and the other financial.

To take the constitutional angle first: one frequently noted rejoinder during debates on the politics of the European Union is to ask whether anyone has in fact read the EU constitution. Few have. The EU constitution is some four hundred pages long (at seventy thousand words, it is seven times as long as the French and Dutch constitutions), and it is unlikely that many Europeans have read it or that they keep a copy close to hand. Nor are they likely to be aware of the detail in the shorter, though important, Charter for Fundamental Rights. Lawyers and academics will tell us that constitutions are legal documents and as such are long and complicated. Still, long, complex texts like the European Constitution put distance between people and those who govern over them.

This is one of the ways in which politics today has created a sense of disconnect between insiders and outsiders. There is a small community in Brussels (lawyers mostly) who know the workings of the EU constitution, but the vast majority of EU citizens have little sense of it. From a social and political point of view, it is a disturbing divide because Europeans are losing confidence in the European Union, and as multiple economic and humanitarian crises take their political toll, Europeans are losing their sense of what Europe stands for.

This is where Hamilton comes in. He would be familiar with the powerful simplicity of the US Declaration of Independence and Bill of Rights, both of which echo the values and recommendations in the

Levellers' Agreements of the People.[3] Hamilton, as a key author of the *Federalist Papers*, actively campaigned in states like New York for the ratification of the Constitution, explaining the practical need for it and the benefits it would create in the long run. His energy and focus are reminders that lofty legal documents, however important they are to a country, need to be brought home to people in a very real way.

An example that often comes to my mind is the promotion of Eritrea's 1997 Constitution. According to Professor Bereket Selassie, one of its authors, the key elements of the new constitution were broadcast daily on state radio, in nine different local languages.[4] It is a good example of a legal document, a constitution, being communicated in a practical way.

In this respect, Hamilton might try a few approaches. One thoroughly modern one might be to use artificial intelligence to optimize the constitutions of the various European states and to condense them into one, meaningful page. I have tried but so far have failed in this approach. What I had in mind was to use an algorithm to extract core beliefs and principles from the constitutions of a range of countries and boil them down into a single, short document. Another approach is to follow the work of the Comparative Constitutions Project, whose team has done a much better job.

A more straightforward tack that a modern-day Hamilton could try is to produce a very short document that highlights the meaning and relevance of the European Union to its many citizens. Constitutions, as legal documents, are often unwieldy from a more popular point of view. In Europe there is a need for something that distills the purpose of the European Union, the characteristics of being an EU citizen, a list of the essential European factors that might be found in common from a Dutch man to a Sicilian woman to a Danish child to a Polish grandmother. One exercise that might help this process along is to have those citizens run pilot projects to discover what they feel they have in common, where they feel they are different, and what policies might, to their advantage, draw them together. In the spirit of the seventeenth century, let's call it something like the Doctrine of Common Understanding, and the initial pilot project could be based on the participation of a retired Portuguese teacher, a Polish bank clerk, a German policewoman, a Latvian student, an Italian pensioner, and a Swedish nurse. Their goal is to produce, on a single sheet of paper, the answers to the following questions: What do they, as Europeans, have in common? And commensurately, what differences do they have as Europeans? Then we might ask them to stress some common values and aspirations. Finally, they would be asked to note policies that would bring them closer together as Europeans (one example I have in mind is the Erasmus pan-European student-exchange program).

The answers might start off with the fact that most Europeans have a common history, one that has been marked by wars (including the bloodiest in history), scarred by the rise and fall of empires (nearly every European country—with the exception of Ireland—has had an empire), shrouded in Christianity, and shaped by the passage of monarchy to democracy and autarchy, the rise of learning and culture, and, from the thirteenth century onward, the evolution of great cities. This is an altogether broad and historical view of European identity, and it might well permit the inclusion of countries, such as Russia, that are not considered part of Europe today. The sum total of this historic experience might well inspire citizens to say that they have the following common values: peace (not to have another European war), the influence of the Christian church(es), democracy, recognition of the benefits of social democracy, and free movement of EU citizens.

Unlike the citizens of large economies like the United States or China, EU citizens do not have a common language. Also, they have very different educational experiences, very strong city or regional attachments, different approaches to doing business and making policy, and varying levels of corruption and transparency in public life. There is, however, a new trend across Europe of mixed marriages and relationships between people from different European countries (and from countries outside the European Union), which is creating the makings of a large cohort of people who, with their children, have a pan-European identity. It may be that this group will be the one to properly flesh out the Doctrine of Common Understanding.

In addition, clarity is required on the responsibilities and behaviors demanded by the European Union from those who wish to become EU citizens and on the principles that govern the economic management of the European Union. This is a short list and it can easily grow. Hamilton might be tempted to produce essays on the topic, but in an age of social media, he might better opt for a short note that sets out the common factors that define what it is to be "European."

With this project in train, Hamilton might turn his attention to Europe's faulty financial system. Just over a year after the publication of the *Federalist Papers* (1787–1788), Hamilton was appointed as the first secretary of the US Treasury. The institution that he shaped remains one of the most influential bodies in the world. By analogy, one might say that the eurozone will only be complete once it has its own treasury secretary and once it has found someone of Hamilton's caliber to lead it. Mario Draghi, the ECB president, is a rare example of a leader who can bring force and direction to an institution in Europe.

The creation of a super finance ministry, or EU Treasury, by the mid 2020s is one of the stated goals of the European Commission, among a number of other institutional initiatives.[5] These are to be welcomed, but they must not be carried out for the sake of giving politicians greater powers; rather, they should be implemented with a sense for how Europe's economies work in harmony with each other. With his genius for communication, Hamilton might recommend that Europe's leaders examine its financial system as if it were a system of pipes. A flow-based view of an economy is an intuitive one, and it has some credence.

Readers might be familiar with the term "Phillips Curve," which is based on the research that New Zealand economist Bill Phillips carried out on the link between unemployment and inflation. Well before he was celebrated for this, however, Phillips built an extraordinary machine that pumped colored water through glass vessels in order to demonstrate how money flows around an economic system. Levers in the machine permitted users to simulate the effect on the system of fiscal (budget) policy changes, and such was the intuitive appeal of the machine that major universities like Harvard and Oxford ordered their own versions.

In today's algorithmic, QE-driven economies and markets, such a simple contraption might seem well out of place, but given the way the eurozone crisis has habitually reared its head, Hamilton might feel that policy makers in Brussels could do a lot worse than build their own version of Phillips's machine. Such a device might encourage a much-needed period of introspection into the workings of the euro and might shine light on the areas missed by the European Commission's rather tame 2015 "Five Presidents' Report," whose aim was to outline some of the measures that would complete Europe's economic and monetary union.[6]

In the spirit of Phillips's machine, picture the eurozone as a system where liquidity passes through nineteen different vessels, at different speeds and causing very disparate pressures in each of them. A few, like Greece, are too weak economically and politically to withstand these pressures.

More broadly, the example of Phillips's machine shows that in the absence of counterbalancing mechanisms or safety valves, a common monetary policy can have different impacts on, say, the Portuguese economy and the Finnish one. This much was clear early in the first decade of the twenty-first century when a monetary policy that was set for a recovering German economy granted very, very low interest rates to Ireland and Spain, where banks and consumers then deployed cheap cash with vigor. Hamilton would be familiar with the different behavior of local economies from his experience in late-eighteenth-century America, where local currencies gave way to the dollar and a more centralized tax system took hold. Though he also had to deal with local and state assemblies, he did not have to contend with so many different legal systems, economic structures, languages, and cultural exceptions.

In this respect, with an eye on the very ambitious plans the European Commission must develop for the eurozone, the engineers of the euro need to figure out how to accommodate a single monetary policy within different economies and financial systems. They need to figure out what works well at a pan-European level and what flexibility needs to be granted at the local level. The commission should consider the chronic Greek crises as a warning to resist the urge to smother its adherents with fiscal uniformity. Instead, it must cleverly redevelop the way the eurozone is engineered so that it is harmonious within its existing member economies and transmission mechanisms.

The principal suggestion here is to revise the restrictive set of fiscal rules to give more emphasis to a framework where national governments have fiscal flexibility. Importantly, they would be bound by the advice of independent fiscal councils and, through restrictions on debt issuance, bound to run fiscal policies that are on balance countercyclical to eurozone monetary policy (so that when monetary policy adds fuel to the economic fire, fiscal policy dampens it down) and that are economically productive rather than political in their aim. Using fiscal policy to complement monetary policy would help ensure that the eurozone's economies, especially the smaller ones, like Clinton's Goldilocks economy, do not become "too hot" or "too cold."

In practice, this will demand lots of innovations in the area that policy wonks call "macroprudential policy"—that is, efforts to reduce financial risks to an economic system. For example, if eurozone interest rates were very low by the standards of the Irish economy and produced a housing bubble, the Irish central bank then could increase the deposit-to-loan ratio on mortgages or the finance ministry could increase the tax on property transactions so as to dampen the risk of a housing bubble. In a sign that Ireland has not fully learned the lessons of its housing crisis, it is now enduring its second housing bubble in ten years, with housing affordability very stretched and homelessness a very public social problem.

Allowing, encouraging, and helping individual states to use policy tools like this would allow them to exist in the eurozone in a more stable way. Such policies could be coordinated by the EU Treasury. Part of its mandate would be recognition that not all eurozone economies are created equal and that many of them behave differently under different conditions (France is less sensitive to fluctuations in the euro than Germany, for example). An EU Treasury with a figure like Hamilton at the top would also give some credibility to the European Union's policies; the European Union does not lack for rules, regulations, and directives, but it rarely finds the political will to enforce them.

One of the Hamilton's triumphs was to persuade individual states (especially wealthier ones like Virginia) that the Treasury should be able to issue debt and collect taxes at a federal level. He might also point Europe down this route. At first, the idea of a pan-European Union tax will face resistance, which may lessen if the need for pan-European public goods becomes clearer. Military hardware projects—in the form of either transport planes or an EU cyberwarfare unit (which would need up to ten thousand personnel)—are among the projects that might attract pan-European funding.

A less controversial means of raising taxes and spending them in a way that spreads growth across the European Union would be a stabilization levy. This is one of the missing ingredients in the eurozone, and it could be put in place to distribute the gains from countries that benefit abnormally from attractive financial market conditions to those who do not. For example, the policies of the ECB drove German interest rates to historically low levels (about a mere 0.4 percent for much of 2018) and, for some time, into negative territory. Germany has benefited greatly in that it barely pays any interest on its debt because of the ECB's policy.

Germans might argue back that Germany gives the ECB its credibility, so it (Germany) deserves a fee in the form of low interest rates. Under the framework of a stabilization levy, the EU Treasury could arbitrate this. In technical terms, it might set a low but less abnormally low neutral rate of interest for Germany, say, 1 percent instead of thirty basis points, and Germany would (depending on the size of its debt) pay the difference to the EU Treasury.

The EU Treasury (rather than national governments) would then invest this money in infrastructure and other economically meaningful investment projects around the eurozone. An investment council or the board of the European Investment Bank would oversee the investment projects, and potentially the countries that pay the highest surcharges would have greater say over how the capital is invested, outside their own countries. One might think of the same being done in situations where, because of ECB policy, the euro weakens sharply, and companies who benefit, such as large exporters, would pay the EU Treasury a low-euro surcharge, which would then be invested as described earlier.

This approach would have several effects. First, the ability of such a system to reflate and redistribute in a transparent, economically meaningful way would mean that in a crisis, markets would react less violently toward the eurozone, and interest rates and single currency may not be as volatile. Second, this approach would, in economist speak, help monetize the policies of the ECB, or in plain English, help ensure a real economic impact (arguably less wealth inequality, a greater fiscal stimulus in the periphery countries, and better infrastructure, to highlight a few potential benefits) from policies such as quantitative easing. Third, this approach would curb imbalances in capital accounts across the eurozone and to a degree take some infrastructure spending decisions out of the hands of politicians (especially in the periphery states). Hamilton might regard it as a tidy solution, and one that would provide a worthy start to the new EU treasury secretary.

Large institutions like a treasury are not always known for their encouragement of innovation, but they can use their power to support good ideas. One might be to foster uniformity of policies where they can make a difference. One such proposal would be to harmonize processes, notably the processes involved in setting up a business. The European Union could establish an EU-level process whereby entrepreneurs could adopt an EU template for setting up a business such that it would take the same amount of time to establish a business anywhere in the European Union. This might be one of a number of responses to Brexit and would help shock national governments, such as France's, into a more business-friendly attitude. As it stands, the World Bank "time to start up a business" statistics vary greatly across Europe: in Belgium it takes four days but in Austria it takes twenty-one days. Of course, setting up a business is only the first and relatively easy stage. The EU entrepreneur template should ideally make the early stages of the life of a business as uncomplicated as possible. Such an approach might well force a more business-oriented approach across Europe and will show the power of the EU Treasury to work around governments on issues like regulation, corruption, and growth. If this approach is taken up and is successful, it might well be extended to other areas, such as legal and justice systems. If one compares the access to, complexity of, and transparency of legal systems across the European Union—from Serbia to Italy to Finland to Belgium—there is potential to harmonize laws across specific topics, such as bankruptcy, prosecution of corruption, and labor laws. This would be a much more meaningful reform than deeper political uniformity.

China

Once finished with Europe, Hamilton might cast an eye over the geopolitical atlas and turn to China. He would appreciate that when he became treasury secretary the United States was but an emerging, even frontier economy and that at that time China accounted for nearly 40 percent of the world economy. In 1950, 150 years later, America made up a third of world economy, and China's share had shrunk to 10 percent, according to the Maddison Historical Statistics database.[7] In a nutshell, the idea of the Chinese Dream is to reestablish China as a world power to the magnitude it enjoyed when Hamilton was alive.

Correspondingly, many accounts of China from an American perspective paint it as a threat, a view that was made official in the 2017 document "National Security Strategy of the United States of America."[8] There is also a growing sense that the American public is becoming alert to the rise of China and to the strategic threats it poses and that the trade dispute between the United States and China is a manifestation of this realization.[9] A speech in October 2018 by Vice President Mike Pence underlined the harsh and uncompromising view of the Trump administration on China, and as a diplomatic statement it will probably prove to be a milestone.[10]

If Hamilton were to study China today, he would probably see a rival to the United States. He might appreciate that, like his own approach, the Chinese way of doing things takes into account the interlinkages among economics, technology, and hard military power. He might have several pieces of advice for the Chinese.

To start with its economy, Hamilton would point out that China's path into the future may need to surmount a few obstacles. The first is the need to become used to a lower trend rate of economic growth and to understand the implications this has for government spending, wage growth, and consumer behavior. The manner in which China digests and overcomes its debt and property bubbles will have enormous consequences for the internal and international narrative of its future.[11] If China can vault the hurdle of high indebtedness, then it will reemerge with confidence and momentum. If not, it may have to contend with a very large cohort of disenchanted citizens, in the same way that the aftermath of the eurozone crisis has bred disenchantment in countries such as Italy, Ireland, and Greece.

The second, more human obstacle relates to the consequences of the development of a consumer culture in China. Though the political instincts and desires of the Chinese people have been curbed during the course of the rise of its economy, the flourishing of consumer tastes is beginning to unleash genies: a more open approach to sex and sexuality, curiosity for Western brands and media, and, it should be said, the reinforcement of a Chinacentric culture.

In Western societies over the past eighty years, economic growth and the development of a consumer culture have gone hand in hand with a greater desire for a more open society and for a more sophisticated and generally open political system. The emergence of a consumer culture in the West has also brought counterreactions, such as the rise of more radical political parties. In particular, in China today there is a deeper consciousness of environmental issues, which can be seen as a reaction and a consequence of a rise in consumer culture and industrialization.

China has so far, to its credit in many respects, not followed the pattern of development of Western nations in that it has, remarkably, so far failed to mimic the boom and bust of Western economic cycles,[12] nor has it followed the pattern of political development of Western nations. It may well continue to confound its Western skeptics, but at some point the tension between control, economic growth, and stability may become acute. The challenge for the Chinese authorities, then, in the context of China's goal of winning greater national prestige, is to maintain social stability. Historically, political leaders and some governments have co-opted the forces of nationalism and religion, the dream of economic progress, and the fear of external threat to corral societies. In China's case, the underlying social, technological, and economic changes may be too great to be contained by words and images alone. China is already investing heavily in technologically based social control mechanisms that employ algorithms and facial and pattern recognition to gauge which citizens are misbehaving, or are likely to misbehave.

Another, perhaps less heavy-handed approach is to develop social infrastructure that encompasses many of the elements of intangible infrastructure, such as health-care spending, education, pension plans, and broader financial services. One indicator of the lack of social infrastructure in China is the very high household savings rate (as a proportion of GDP), which, at close to 37 percent according to the OECD, is nearly six times higher than that of many developed countries (6 percent in the United States). The high rate of savings suggests that many Chinese save on a precautionary basis in order to be able to meet health or proxy pension costs in the future. Consider that in China today out-of-pocket health-care expenses are 72 percent of GDP (compare this to just over 27 percent in France) and that from a pensions point of view China has the lowest pension and mutual fund assets as a proportion of GDP (in the low single digits) of the major emerging markets and significantly lags developed economies.[13]

Motivation for building social infrastructure in China may come from stress points uncovered during China's next recession, which will probably diminish property values, cause controversy with the collapse of wealth-management products, see unemployment rise, and consequently see many people questioning the willingness and ability of the government or Communist Party to maintain order and social cohesion. The call by President Xi at the 2017 Communist Party Congress for the party to focus more on providing people with a "better, happier life" is a nod in this direction.[14] As such, it would be a logical chapter in China's path to development, and not at all unlike Franklin D. Roosevelt's New Deal. The New Deal was a watershed in the United States in many respects, one of which was that it marked the full evolution of the United States from an emerging to a developed nation.

Some of the measures proposed by Roosevelt administration members such as Frances Perkins—a minimum wage and unemployment compensation, for example[15]—are already in place in China or are incarnated in the form of "iron rice bowls."* But the Chinese system is not as comprehensive, or one might say generous, as those in other developed countries. China's Ministry of Civil Affairs website shows that a relatively low number of rural households (approximately 20 million) receive subsistence allowances (about USD 50 per month).[16] This is tiny compared to the benefits in more developed socioeconomic models (e.g., Denmark) and underlines the fact that very high saving rates in China exist on a precautionary basis, so that people have cash available for medical and economic emergencies.

---

* Jobs "for life."

Broadening financial services in simple, transparent savings and mortgage segments (in financial technology and traditional banking areas), broadening health-care coverage, and sponsoring reskilling within social security programs are some ways in which new forms of growth can be stimulated and newer sections of the Chinese economy opened up in a postcrisis or postrecession economic climate.

Such a plan may also be the political consequence of a slowing Chinese economy and of evolving views and factions within the Communist Party. In light of the postcrises experiences of the United States and Europe, a political response that addresses the absolute losers in a recession would appear expedient. It may also offer Chinese authorities an opportunity to redress some of the economic and wealth imbalances across regions of China and between some of its cities.

China faces another challenge. In recent decades it has had the luxury of sitting back and studying the complexity of other regions' engagements in Syria, Ukraine, and Iraq, to name a few trouble spots. China's imperial past is sufficiently well buried in history that relations between China and emerging countries (notably those in Africa) do not (yet) have an imperial veneer. (Compare that to, say, an economic engagement between the Democratic Republic of the Congo and its former colonizer, Belgium.) China is now more confidently proposing a "China solution" to issues beyond its borders. However, as its economic imprint in Africa grows and as the One Belt, One Road project rolls forward, it may find that in many developing countries, it will become a focus for friction and resentment, and indebtedness. Hamilton, who was instrumental in sharpening the military tactics that helped George Washington during the American Revolution and in shaping the role of the US Navy and Coast Guard, might have some advice to add.

From a technical point of view, Hamilton—were he to take the Chinese view of the world—would be excited by the acceleration in the buildup of the Chinese navy: its experimentation with fitting out aircraft carriers, with ultra-high-speed shore-to-ship missiles, with rail guns on ships, and with the use of swarming drones. He might at the same time point out that the growing presence of a large and increasingly sophis-ticated Chinese navy creates its own risks. Unlike during the eighteenth and nineteenth centuries, much of the world's trade today does not need naval protection (arguably, it does require cyberprotection).

Though China will feel that, like the other large regions of the world, it is entitled to a sizable naval fleet, development of the Chinese navy may cause other nations—from Vietnam to India—to react in kind. India, as mentioned, is now part of a relatively new defense group, the Quad.

Bearing this in mind, Hamilton, were his advice sought in Beijing, might advise two related approaches. The first would be for China to set out very clearly the role of its navy and, where it could, to use the navy to solve regional collective action problems, such as piracy, humanitarian missions, and environmental protection. The second would be for China to position itself better in terms of its role as a diplomatic power. Amer-ica has built its diplomatic power as the supporter and architect of many of the world's public goods—institutions like the United Nations are an example. Robert Kagan's book *The World America Made* discusses this in fine detail, sketching the accomplishment of the world order crafted by America and then warning of the dangers to this order, and to the world in general, of a more isolationist and insular American foreign policy. Kagan, in fact, compares the consequences of an American re-treat from global diplomacy to the disintegration of relations among European countries before the First World War and, dramatically, to the collapse of the Roman Empire.

The beginnings of American power struck a very different note. In 1906 the Nobel Peace Prize was awarded to President Theodore Roos-evelt, the first time an American was granted any Nobel Prize. Roosevelt's contribution to peace was the clever way he brokered the Treaty of Ports-mouth in 1905, between the two parties in the Russo-Japanese War. At the time, the award was controversial because America's power was rising across the world stage (notably in South America) and also because many suspected that the awarding of the prize by the Norwegian government helped bolster the place of Norway, then newly independent from Sweden.

Today it is worth considering the words of Norwegian statesman Gunnar Knudsen during the award ceremony (Roosevelt didn't make it to the Nobel Foundation until 1910): "The United States of America was among the first to infuse the ideal of peace into practical politics. Peace and arbitration treaties have now been concluded between the United States and the governments of several countries."[17]

Yet with America now pulling back from an internationalist stance— for example, recently cutting its contribution to the United Nations, pulling out of the Paris Climate Accord, effectively ignoring Latin America (e.g., ignoring the Venezuelan refugee crisis), degrading relations with neighbors and trading partners from Canada to the European Union, and maintaining ambivalent relations between the White House and Russia, to name just a few developments—it may fall to China to perform the role of underwriter of international public goods. Or, at the very least, there is a lacuna opening up in international relations that China may choose to fill. Some experts, such as Harvard professor Joe Nye, fear that in this respect China may be wanting. He refers to this as "the Kindleberger Trap."[18] Charles Kindleberger, whose book *Manias, Panics, and Crashes* I have already commended, was one of the intellectual architects of the Marshall Plan and was devoted to the idea of public goods and international institutions. The trouble is that, though China is intent on increasing its international influence, it is yet not well practiced in soft power. In this respect, the One Belt, One Road project, though economically impactful, may prove double-edged. For example, the financial quid pro quo for countries (notably Pakistan, Sri Lanka, and Cambodia) that participate in the project is that they are obliged to take on cripplingly large amounts of debt to finance construction projects and as a result may end up losing control of strategic assets such as ports.[19]

Finally, though Hamilton may accept that in a multipolar world large countries will develop their own approaches to governance, he might remind China that the system of checks and balances he put in place, and the institutions that govern the United States, have in general stood the test of time. He would emphasize that these checks and balances, and the very clear approach to the rule of law, are greater than any individual and that once an individual begins to rise above the institutions of state, the state itself becomes compromised.

The United States

Should Hamilton return to the United States, the above-mentioned checks and balances might be one of the first things to come to his mind, and he would be pleased that they still work well today. Indeed, he would still have much to admire in his own handiwork. He might not be surprised to discover America's rise to primus inter pares during the twentieth century, and he would be pleased that vital elements of its power, such as its navy, army, and the Treasury, were of his making. Some complain about the tone and ferocity of political debate in the United States today; Hamilton might also deplore it but would recognize that little has changed from his time.

Should he survey the land today, he would be concerned about the dip in and threats to world trade and the rise of the indebtedness of nations. He might also side with those who in today's world see immigration as a necessary part of international economic vitality. He might also recognize the need to rebuild physical infrastructure across the United States (fast trains, sleek airports, and smooth roads) but could see that achieving that is probably just a matter of time. What might pique his curiosity are the laws and institutions that need to be built in the United States to equip it for the twenty-first century. The legal frameworks around technology, impactful investment, and equality are just some of things he might focus on.

To start with, given that he was a military man, Hamilton would be impressed that America has become so mighty militarily, but, to follow his writings in the *Federalist Papers*, he might argue that a strong president should balance might with a sense of diplomacy, at least when relations with conventional foes are considered. Military power is one of the areas where the United States is predominant,[20] though conflicts in Iraq and Afghanistan have shown that when pitted against military might, unconventional warfare can produce an outsized impact. Against this, the US military is outstanding for the schooling of its soldiers and officers in strategy, history, and tactics and for the ways in which sociology and economics are considered as elements that can shape modern battlefields.

In the United States today, the expansion of the military appears set to continue under President Trump, and in time the United States, with perhaps Russia, China, the United Kingdom, and France following behind, will be the only country to have a suite of "total warfare" capabilities. Some countries, such as Russia, are already practicing war by "many means"—that is, where traditional military force is mixed with covert action, propaganda, and disinformation. The Russian doctrine of *maskirovka* has roots that go back to the fourteenth-century Battle of Kulikovo and was further developed more recently, beginning with its use in the Second World War. In a very basic sense, it involves the use of decoys and deception to distract and destabilize an enemy, though the doctrine of *maskirovka* has broad applications, stretching to disinformation, propaganda, and politically related tactics. A significant element of the thinking that reflects the new doctrine of warfare in Russia is that wars do not follow the same boundaries and time lines as they did historically.[21] This means that they are not officially declared—in the way cyberattacks happen—and that they can rely on many different types of force (e.g., information, humanitarian, and media) and can rely on the subversion of states on a continual basis using mercenaries and special operatives. The United States has the capability to take this to a higher level, adding a financial arsenal, space-based warfare, private military contractors, massive cyberwarfare, and robotic military capabilities to its already formidable set of capabilities.[22]

What is not so clear, and where Hamilton might be curious, is how the rise of new military or strategic capabilities and the way in which these are deployed together change the rules of war, the realities of trade, and the international flow of information. In particular, the possession of such a vast capability by a democracy places the onus on the United States to lead the recrafting of a modern Geneva Convention on rules of war. Such a convention could touch on many topics, such as the extent to which cyberwarfare can be used (what right does a country have to retaliate with a conventional military response following a cyberattack?), the rules governing space war, and the legal framework governing the deployment of robots in the battlefield.

On a similar basis, there is room for the United States to take the lead, perhaps with Europe, in crafting the legal and philosophical frameworks that will oversee the rise in the use of new technologies. Consider the potential for robots to disrupt many forms of employment or to bolster demographics by allowing older people to live more comfortably for longer (consider advances in home care or driverless cars), or consider the way in which algorithms entrench inequalities.

Think also about advances in science in the realm of DNA and genetic experimentation, which may allow some people to enjoy long lives. As with many advances in medical technology, the benefits of advances in the areas of genetic editing (a leading area here is Clustered Regularly Interspaced Short Palindromic Repeats [CRISPR], which is effectively a DNA-based approach to managing bacteria and viruses), gene sequencing, and the manipulation of reproductive cells are going to be enjoyed by the better-off; more worryingly, they are not yet bound by internationally recognized laws. This creates an incentive for some states to position themselves as leaders in the field of gene manipulation, though there will be a very strong temptation for them to participate in forms of genetic engineering that are considered ethically unacceptable and that can conjure up thoughts of eugenics and natural selection.

The introduction of binding global standards and legal frameworks in this area will help prevent a practice of ethical arbitrage by more opportunistic states that may look to create ethical paradises in the same way that others create fiscal paradises (e.g., tax havens like Bermuda and the Cayman Islands). A number of codes and standards already exist, but they largely rely on scientists' willingness to follow them.[23] In a context where privately funded research competes with government research institutes and universities, and where governments are competing with each other, observance of these codes may be scant. One aim would be to halt states that seek to provide terrain for experimentation in health technology, genomics, and eugenics, to name a few areas where advances in science could have profound social and ethical consequences. For example, China's Institute of Neuroscience of the Chinese Academy of Sciences in Shanghai has cloned monkeys and pays large rewards to scientists who can advance it in the area of genetics. China has a policy of World Class 2.0, with a plan to boost its best universities into the top rankings of world academes. It is now close to matching the United States in terms of spending on science research and development. It may seem far-fetched that science can stretch and subvert existing legal frameworks, but science opens up many philosophically unanswered questions. Consider another example: space. There are projects ongoing (the Overview Institute, for instance) to craft the rules of a space-based society. Hamilton might well be impressed that the law would stretch so far and would probably also see the need for rules of the road in uncharted territory.

Hamilton, if he were present today, might also have caught up on world history. He would realize that, like Germany in the early part of the twentieth century, the United States is the world leader in technology and the sciences (social sciences as well). He would emphasize that this leadership brings with it a responsibility to use science for the public good, as conceived in a global sense and within agreed ethical parameters. By taking the leadership in areas such as the ethics of genomics, the United States can, if it wishes, take the lead in setting the rules of the road of the evolving multipolar system. Hamilton would also recognize two dangers: first, the power that such leadership brings, and, again with the example of Germany of the 1910s in mind, the possibility that leadership will lead to hubris; and second, the dual risk that such powerful technologies are increasingly owned and accessed by elites and, concurrently, that people lower down the pyramid are deprived of their benefits. Consider the prices of new drugs and therapies for the treatment of cancer and hepatitis.

To follow this line of argument even further, one development that Hamilton might find curious is that inequality has become a hallmark of American society and that this is manifest in many ways, such as treatment for mental health, the prevalence of obesity in people with low income, and inequalities in access to education. As an issue, inequality has few friends in the mainstream of American politics. Hamilton, as one of the intellectual founders of central banking in America and as someone from a very poor background, might feel that policy makers are remiss in ignoring this important issue. He would regard it as a failure that the only policy maker in recent times to speak to issues such as long-term unemployment and to try to address them was Janet Yellen, the previous chair of the Federal Reserve.

In several policy speeches and policy moves, Yellen expressed the view that extremely accommodative monetary policy was required in order to ease long-term unemployment, and several Federal Reserve economists have also advocated very low interest rates as a means of pushing economic activity out to the furthest reaches of an economy still shocked by the Great Recession.[24] Hamilton might be surprised by this in that a Hamiltonian view of economics would determine that institutions, clever fiscal policy, and human development were the ways to address long-term unemployment, as is often the prescription in Europe, rather than monetary policy. The reasoning here is that long-term unemployment is a complex socioeconomic issue whose remedy is found in the patient use of reskilling, education, proper incentivization, and other measures that are far more fine-tuned than the bazooka of monetary policy. To some extent, the fact that the Fed chair was (nobly) driven to consider using an overly accommodative form of monetary policy shows the failure of fiscal policy in the United States to address long-term unemployment. There is no sign that the current administration shares this view. Lowering corporate taxes and cutting education spending and benefits is not the prescribed way to approach such a problem, and measures such as protectionism and moral suasion (such as the threat to tax the Harley-Davidson Motor Company following its announcement that it would shift some production overseas) make the task of job creation even more challenging.

There are alternatives, and Hamilton might make at least two suggestions, one in banking and the other in labor-related taxes. The first might be a Revival Bank, an idea that comes from the observation that banking systems will increasingly lend capital to those who don't necessarily need it and will ration it to those who do require financing. The seven-year period from 2011 to 2018 in Europe is a case in point. In addition, in the case of development, or more particularly in the notion of "revival," there is a need for coordination among economic actors by getting local government, businesses, and educational institutions to work together. A Revival Bank could fill this role and might also function as a sort of bottom-up policy specialist for microlevel economic policy, at the level of communities and cities.

The most notable component of a Revival Bank would ensure adoption of a long-term approach to lending. Then lending conditions could be based on a combination of financial returns and social returns (i.e., those with an impact on poverty or the environment), and loan holders would be held stringently to those conditions. In this way it should combine making money and putting it to good use. Unlike in many other retail and mortgage banks, loan officers would be more specialized than "ordinary," property-led loan officers in the way they appraise projects. Correspondingly, a body related to the Revival Bank would coach entrepreneurs and businesspeople in the sourcing of funding and in how to prepare funding proposals.

In many revival-type projects, individual projects will only work where there is an upgrade of infrastructure. Thus, the Revival Bank might identify infrastructure needs, might coordinate the funding of these, and could formally involve local governments or entrepreneurs. Elsewhere,

Hamilton might observe that in the context of low productivity, not enough capital is invested in human capabilities and that, in many industries, graduates are drawn to jobs that pay well but have no social value. He might propose two new approaches to reversing low productivity.

The first would be focused on providing incentives for skill development for workers in small to medium enterprises (SMEs), partly because large companies can avail themselves of other tax benefits, in start-ups business metrics like productivity and profitability are harder to measure, and SMEs are a crucial engine of economic activity. This could be done in the same way that companies can depreciate fixed investments: by allowing tax breaks for the fostering of medium-term to long-term development of skills in employees.

So for measurable increases in an employee's capability (measured by completion of training courses, education, and formal reskilling courses), a company would be allowed to offset part of the human value added. This has several advantages: it encourages longer-term employment relationships between companies and employees; rather than replacing people with technology, it should give companies an incentive to teach existing workforces to use technology better and so become more productive; and in aggregate it produces a smarter workforce.

The second and probably controversial idea relates to income tax. One of the tensions between economic activity and society is that they diverge in their aims and outcomes, something underlined by the work of Karl Polyani. Polyani was an Austro-Hungarian economist whose book *The Great Transformation*, published in 1944, tracked the impact that the introduction of the market economy had on British society through the nineteenth century. His broad thesis is that the development of markets should occur in a harmonious way that balances social change. Today, many people earn vast amounts of money doing jobs that have little social impact, or in some cases, a negative social impact. This is not to say that all jobs should affect society in a positive way, but that channels should be found to balance rewards between, say, soldiers, police officers, and doctors, on the one hand, and derivative traders and people selling luxury goods, on the other. In addition, such channels might also help the labor market, where young people can feel rewarded for working as, say, a teacher rather than a management consultant. A Hamilton-type figure might ask a body like the OECD to draw up a broad, internationally recognized code of job roles, categorized by social impact. Then governments could add (or subtract) a tax depending on the social relevance of specific jobs. In such a system, a plastic surgeon might pay higher taxes, but more young doctors might be incentivized to work as accident and emergency surgeons.

Stability and Capability

Having done all this, Hamilton deserves a rest. Given what he did for the United States in the late eighteenth century, I have invoked him for a number of reasons. The first is to paint a road map of how, through the levelling, the large poles of the emerging multipolar order—the United States, Europe, and China—might develop. The second is to emphasize that the idea of a country or a region being "great" and strong does not necessarily have to be interpreted in a belligerent way; rather, it can be taken in the sense that the country should be stable and capable, with appropriate, functioning institutions and the people to run them. The third element is to point out that the more developed, robust, and institutionally complete the major regions are, the less prone they are to conflict, and the less likely they are to upset relatively smaller countries in their geopolitical hinterland. In this way, the evolving, levelling world order has a sounder basis.

ELEVEN

LOOKING AHEAD

From Noise and Disruption to . . . What?

I T'S AUGUST 2018 AND I AM JUST FINISHING THE FINAL EDITS TO THIS book, hoping dearly that nothing too dramatic happens in the world between now and publication date—though political, economic, and geopolitical volatility across the word is rising noticeably. I have lost count of the number of times people have told me, "We live in interesting times."

With some holiday to salvage and with the best part of one hundred thousand words trawled through, I am tempted to close my laptop, but a few things still bother me.

The first is that, with the passing of the headline-grabbing events I mentioned in the book's very first paragraph—the election of Donald Trump, Brexit, the advent of new governments in Mexico and Italy—sooner or later people will realize that the deep, persistent, underlying issues in our world are the need to reduce imbalances in indebtedness globally, the need to decommission the vast power of central banks, wealth inequality, the role of women in economies, the search for a new model for economic growth, and the rise of emerging countries (e.g., China) to rival incumbent powers (e.g., the United States).

In that light, my aim in this final chapter is to briefly summarize and restate the aims and arguments of the book. The first is to bring readers, and hopefully others, to realize that the events we are observing are part of a process of paradigm shift: the passage from the globalization-driven world order of the last forty years to a new one. I call this process the levelling. We are simply at the early, first stage of the levelling, a stage that is noisy and disorderly.

The passage to something more stable, and new, will entail several challenges. One is that geopolitics will change; the world will be less interconnected, more multipolar, and thus dominated by three large regions or poles: the US-led Americas, the European Union, and China-centric Asia. India has the capability to be a pole, but it is not there yet.

As a result, middle powers like Russia, the United Kingdom, Australia, and Japan will struggle to find their places in this world. World institutions, built for the twentieth century—the IMF, the World Bank, the WTO, and to an extent the United Nations—will fade and lose their relevance. New formations of states will become more prominent; expect to hear more about the Quad and the SCO. Small advanced economies will form a policy body—let's call it the "g20," with a lowercase g—and will become the policy model for stable economic growth and democracy.

Economically (and our world is dominated by economic forces) the trail through the levelling will be marked by several trials. The first is (with excuses for my forecasting) that political volatility within and between countries will be heightened by the probable onset of a recession by early 2020, driven by downturns in the United States and China.

Second, radical action is needed to reduce the extremes across economies. Two in particular—the record levels of indebtedness globally and the dominant imprint of central banks on economies—can only be resolved by historic levels of coordination between countries. Such cooperation only happens when things get bad or when other, milder approaches have been exhausted. I propose a world debt conference, to take place in 2024, to pare back debt levels and a treaty on risk taking to curb the use of extraordinary monetary policy in all but the most extreme circumstances.

The third and most important economic issue will revolve around the need to accept expectations that the trend level of growth worldwide will be lower in the next ten to twenty years than it has been over the past forty. Once these new expectations have been acknowledged, the search for a sustainable model of growth will start. I propose that a framework for this new model should be centered on the concepts of country strength (i.e., the stability and resilience of economies) and intangible infrastructure.

Intangible infrastructure is based on the things that matter to human development: health care, education, laws, and institutions. I fundamentally believe that a very significant element of the political dislocation seen across the world results from a lack of focus on intangible infrastructure in particular, ranging from a lack of clear, fair laws to a lack of accessible, high-quality education. The United States is an example, spending enormous political energy on cutting corporate tax rates as spending on education falls and student debt balloons. The features of country strength and intangible infrastructure are manifest in small, advanced economies, but they may also provide a basis for other countries. Post-Brexit "global Britain" is one, a post–Vladimir Putin Russia (he is due to retire in 2024) is another, and a final example is the many smaller, emerging economies that are looking to make the next step forward in their development.

To say that politicians should focus on human development is to state the obvious and is perhaps trite, but the reality is that it is not done in practice. It is one component of the distance between politicians and their electorates. Ultimately this distance will produce a greater rupture, and hopefully a more positive political environment in which new parties will spring up to constructively represent the needs and aspirations of people in the twenty-first century. At the time of this writing, the Democrats and Republicans in the United States, as well as Tories and Labour in the United Kingdom, could feasibly split. My view is that new parties are part of the regeneration process in politics, and I have sketched out some possible examples.

There are two other components of the revival of public life. The first is to attract new blood into politics, so that there is a greater focus on policy decision making. Part of the challenge here is to make the political game less unattractive to, say, mothers or people from non-politics-related walks of life. In the future, the great issues or fights in politics will address the environment to a greater extent, as well as new policy issues such as mental health and the interaction between humans and technology.

A profound axis around which international politics will rotate is the tension between the leveller view of the world (democratic, open societies with a focus on rule of law and in which institutions and investment in humans are the central pillars of economic growth) and the Leviathan view (societies in which freedom is surrendered in exchange for social order and the prospect of greater national prosperity).

The final element in the levelling is my challenge to voters. Today politics is discredited, debate around politics is contaminated, and political outcomes are increasingly hurtful and negative. The challenge is to ask people what, coherently, they want from politics and to express that in a constructive and positive way. It has been done before. The Levellers' Agreements of the People are a hidden gem, and it is time to discover and recast them for the twenty-first century.

ACKNOWLEDGMENTS

IN CHAPTER 11, I MENTIONED FINISHING *THE LEVELLING* WHILE ON HOLI-day, and my first and greatest acknowledgment is to my family for their support through this project. I started to write *The Levelling* a couple of years ago in the remote reaches of Achill Island, County Mayo, and now finish it in slightly less remote, equally beautiful, and sunnier Corsica.

I initially "finished" the book in April 2017—or, rather, I thought then that the book was finished. When I fired it off to a number of publishers, I was crestfallen to learn that many of them now require writers to submit scripts through literary agents. This was another hurdle to surmount, but I'm glad I persisted.

I had the very good fortune to find Don Fehr. He politely told me what I had suspected, that the first version was incoherent, and over the course of a couple of months he helped me enormously in restructuring the book and making sense of my thoughts.

Through Don, the book was picked up by PublicAffairs, which delighted me given their reputation for producing serious and thoughtful work. John Mahaney, an editor at PublicAffairs, has edited some of the key books I mention in this text, and I was tremendously excited to have the benefit of his experience and judgment. He has helped me to bring color to the book and strength to its arguments and to make it more real and relevant to readers across countries and political divides. The editing of Kathy Delfosse has greatly improved the book, and I appreciate her patience and eye for detail.

Much of the work in this book is the product of years of writing, thinking, and researching. One person who has been instrumental as a collaborator is David Skilling, with whom I have written and researched extensively on the secret sauce behind the stability and strong economic performance of small advanced economies like Ireland, Switzerland, New Zealand, and Singapore. My friend Nicholas Benachi has also fed my mind through our discussions and exchanges on books and current affairs.

NOTES

Chapter 1: The Levelling

1. Christian Hacke, "Eine Nuklearmacht Deutschland stärkt die Sicherheit des Westens" [A nuclear Germany strengthens the security of the West], *Die Welt*, July 29, 2018, https://www.welt.de/politik/deutschland/plus180136274/Eine -Nuklearmacht-Deutschland-staerkt-die-Sicherheit-des-Westens.html.

2. Swedish Civil Contingencies Agency, *If Crisis or War Comes*, May 21, 2018, https://www.msb.se/Forebyggande/Krisberedskap/MSBs-krisberedskapsvecka /Fakta-om-broschyren-Om-krisen-eller-kriget-kommer-/.

3. Taylor Downing's book *1983: The World at the Brink* tells of Russia's near-misreading of the intent behind a NATO war game, a misunderstanding that could have triggered war.

4. The film *Amazing China* gives a sense of this and of what is ahead. CCTV Video News Agency, *Amazing China*, October 22, 2017, https://www.youtube .com/watch?v=tYjozY41OnM. More formally, the Chinese president laid out his vision of the Chinese Dream in a speech when visiting the National Museum of China in November 2012, having taken the office of general secretary. "Full Text: China's New Party Chief XI Jinping's Speech," *BBC News*, broadcast November 15, 2012, https://www.bbc.com/news/world-asia-china-20338586.

5. Marie Ng, Tom Fleming, Margaret Robinson, et al., "Global, Regional, and National Prevalence of Overweight and Obesity in Children and Adults during 1980–2013: A Systematic Analysis for the Global Burden of Disease Study 2013," *Lancet*, August 30, 2014.

6. Diamond, "Facing Up to the Democratic Recession."

7. R. Miller and M. O'Sullivan, *What Did We Do Right?* (Blackhall, 2011), 7.

8. The World University Rankings, *Times Higher Education*, October 17, 2018. https://www.timeshighereducation.com/.

Chapter 2: The Tide Goes Out

1. A. Guterres, "An Alert for the World," 2018 New Year Video Message, http://webtv.un.org/watch/sg-new-year-vm-en/5693250482001.

2. R. Foroohar, "The Dangers of Digital Democracy," *Financial Times*, January 28, 2018.

3. Victor Lukerson, "Fear, Misinformation, and Social Media Complicate Ebola Fight," *Time*, October 8, 2015, http://time.com/3479254/ebola-social-media.

4. World Bank regionally aggregated poverty data, PovcalNet, http://iresearch.worldbank.org/PovcalNet/povDuplicateWB.aspx.

5. In general, definitions of, objections to, and perspectives on globalization span many fields. Often it is not easy to identify whether specific problems arise as a result of globalization or whether globalization simply exacerbates them. Measuring globalization and, in particular, the causality of its effects is difficult, though perhaps the least problematic aspect of analyzing globalization is measuring its economic effects. Measures that economists often examine are the relation between a country's savings and its investment activities, its current account (part of a country's balance of payments; it measures the flow of trade and income into a country) relative to its output, and levels of foreign direct investment (FDI). A number of other more idiosyncratic measures can be examined as well, such as the change in the number of foreign firms located in a country, differences between domestic and national products and between the research-and-development activities of foreign and indigenous corporations. Measures of migration are useful too, though the flow of labor was more widespread during the first wave of globalization than it is now.

6. Organisation for Economic Cooperation and Development (OECD), "G20 International Merchandise Trade Statistics," news release, August 29, 2018, http://www.oecd.org/sdd/its/OECD-G20-Trade-Q22018.pdf.

7. P. Conconi, G. Facchini, and M. Zanardi, "Policy Makers Horizon and Trade Votes," CEPR Discussion Paper DP 8561, September 2011.

8. S. J. Evenett and J. Fritz, "Global Trade Plateaus," Nineteenth Global Trade Alert Report, July 13, 2016, Global Trade Alert, https://www.globaltradealert .org/reports/15.

9. Autor, Dorn, Hanson, and Majlesi, "Importing Political Polarization?"

10. Che, Lu, Pierce, and Schott, "Does Trade Liberalization with China Affect US Elections?"

11. Lang and Mendes, "The Distribution of Gains from Globalization."

12. R. Dobbs, A. Madgavkar, J. Manyika et al., "Poorer Than Their Parents?"

13. Jeff Desjardins and Visual Capitalist, "This Is What Countries around the World Think about Globalization," World Economic Forum, November 13, 2017, https://www.weforum.org/agenda/2017/11/what-your-country-thinks -of-globalization.

14. Pew Research Center, Global Indicators Database, http://www.pewglobal .org/database/indicator/5/.

15. Another interesting viewpoint appears in Walter Schneider's book The Great Leveller, which points out that often a crisis or regime change is required to alter the sociopolitical landscape.

16. A paper by Thomas Piketty and his colleagues shows that inequality in China may be higher than thought. See Piketty, Yang, and Zucman, "Capital Accumulation, Private Property, and Inequality in China, 1978–2015."

17. World Bank, Visualize Inequality, http://www1.worldbank.org/poverty /visualizeinequality/; OECD Data, Income Inequality, https://data.oecd.org /inequality/income-inequality.htm; Milanovic, Global Inequality.

18. E. Sommellier and M. Price, "The New Gilded Age—Income Inequality in the USA by State, Metropolitan Area and County," Economic Policy Institute, July 19, 2018, www.epi.org/publication/the-new-gilded-age-income-inequality-in -the-u-s-by-state-metropolitan-area-and-county/.

19. World Bank Group, Poverty and Shared Prosperity 2016: Taking on Inequality, World Bank, October 2, 2016, https://openknowledge.worldbank.org /handle/10986/25078.

20. Shorrocks and Davies's book Personal Wealth from a Global Perspective is the key text on wealth data. Their wealth data set is now updated and analyzed annually in the Credit Suisse Wealth Report, https://www.credit-suisse.com /corporate/en/research/research-institute/global-wealth-report.html.

21. Credit Suisse Research Institute, "Global Wealth Report 2018," https:// www.credit-suisse.com/corporate/en/research/research-institute/global-wealth -report.html.

22. Pew Research Center, "The American Middle Class Is Losing Ground," December 9, 2015, http://www.pewsocialtrends.org/2015/12/09/the-american -middle-class-is-losing-ground/.

23. Credit Suisse Research Institute, "Global Wealth Report 2015," October 18, 2015, www.credit-suisse.com/media/assets/corporate/docs/about-us/research /publications/global-wealth-report-2015.pdf.

24. Engen, Laubach, and Reifschneider, "The Macroeconomic Effects of the Federal Reserve's Unconventional Monetary Policies."

25. Kate Versho-Downing, "Letter of Resignation from the Palo Alto Planning and Transportation Commission," *NewCo Shift*, August 10, 2016, https://shift .newco.co/letter-of-resignation-from-the-palo-alto-planning-and-transportation -commission-f7b6facd94f5#.sw0wd0p1f.

26. Khatya Chhor, "French Students Most Affected by Social Inequality, OECD Finds," *France 24*, December 14, 2016, https://www.france24.com/en /20161207-french-students-most-affected-socioeconomic-disadvantages-oecd -pisa-study.

27. Data collected at Centers for Disease Control and Prevention, Data & Statistics, https://www.cdc.gov/datastatistics/index.html.

28. Currie, Schwandt, and Thuilliez, "When Social Policy Saves Lives."

29. Council of Economic Advisers, "The Underestimated Cost of the Opioid Crisis," November 2017, https://www.whitehouse.gov/sites/whitehouse.gov/files /images/The%20Underestimated%20Cost%20of%20the%20Opioid%20Crisis.pdf.

30. Add Health: The National Longitudinal Study of Adolescent to Adult Health, UNC Carolina Population Center, http://www.cpc.unc.edu/projects/addhealth.

31. Ferrie, Massey, and Rothbaum, "Do Grandparents and Great-Grandparents Matter?"

32. Barrone, and Mocetti, "What's Your (Sur)Name?"

33. Data collected at CHNS: China Health and Nutritional Survey, UNC Carolina Population Center, https://www.cpc.unc.edu/projects/china.

34. T. Marshall, "Physical Activity: Policy Statement," Arthritis Research UK, March 2018, www.versusarthritis.org/media/2075/physical-activity-policy -statement-march-2018.pdf.

35. Analysis drawn from data at Centers for Disease Control and Prevention, Arthritis: Data and Statistics, https://www.cdc.gov/arthritis/data_statistics/index .htm?CDC_AA_refVal=https%3A%2F%2Fwww.cdc.gov%2Farthritis%2Fdata _statistics.htm.

36. M. Rodell, J. S. Famiglietti, D. N. Wiese, et al., "Emerging Trends in Global Freshwater Availability," *Nature* 557 (2018): 651–659, https://www.nature.com /articles/s41586-018-0123-1.

37. NASA, "NASA Satellites Reveal Major Shifts in Global Freshwater," press release 18-008, May 16, 2018, https://www.nasa.gov/press-release/nasa -satellites-reveal-major-shifts-in-global-freshwater.

38. McCarthy, *The Moth Snowstorm*.

39. US Postal Service, A Decade of Facts and Figures, https://facts.usps.com/table-facts/.

40. Statista: The Statistics Portal, "Mobile Social Media Usage in the United States—Statistics & Facts," https://www.statista.com/topics/4689/mobile-social-media-usage-in-the-united-states/.

41. P. Hergovich and J. Ortega, "The Strength of Absent Ties: Social Integration via Online Dating," research paper, September 17, 2018, https://arxiv.org/pdf/1709.10478.pdf.

42. Bureau of Labor Statistics, "American Time Use Survey—2017 Results," news release, June 28, 2018, https://www.bls.gov/news.release/pdf/atus.pdf.

43. C. Kobayashi and R. Evans, "No Sex, Please," BBC Radio 4, broadcast July 13, 2018, https://www.bbc.co.uk/programmes/b0b01vgv.

44. M. Brenan, "Nurses Keep Healthy Lead as Most Honest, Ethical Profession," Gallup News, December 26, 2017, https://news.gallup.com/poll/224639/nurses-keep-healthy-lead-honest-ethical-profession.aspx.

45. Mair, *Ruling the Void*, 105.

46. European Commission, Standard Eurobarometer, 89, Spring 2018, Public Opinion, http://ec.europa.eu/commfrontoffice/publicopinion/index.cfm.

47. Edelman, "2018 Edelman Trust Barometer," January 21, 2018, https://www.edelman.com/research/2018-edelman-trust-barometer.

48. Institute for Democracy and Electoral Assistance, Voter Turnout Database, https://www.idea.int/data-tools.

49. "MEPs," European Parliament, updated February 11, 2019, www.europarl.europa.eu/meps/en/search/chamber.

50. R. Dalio, Bridgewater Daily Observations (not publicly available), March 22, 2017.

51. According to the Angus Maddison database, in 1600 India and China had 22.4 percent and 29 percent of world GDP, respectively, and by 1700, 24.4 percent and 22 percent, respectively. Maddison Historical Statistics, University of Gronigen, Gronigen Growth and Development Centre, https://www.rug.nl/ggdc/historicaldevelopment/maddison/.

Chapter 3: What's Next?

1. Keynes, *The Economic Consequences of the Peace*, 4.

2. Chambers, Dimson, and Foo, "Keynes the Stock Market Investor," 431–449.

3. K. O'Rourke, "Europe and the Causes of Globalization, 1790 to 2000," in *Europe and Globalization*, ed. H. Kierzkowski, 64–86.

4. Findlay and O'Rourke, *Power and Plenty*, 405.

5. Findlay and O'Rourke, *Power and Plenty*, 3.

6. Findlay and O'Rourke, *Power and Plenty*, 381.

7. D. Rodrik, *Has Globalization Gone Too Far?* (Institute for International Economics, 1997), 7.

8. Rajan and Zingales, "The Great Reversals."

9. Credit Suisse Research Institute, *Credit Suisse Investment Returns Yearbook 2018*, https://www.credit-suisse.com/corporate/en/research/research-institute/publications.html.

10. An NBER working paper by Grace Xing Hu, Jun Pan, and Jang Wang gives a very good overview of the development of China's capital market development. Hu, Pan, and Wang, "The Chinese Capital Market."

11. "Trump's Trade Folly," editorial, *Wall Street Journal*, March 1, 2018.

12. Analysis drawn from data in Robert Shiller's historic stock market data found at http://www.econ.yale.edu/~shiller/data.htm.

13. See, for example, Bernanke, "The Macroeconomics of the Great Depression."

14. One of Ben Bernanke's fields of expertise is the Great Depression; see, for example, his *Essays on the Great Depression*.

15. Buckles, Hungermann, and Lugauer, "Is Fertility a Leading Economic Indicator?."

16. Freedman, *The Future of War*, 264.

17. R. Dornbusch, "Expectations and Exchange Rate Dynamics," *Journal of Political Economy* 84 (1976): 1161–1176; R. Dornbusch, "Exchange Rate Expectations and Monetary Policy," *Journal of International Economics* 6 (1976): 231–244.

18. A. Pierce, "The Queen Asks Why No One Saw the Credit Crunch Coming," *Daily Telegraph*, November 5, 2008.

19. P. Krugman, "How Did Economists Get It So Wrong?," *New York Times Magazine*, September 2, 2009, http://www.nytimes.com/2009/09/06/magazine/06Economic-t.html.

20. P. Romer, "The Trouble with Macroeconomics," working paper, September 14, 2016, 15, https://paulromer.net/wp-content/uploads/2016/09/WP-Trouble.pdf; N. Taleb, "The Intellectual Yet Idiot," *Incerto* (blog), *Medium*, September 16, 2018, https://medium.com/@nntaleb/the-intellectual-yet-idiot-13211e2d0577#.hicytcdpb; K. Warsh, "The Federal Reserve Needs New Thinking," *Wall Street Journal*, August 24, 2016, http://www.wsj.com/articles/the-federal-reserve-needs-new-thinking-1472076212.

21. D. Vines and S. Willis, "The Rebuilding Macroeconomic Theory Project: An Analytical Assessment," *Oxford Review of Economic Policy* 34, nos. 1–2 (January 5, 2018): 1–42.

22. Many of the articles on this topic by the *Financial Times*'s Gillian Tett are useful here; see, for example, G. Tett, "An Anthropologist in the Boardroom," *Financial Times*, April 21, 2017.

23. On development economics, see, for example, Rodrik and Rosenzweig, *Handbook of Development Economics*. And Sir Thomas Bingham's *The Rule of Law* is worth a read.

24. Berlin, *The Power of Ideas*.

25. One of the Santa Fe Institute's leading scholars, Geoffrey West, gives a good account of it: "What a fantastic melting pot. There is almost no hierarchy, and its size is sufficiently small that everyone on-site gets to know everyone else, the archaeologist, economist, social scientist, ecologist and physicist all freely interact on a daily basis to talk, speculate, bullshit and seriously collaborate on questions big and small." West, *Scale*, 433.

26. N. Wade, *A Troublesome Inheritance: Genes, Race, and Human History* (Penguin, 2014). This debate may have already begun; see G. Coop, M. Eisen, R. Nielsen, et al., letter to the editor, *New York Times*, August 8, 2014, https://www.nytimes.com/2014/08/10/books/review/letters-a-troublesome-inheritance.html?

Chapter 4: The Levellers

1. Rees, *The Leveller Revolution*, 210. The complete quotation goes, "For really I thinke that the poorest hee that is in England hath a life to live as the greatest he; and therefore truly, Sir, I thinke itt's cleare, that everyman that is to live under a Government ought first by his owne consent to putt himself under that Government; and I doe thinke that the poorest man in England is not at all bound in a strict sense to that government that he hath not had a voice to put himself under."

2. Rees, *The Leveller Revolution*, 37.

3. See Rees, "Leveller Organization and the Dynamic of the English Revolution."

4. The A. S. P. Woodhouse version of the transcripts lists the many debates and petitions of the Levellers. See Woodhouse, *Puritanism and Liberty*.

5. Le Claire, cited in Mendle, *The Putney Debates of 1647*, 19–35.

6. Mendle, *The Putney Debates of 1647*, 268.

7. Overton's lengthy pamphlet *An Arrow Against All Tyrants* is also worth a read. Overton especially expresses a doctrine of self-directed rights and individual responsibility: "To every individual in nature is given an individual property by nature, not to be invaded or usurped by any: for everyone as he is himselfe, so he has a self-propriety, else could he not be himselfe." Both *A Remonstrance of Many Thousand Citizens* and *An Arrow Against All Tyrants* can be found at the Constitution Society website: *A Remonstrance of Many Thousand Citizens*, http://www.constitution.org/lev/eng_lev_04.htm; *An Arrow Against All Tyrants*, http://www.constitution.org/lev/eng_lev_05.htm.

8. Overton, *Remonstrance of Many Thousand Citizens*, 3.

9. Overton, *Remonstrance of Many Thousand Citizens*, 5.

10. Overton, *Remonstrance of Many Thousand Citizens*, 5.

11. Overton, *Remonstrance of Many Thousand Citizens*, 6.

12. Pettit, *Republicanism*.

13. Overton, *Remonstrance of Many Thousand Citizens*, 12.

14. Overton, *Remonstrance of Many Thousand Citizens*, 14.

15. "An Agreement of the People for a Firm and Present Peace upon Grounds of Common Right and Freedom," October 28, 1647, Constitution Society, http://www.constitution.org/lev/eng_lev_07.htm.

16. Woodhouse, *Puritanism and Liberty*, 444.

17. "An Agreement of the Free People of England" (third agreement), May 1, 1649, Constitution Society, http://www.constitution.org/eng/agreepeo.htm. Hereafter "Third Agreement of the People."

18. "Third Agreement of the People."

19. "Third Agreement of the People."

20. For example, Richard Beeman writes that the Levellers did not want to abolish all distinctions in society, only hereditary political institutions, making Parliament more representative and accountable to constituents and to the rule of law. Beeman, *The Varieties of Political Experience in Eighteenth-Century America*, 16.

21. "Third Agreement of the People."

22. On probity in office, the agreement states, "That the next, and all future Representatives shall exactly keep the publike Faith, and give ful satisfaction, for all securitie, debts, arrears or damages, (justly chargeable) out of the publike Treasury; and shall confirm and make good all just publike Purchases and Contracts that have, been, or shall bee made; save that the next Representative may confirm or make null in part, or in whole, all gifts of Lands, Moneys, Offices, or otherwise made by the present Parliament, to any Member of the House of Commons, or to any of the Lords, or to any of the attendants of either of them." "Third Agreement of the People."

23. "The Petition of 11 Sept. 1648: Anon, The Petition of 11 September 1648," An Anthology of Leveller Tracts: Agreements of the People, Petitions, Remonstrances, and Declarations (1646–1659), July 14, 2016, Online Library of Liberty, https://oll.libertyfund.org/pages/leveller-anthology-agreements.

24. "Third Agreement of the People."

25. Daniel Rolph, "'Levellers' in American Politics," *History Hits* (blog), Historical Society of Pennsylvania, May 6, 2013, https://hsp.org/blogs/history-hits/levellers-in-american-politics.

26. Woodhouse, *Puritanism and Liberty*, 335.

27. Analysis drawn from data at "Religion," Gallup, http://www.gallup.com/poll/1690/religion.aspx; "Religion and Public Life," Pew Research Center, http://www.pewforum.org/; "The Future of World Religions," Pew-Templeton Global Religious Futures Project, http://www.globalreligiousfutures.org/.

28. Paraphrase of Giuseppe Tomasi di Lampedusa, *The Leopard*, translated by Archibald Colquhoun (Pantheon Books, 1960), 40. The exact English translation is "If we want things to stay as they are, things will have to change."

29. Hill, *The World Turned Upside Down*, 361.

30. Overton, quoted in Rees, "Leveller Organization and the Dynamic of the English Revolution," 177.

31. Inglehart and Norris, "Trump, Brexit and the Rise of Populism"; Mudde, "The Populist Zeitgeist."

32. K. Popper, "The Open Society and Its Enemies Revisited," *Economist*, April 23, 1988, as reprinted at "From the Archives: The Open Society and Its Enemies Revisited," Democracy in America, *Economist*, January 31, 2016, https://www.economist.com/democracy-in-america/2016/01/31/from-the-archives-the-open-society-and-its-enemies-revisited.

33. Lindsay, quoted in Mendle, *The Putney Debates of 1647*, 245.

34. L. S. Feuer, *Spinoza and the Rise of Liberalism* (Transaction, 1987).

35. M. Loughlin, "The Constitutional Thought of the Levellers," 2.

36. Another interesting take on civil wars comes in Francis Fukuyama's elaboration of the echo of civil war through English history. His thesis, which may also inform the debate on Brexit, is that civil wars in England came to a halt in the late seventeenth century after the Glorious Revolution because from that point on people started to believe in the law, and the rule of law began to flourish. See Fukuyama, "The Last English Civil War," *Daedalus* 147, no. 1 (Winter 2018): 15–24, https://www.amacad.org/multimedia/pdfs/publications/daedalus/winter2018/18_Winter_Daedalus_03_Fukuyama.pdf.

37. J. W. Müller, *What Is Populism?*, 3.

Chapter 5: Can They Do It?

1. For example, Mudde, "The Study of Populist Radical Right Parties."

2. Funke, Schularick, and Trebesch, "Going to Extremes."

3. Analysis based on data at National Consortium for the Study of Terrorism and Responses to Terrorism, University of Maryland, https://www.start.umd.edu/.

4. The Economist Intelligence Unit, "Democracy Index 2017: Free Speech Under Attack," January 31, 2018, www.eiu.com/public/topical_report.aspx?campaignid=DemocracyIndex2017.

5. "BTI 2018: Global Findings," Transformation Index BTI, Bertelsmann Stiftung, accessed February 13, 2019, www.bti-project.org/en/key-findings/global/.

6. Rovny, "Where Do Radical Right Parties Stand?," 1–26.

7. "2014 Chapel Hill Expert Survey," Chesdata, accessed February 13, 2019, www.chesdata.eu/2014-chapel-hill-expert-survey/. Published analysis available via J. Polk

et al., "Explaining the Salience of Anti-elitism and Reducing Political Corruption for Political Parties in Europe with the 2014 Chapel Hill Expert Survey Data," *Research & Politics* 4 (January 1, 2017): 1–9, https://doi.org/10.1177/2053168016686915.

8. Mair, *Ruling the Void*, 67.

9. A. Blinder, "Is Government Too Political?" *Foreign Affairs*, November–December 1997, 115–126.

10. Van Reybrouck, *Against Elections*, 12.

11. Van Reybrouck, *Against Elections*, 43.

12. Deschouwer, *New Parties in Government*; Bolleyer and Bytzek, "Origins of Party Formation and New Party Success in Advanced Democracies"; Harmel and Robertson, "Formation and Success of New Parties."

13. "2018 Edelman Trust Barometer," February 2018, p. 16, https://www .edelman.com/sites/g/files/aatuss191/files/2018-10/2018_Edelman_Trust _Barometer_Global_Report_FEB.pdf.

14. Credit Suisse Research Institute, "Emerging Consumer Survey 2018," March 2018, https://www.credit-suisse.com/media/assets/corporate/docs/about -us/research/publications/ecs-2018.pdf.

15. R. B. Reich, *Locked in the Cabinet* (Vintage, 1998), 28.

Chapter 6: Great Countries or Strong Countries?

1. I did not quite make up the character of Katherine Chidley. One of the most important female Levellers, Katherine Chidley was born in 1616 and was perhaps one of the most eloquent and prominent women in public life in mid-seventeenth-century England. At a time when women had no rights, she was one of the very first to broach the topic of the independence of women. She wrote widely on religion and authored petitions arguing for the Levellers' positions. In addition, she ran a business (selling socks to the army) and was the mother of seven children.

2. This particular statement is from the 2016 Hangzhou (China) Summit. See "G20 Hangzhou Summit," Ministry of Foreign Affairs of Japan, updated September 5, 2016, www.mofa.go.jp/ecm/ec/page3e_000583.html.

3. The Brookings Institution Tracking Indices for the Global Economic Recovery (Tiger) at www.brookings.edu is a useful resource here.

4. World Bank, "Global Economic Prospects: The Turning of the Tide?," World Bank Flagship Report, June 2018, http://www.worldbank.org/en/publication /global-economic-prospects.

5. National Bureau of Economic Research, "US Business Cycle Expansions and Contractions," http://www.nber.org/cycles.html.

6. L. Summers, "The Age of Secular Stagnation: What It Is and What to Do About It," *Foreign Affairs*, March–April, 2016, https://www.foreignaffairs.com

/articles/united-states/2016-02-15/age-secular-stagnation. In addition, a speech by Claudio Borio, chief economist at the Bank for International Settlements, examines some of the financial and monetary factors associated with low interest rates and, by association, low growth. Borio, "Secular Stagnation or Financial Cycle Drag."

7. Gordon, "Is U.S. Economic Growth Over?"

8. Bloom, Jones, van Reenen, and Webb, "Are Ideas Getting Harder to Find?," 1.

9. The Long-Term Productivity database at the Banque de France is a very useful resource here; see "About the Database," http://www.longtermproductivity .com/about.html.

10. Eichengren, Park, and Shin, "The Global Productivity Slump," 1–8.

11. A good treatment of the impact of robotics on work comes from philosopher Michael Sandel; see Sandel, "Would Life Be Better if Robots Did All the Work," *The Public Philosopher*, BBC Radio 4 program, broadcast March 7, 2017, http://www.bbc.co.uk/programmes/b08gxndc.

12. A. Haldane, "Work, Wages and Monetary Policy," speech at National Science and Media Museum Bradford, June 21, 2017, https://www.bankofengland .co.uk/speech/2017/work-wages-and-monetary-policy.

13. Many of those involved in the original Boston Tea Party were descendants of the Levellers, both intellectually and also in terms of family connections. Volo, *The Boston Tea Party*.

14. Analysis drawn from data at Overview of BLS Productivity Statistics, Bureau of Labor Statistics, http://www.bls.gov/bls/productivity.htm.

15. Analysis drawn from data at OECD Data site, https://data.oecd.org.

16. Maestas, Mulle, and Powell, "The Effect of Population Ageing on Economic Growth, the Labor Force and Productivity."

17. Gagnon, Johannsen, and Lopez-Salido, "Understanding the New Normal."

18. IMF World Economic Outlook, "Too Slow for Too Long," International Monetary Fund, April 2016, http://www.imf.org/external/pubs/ft/weo/2016 /01/; "GDP Long-Term Forecast," OECD Data, https://data.oecd.org/gdp/gdp -long-term-forecast.htm.

19. This IMF Staff Discussion Note is worth looking at: V. Gaspar, M. Obstfeld, R. Sahay, et al., "Macroeconomic Management When Policy Space Is Constrained: A Comprehensive, Consistent, and Coordinated Approach to Economic Policy," September 2016, http://www.imf.org/external/pubs/ft/sdn /2016/sdn1609.pdf.

20. Elizabeth Drew, "A Country Breaking Down," *New York Review of Books*, February 25, 2016, http://www.nybooks.com/articles/2016/02/25 /infrastructure-country-breaking-down/; Woetzel, Garemo, Mischke, et al., "Bridging Global Infrastructure Gaps."

21. Ansar, Flyvbjerg, Budzier, and Lunn, "Does Infrastructure Lead to Economic Growth or Economic Fragility?," 360–390.

22. For example, see the website of the National Infrastructure Commission, www.nic.org.uk.

23. Credit Suisse Research Institute, *Global Investment Returns Yearbook 2018*, https://www.credit-suisse.com/corporate/en/research/research-institute/publications.html.

24. Eichengreen, Mehl, and Chitu, "Mars or Mercury?" Eichengreen has written some splendid material on currencies and is recognized as the academic expert in this area. Two works that are worth examining are *Golden Fetters: The Gold Standard and the Great Depression, 1919–1939* (Oxford University Press, 1992) and *Exorbitant Privilege: The Rise and Fall of the Dollar* (Oxford University Press, 2012).

25. Perón is quoted here from A. Velasco, "How Economic Populism Works," *Project Syndicate*, February 7, 2017, https://www.project-syndicate.org/commentary/economic-populism-temporary-success-by-andres-velasco-2017-02?referrer=/FzT7pl2CCa.

26. For example, Richard Easterlin, whose early work on happiness is credited with sparking academic interest in the issue by economic researchers, sums up the literature: "Life events in the non-pecuniary domain, such as marriage, divorce and serious disability, have a lasting effect on happiness" and "an increase in income, and thus in the goods at one's disposal, does not bring with it a lasting increase in happiness." Easterlin, "Explaining Happiness," 11177.

27. Marx quoted in R. Layard, *Happiness: Has Social Science a Clue?*, Lionel Robbins Memorial Lectures (London School of Economics, 2003), lecture 1, p. 13. Layard is also the author of *Happiness: Lessons from a New Science* (Penguin, 2005).

28. Somewhat related to this view, a recent study from the World Bank takes a broader view of country prosperity, looking at human capital, environmental resources, and country balance sheets. G.-M. Lange, Q. Wodon, and K. Carey, eds., *The Changing Wealth of Nations, 2018: Building a Sustainable Future* (World Bank Group, 2018), https://openknowledge.worldbank.org/bitstream/handle/10986/29001/9781464810466.pdf?sequence=2&isAllowed=y.

29. See David Skilling's article "The Future of Small Economies in a Changed World," *Straits Times*, September 26, 2017, https://www.straitstimes.com/opinion/the-future-of-small-economies-in-a-changed-world.

30. Credit Suisse Research Institute, "Getting Over Globalization," 2017, https://www.credit-suisse.com/ch/en/about-us/research/research-institute/publications.html.

31. Analysis drawn from data at "2018 Key Findings: Prosperity Is Growing, but Not Equally," Legatum Prosperity Index 2018, www.prosperity.com.

32. The subcomponents of intangible infrastructure are as follows: in education: secondary and tertiary enrollment ratio; in health care: infant mortality, life expectancy, and health spending per capita; in technology: cellphone users (per 100), telephone lines (per 100), secure servers (per million), internet users (per 100), research-and-development expenditure (percent of GDP); in financial services: credit information score, legal rights score, lending risk premium, equity market capitalization (percent of GDP); in business services: ease of doing business rank, import delays, mean tariff rates, procedures needed to register a business.

33. Diamond, "Facing Up to the Democratic Recession."

34. Data collected from World Bank World Governance Indicators, http://info.worldbank.org/governance/wgi/?xyzallow#home.

35. On the UN Human Development Index, see United Nations Development Programme, "Human Development Reports," http://hdr.undp.org/en/composite/HDI. Quality of governance is expressed by the average of Transparency International's Corruption Perceptions Index and the Center for Systemic Peace's State Fragility Index. In assessing an economy's macroeconomic volatility, two variables are important: standard deviation of GDP growth rates and inflation, taken from the World Bank database, from 1960 onward. World Bank, "Open Data," https://data.worldbank.org/?xyzallow.

36. Fukuyama, *Political Order and Political Decay*, 14.

37. The miniconference was the Credit Suisse Entrepreneur Summit, June 2017.

38. Harvard Law School, Access to Justice Lab, "Spotlight: Drug Courts" (blog), February 6, 2018, http://a2jlab.org/spotlight-drug-courts/; P. Waldmeir, "None of These People Ever Gave Up on Me: America's Drug Courts," *Financial Times Magazine*, August 24, 2018, https://www.ft.com/content/8a1ee8f0-a593-11e8-926a-7342fe5e173f.

Chapter 7: A Westphalia for Finance

1. US Securities and Exchange Commission, *A Plain English Handbook: How to Create Clear SEC Disclosure Documents*, August 1998, https://www.sec.gov/pdf/handbook.pdf.

2. Meiksins Wood, "Why It Matters."

3. M. El-Erian, *The Only Game in Town: Central Banks, Instability and Avoiding the Next Collapse* (Yale University Press, 2016).

4. Mallaby, *The Man Who Knew*.

5. "What's in Greenspan's Briefcase?," Fall 2000, Inside the Vault, Federal Reserve Bank of St. Louis, https://www.stlouisfed.org/publications/inside-the-vault/fall-2000/whats-in-greenspans-briefcase.

6. "Verbatim of the Remarks Made by Mario Draghi," speech at the Global Investment Conference in London, July 26, 2012, European Central Bank, https://www.ecb.europa.eu/press/key/date/2012/html/sp120726.en.html.

7. P. L. Siklos, *Central Banks into the Breach: From Triumph to Crisis and the Road Ahead* (Oxford University Press, 2017), 188.

8. J. Bhagwati, *In Defense of Globalization* (Oxford University Press, 2007), 4.

9. Even the Riksbank has struggled in recent years. See M. Goodfriend and M. King, "Review of the Riksbank's Monetary Policy, 2010–2015," http://data.riksdagen.se/dokument/RFR-201516-RFR7.pdf.

10. Here is a modern interpretation of the dictum: B. F. Madigan, "Bagehot's Dictum in Practice: Formulating and Implementing Policies to Combat the Financial Crisis," speech at Federal Reserve Bank of Kansas City Annual Economic Symposium, Jackson Hole, Wyoming, August 21, 2009, https://www.federalreserve.gov/newsevents/speech/madigan20090821a.htm.

11. The "Committee to Save the World," with Alan Greenspan as the architect, was the subject of a *Time* magazine cover story in the February 15, 1999, edition, http://content.time.com/time/magazine/0,9263,7601990215,00.html.

12. Greenwood, Shleifer, and Yang, "Bubbles for Fama." See also B. Jones, "Asset Bubbles: Re-thinking Policy for the Age of Asset Management," International Monetary Fund Working Paper WP/15/27, February 2015, https://www.imf.org/external/pubs/ft/wp/2015/wp1527.pdf.

13. Though the Bank of Japan adopted quantitative easing in 2001, the wave of QE that has come to dominate markets started with the Federal Reserve's first QE program in November 2008, when they bought close to USD 600 million in mortgage-backed securities. The second program started in November 2010, and a third and final round, begun in September 2012, was then slowly disengaged or "tapered." In the United Kingdom, the Bank of England launched its QE program in March 2009, followed some five years later by the European Central Bank (they also bought covered bonds in 2011). A helpful guide to QE comes from the Federal Reserve Bank of Richmond: R. Haltom and A. L. Wolman, "A Citizen's Guide to Unconventional Monetary Policy," economic brief, December 2012, https://www.richmondfed.org/~/media/richmondfedorg/publications/research/economic_brief/2012/pdf/eb_12-12.pdf.

14. D. Greenlaw, J. Hamilton, E. Harris, and K. West, "A Skeptical View of the Impact of the Fed's Balance Sheet," Chicago Booth Working Paper, February 2018, https://research.chicagobooth.edu/igm/usmpf/usmpf-paper.

15. D. Andrews, M. A. McGowan, and V. Millot, "Zombie Firms and Weak Productivity: What Role for Policy?," *OECD Ecoscope* (blog), Organization for Economic Cooperation and Development, December 6, 2017, https://

oecdecoscope.blog/2017/12/06/zombie-firms-and-weak-productivity-what
-role-for-policy/.

16. Central banks are beginning to be better at communicating with the public. The Bank of England has begun to send its officers to cities around the United Kingdom to explain its policies and has started to experiment with "public friendly" press releases.

17. A paper from staff at the Chicago Federal Reserve shows that unequal access to financial liquidity can carry through to later wealth inequality. Amromin, De Nardi, and Schulze, "Inequality and Recessions."

18. B. M. Smith, *The Equity Culture: The Story of the Global Stock Market* (Farrar, Straus and Giroux, 2003), 5.

19. J. Carville, "The Bond Vigilantes," *Wall Street Journal*, February 25, 1993, A1.

20. M. Fox, "'Bond Vigilantes' Are Saddled Up and Ready to Push Rates Higher, Says Economist Who Coined the Term," February 9, 2018, US Markets, CNBC, https://www.cnbc.com/2018/02/09/bond-vigilantes-saddled-up-and
-ready-to-make-a-comeback-ed-yardeni.html.

21. One such proposal comes from Mike Konczal and J. W. Mason of the Roosevelt Institute: Konczal and Mason, "A New Direction for the Federal Reserve: Expanding the Monetary Toolkit," November 30, 2017, http://rooseveltinstitute
.org/expanding-monetary-policy-toolkit/.

22. One example of this thinking is Kiley and Roberts, "Monetary Policy in a Low Rate World."

23. R. Wrigglesworth, "US Student Debt Balloons Past $1.5tn," *Financial Times*, August 26, 2018, https://www.ft.com/content/18530da6-a637-11e8
-926a-7342fe5e173f; S. Claessens and M. A. Kose, "Financial Crises: Explanations, Types, and Implications," IMF Working Paper WP/13/28, January 2013, https://www.imf.org/external/pubs/ft/wp/2013/wp1328.pdf.

24. Claessens and Kose, "Financial Crises: Explanations, Types, and Implications"; Bank of Korea–IMF Workshop, "Managing Real Estate Booms and Busts," April 11–12, 2011, http://www.imf.org/external/np/res/seminars/2011
/bok/041111.pdf.

25. Chen and Kang, "Credit Booms."

26. Chen, Ratnovski, and Tsai, "Credit and Fiscal Multipliers in China."

27. Mian, Sufi, and Verner, "Household Debt and Business Cycles Worldwide."

28. Congressional Budget Office, "The 2018 Long-Term Budget Outlook," June 26, 2018, https://www.cbo.gov/publication/53919.

29. See Mulford, *Packing for India*. Mulford was also US ambassador to India from 2004 to 2009.

30. On the task of paring down existing debt levels, see IMF, "Fiscal Monitor: Debt. Use It Wisely," World Economic and Financial Surveys, October 2016, https://www.imf.org/external/pubs/ft/fm/2016/02/pdf/fm1602.pdf. One of the original proposals made during the euro crisis was the "Blue Bond" proposal set out by Jakob von Weizsäcker and Jacques Delpla for the Breugel think tank on May 5, 2010. J. Weizsäcker and J. Delpla, "The Blue Bond Proposal," policy brief, May 5, 2010, http://bruegel.org/2010/05/the-blue-bond-proposal/.

31. W. Maliszewski, S. Arslanalp, J. Caparusso, et al., "Resolving China's Corporate Debt Problem," IMF Working Paper WP/16/203, October 2016, https://www.imf.org/external/pubs/ft/wp/2016/wp16203.pdf.

32. Chen and Kang, "Credit Booms: Is China Different?"

33. J. R. Franks and C. Mayer, "Ownership and Control of German Corporations," September 25, 2000, posted December 29, 2000, SSRN, https://ssrn.com/abstract=247501 or http://dx.doi.org/10.2139/ssrn.247501.

34. Alletzhauser, The House of Nomura.

35. One or two dissenting members of the Bank of Japan's board have warned of the risks from the consequences of quantitative easing, notably Takahide Kiuchi. See R. Yoshida and C. Baird, "BOJ Chief Faces Tougher Second Term as Reality of Monetary Easing Program Sinks In," Japan Times, March 5, 2018, https://www.japantimes.co.jp/news/2018/03/05/business/economy-business/boj-chief-faces-tougher-second-term-reality-easing-program-sinks/#.Wp7F2_nyubh.

36. The OECD has done excellent work in trying to develop rigorous global governance standards. See their corporate governance statement at http://www.oecd.org/corporate/.

37. Eisinger, The Chickenshit Club.

38. B. McLean and P. Elkind, The Smartest Guys in the Room: The Amazing Rise and Scandalous Fall of Enron (Penguin Books, 2003).

39. Committee on the Financial Aspects of Corporate Governance, "The Financial Aspects of Corporate Governance," December 1, 1992, https://www.icaew.com/-/media/corporate/files/library/subjects/corporate-governance/financial-aspects-of-corporate-governance.ashx?la=en.

40. "The Agreement of the People," October 28, 1647, Constitution Society, http://www.constitution.org/eng/conpur074.htm.

41. OECD, Toolkit for Risk Governance, https://www.oecd.org/governance/toolkit-on-risk-governance/home/.

Chapter 8: A Multipolar World

1. Rachman, Easternisation; Quah, "The Global Economy's Shifting Centre of Gravity."

2. D. Furceri et al., "Gone with the Headwinds: Global Productivity," International Monetary Fund Staff Discussion Notes 17/04, April 3, 2017.

3. T. Sablik, "Are Markets Too Concentrated?," Richmond Federal Reserve, Economic Focus, First Quarter 2018, https://www.richmondfed.org/-/media/richmondfedorg/publications/research/econ_focus/2018/q1/pdf/cover_story.pdf; G. Grullon, Y. Larkin, and R. Michaely, "Are US Industries Becoming More Concentrated?," last revised May 31, 2015, *Review of Finance*, October 2018, (forthcoming), https://papers.ssrn.com/sol3/papers.cfm?abstract_id=2612047.

4. World Bank, *Multipolarity: The New Global Economy* (Global Development Horizons 2011).

5. The Peterson Institute has a very useful resource on globalization that examines trade, supply chains, and other aspects of globalization; see "What Is Globalization? And How Has the Global Economy Shaped the United States?," Peterson Institute for International Economics (PIIE), https://piie.com/microsites/globalization/what-is-globalization.html.

6. Australian Government, Department of Foreign Affairs and Trade, "Statistics on Who Invests in Australia," https://dfat.gov.au/trade/resources/investment-statistics/Pages/statistics-on-who-invests-in-australia.aspx.

7. United Nations, "International Migration Report 2017: Highlights," p. 14, http://www.un.org/en/development/desa/population/migration/publications/migrationreport/docs/MigrationReport2017_Highlights.pdf.

8. Max Galka Metrocosm data maps: "All the World's Immigration Visualized in 1 Map," June 29, 2016, Metrocosm, http://metrocosm.com/global-immigration-map/; and see also "Here's Everyone Who's Immigrated to the U.S. Since 1820," May 3, 2016, Metrocosm, http://metrocosm.com/animated-immigration-map/.

9. UN Refugee Agency, UNHCR, "Number of Refugees and Migrants from Venezuela Reaches 3 Million," November 8, 2018, https://www.unhcr.org/news/press/2018/11/5be4192b4/number-refugees-migrants-venezuela-reaches-3-million.html.

10. Standard Chartered Bank runs a renminbi globalization indicator, which indicates that the international use of the Chinese currency has flagged in recent years. Standard Chartered, "Renminbi Tracker: How Global Is the Renminbi?," October 10, 2018, https://www.sc.com/en/trade-beyond-borders/renminbi-globalisation-index/. Estimates provided in the Triennial Central Bank Survey of foreign exchange turnover in April 2016, released in September 2016. "Triennial Central Bank Survey of Foreign Exchange and OTC Derivatives Markets in 2016," Bank for International Settlements (BIS), December 2016, https://www.bis.org/publ/rpfx16.htm.

11. T. Taussig, "The Rise of Personalist Rule," *Order from Chaos* (blog), Brookings, March 23, 2017, www.brookings.edu.

12. A. H. Cordesman, "Estimates of Chinese Military Spending," Center for Strategic and International Studies, Working draft, September 21, 2016, https://csis-prod.s3.amazonaws.com/s3fs-public/publication/160928_AHC_Estimates_Chinese_Military_Spending.pdf.

13. The Space Launch Report, for example, highlights the increase in space launches from China, India, and Japan in recent years. *Space Launch Report* (news digest), http://www.spacelaunchreport.com/.

14. J. S. Nye Jr., *Soft Power: The Means to Success in World Politics* (Public Affairs, 2004).

15. J. Desjardins, "The World's Most Respected 'Made In' Labels," October 20, 2017, Visual Capitalist, http://www.visualcapitalist.com/respected-made-in-labels-country/.

16. J. G. Castaneda, "The Forgotten Relationship," *Foreign Affairs*, May–June 2003, 67–81.

17. Xi Jinping, "Address," 12th National People's Congress, March 17, 2013.

18. The governance indicators the World Bank follows are voice and accountability, political stability and absence of violence, government effectiveness, regulatory quality, rule of law, and control of corruption.

19. Allison, *Destined for War: Can America and China Escape Thucydides's Trap?*

20. See, for example, the Beijing Xiangshan Forum, http://www.xiangshanforum.cn/, which is sponsored by the Chinese military; L. Lucas and E. Feng, "China's Push to Become a Tech Superpower Triggers Alarms Abroad," *Financial Times*, March 19, 2017, https://www.ft.com/content/1d815944-f1da-11e6-8758-6876151821a6.

21. Interestingly, a similar term, "Oceana," was coined in the immediate post-Leveller period, in James Harrington's *The Common Wealth of Oceana* (1656), a book that set out a utopian republic and that was probably influenced by the Levellers, the Putney Debates, and the political climate of the pre-Cromwellian era.

22. Stiglitz, *Globalization and Its Discontents*. For example, on page xiv he states that "no one was happy about the suffering that often accompanied the IMF programs, inside the IMF it was simply assumed that whatever suffering occurred was a necessary part of the pain countries had to experience." In a reply to Stiglitz's book, Thomas Dawson, a director at the IMF, points out, "[*The Economist*] said in its review that a more accurate title for the book would have been 'The IMF and My Discontent.'" In addition, he notes that Stiglitz's book has some 64 references to globalization but 340 references to the IMF. See Dawson, "Stiglitz, the IMF and Globalization," speech to the MIT Club of Washington, June 12, 2002, http://www.imf.org/external/np/speeches/2002/061302.htm.

23. H. Chisholm, ed., *Encyclopædia Britannica* 10, 11th ed. (Cambridge University Press, 1910–1911), 869–921.

24. Winston Churchill, "The Russia Enigma," broadcast, October 1, 1939, The Churchill Society, http://www.churchill-society-london.org.uk/RusnEnig.html.

25. Credit Suisse Research Institute, "Global Wealth Report 2018," https://www.credit-suisse.com/corporate/en/research/research-institute/global-wealth-report.html.

26. The influential Fu Ying, chairperson of the Foreign Affairs Committee of the National People's Congress, has stated that "the old way is not working." Fu Ying, "Quo Vadis," Valdai Club, October 25, 2016. She has made similar remarks in the Western press, notably in "The US World Order Is a Suit That No Longer Fits," op-ed, *Financial Times*, January 6, 2016, https://www.ft.com/content/c09cbcb6-b3cb-11e5-b147-e5e5bba42e51.

27. T. Pakenham, *The Scramble for Africa: The White Man's Conquest of the Dark Continent from 1876 to 1912* (Random House, 1990).

28. "Cooperation between China and Central and Eastern European Countries," http://www.china-ceec.org/eng/.

29. On the place of religion in China, see Johnson, *The Souls of China*.

30. E. Feng, "Security Spending Ramped Up in China's Restive Xinjiang Region," *Financial Times*, March 12, 2016.

31. World Bank Data Catalog, "Population Estimates and Projections," https://datacatalog.worldbank.org/dataset/population-estimates-and-projections??xyzallow.

32. T. G. Ash, "Is Europe Disintegrating?," *New York Review of Books*, January 19, 2017, http://www.nybooks.com/articles/2017/01/19/is-europe-disintegrating/.

33. G. Chazan, "Germany Calls for Global Payments System Free of US," *Financial Times*, August 21, 2018, https://www.ft.com/content/23ca2986-a569-11e8-8ecf-a7ae1beff35b.

34. Rodrik, "The Inescapable Trilemma of the World Economy."

35. "Out of Order: The Future of the International System," special issue, *Foreign Affairs*, January–February 2017.

Chapter 9: A New World Order

1. M. O'Sullivan and D. Skilling, "Hanseatic League 2.0 Reflects Changing Shape of EU," *Irish Times*, January 4, 2019, https://www.irishtimes.com/opinion/hanseatic-league-2-0-reflects-changing-shape-of-eu-1.3746896?mode=amp.

2. G. Orwell, "Boy's Weeklies," Orwell Foundation, https://www.orwellfoundation.com/the-orwell-foundation/orwell/essays-and-other-works/boys-weeklies/.

3. J. C. Humes, *Churchill: The Prophetic Statesman* (Regnery History, 2012), 101.

4. L. H. Officer, "Dollar-Pound Exchange Rate from 1791," MeasuringWorth, 2018, http://www.measuringworth.com/exchangepound/.

5. J. Sawyers, "Britain on Its Own Will Count for Little on the World Stage," *Financial Times*, June 20, 2017.

6. See M. O'Sullivan and D. Skilling, "From Great Britain to Little England," *Project Syndicate*, March 29, 2017; also M. O'Sullivan and D. Skilling, "Britain Needs to Find a New Role," *London Times*, February 6, 2018.

7. I set out some of the choices facing these nations in a *Foreign Affairs* article with David Skilling: M. O'Sullivan and D. Skilling, "The Lessons of Little States: Small Countries Show the Way Through Brexit," *Foreign Affairs*, June 8, 2017, https://www.foreignaffairs.com/articles/ireland/2017-06-08/lessons-little-states.

8. "Housing Should Be for Living In, Not for Speculation, Xi Says," *Bloomberg News*, October 18, 2017, https://www.bloomberg.com/news/articles/2017-10-18 /xi-renews-call-housing-should-be-for-living-in-not-speculation.

9. The historian Nicholas Mansergh tracks India's development in his book *Independence Years: The Selected Indian and Commonwealth Papers of Nicholas Mansergh* (Oxford University Press, 2000). And Shashi Taroor's book *Inglorious Empire* is worth a read in this regard.

10. I have developed many of these themes in articles coauthored with David Skilling. For example, see M. O'Sullivan and D. Skilling, "At the G20, Look Beyond the Usual Suspects," *Wall Street Journal*, September 2, 2016; D. Skilling and M. O'Sullivan, "Small Nations—Not the G-20—Lead the Way," *Wall Street Journal*, November 1, 2018, http://www.wsj.com/articles/small-nationsnot-the -g-20lead-the-way-1472771969; D. Skilling and M. O'Sullivan, "Small Countries Are the Canaries in the Coalmine of the World's Economies," *Irish Times*, March 17, 2015, http://www.irishtimes.com/opinion/small-countries-are-the-canaries -in-the-coalmine-of-the-world-s-economies-1.2141952.

11. The Economist Intelligence Unit, "Democracy Index 2017: Free Speech Under Attack," January 31, 2018, www.eiu.com/public/topical_report.aspx?camp aignid=DemocracyIndex2017.

12. For example, the small, northern European states have issued joint opinions on European economic reforms; see Ministry of Finance, "European Finance Ministers' Joint Statement on the Development of the Economic and Monetary Union," http://vm.fi/article/-/asset_publisher/valtiovarainministerien-yhteiskannanotto -euroopan-talous-ja-rahaliiton-kehittamisesta.

13. Kim and Millen, *Dying for Growth*.

14. C. Wyplosz, "When the IMF Evaluates the IMF," VOX CEPR Policy Portal, February 17, 2017, http://voxeu.org/article/when-imf-evaluates-imf.

15. "Recommendations by the Commission of Experts of the President of the General Assembly on Reforms of the International Monetary and Financial System," March 19, 2009, https://www.un.org/ga/president/63/letters/recommendation Experts200309.pdf.

16. C. von Clausewitz, *On War* (Barnes and Noble, 2004), xv.

17. See the *Climate Science Special Report* put together by bodies such as the Department of Energy and NASA: US Global Change Research Program, *Climate Science Special Report: Fourth National Climate Assessment*, vol. 1, edited by D. J. Wuebbles, D. W. Fahey, K. A. Hibbard, et al., 2017, https://science2017.globalchange.gov/.

18. M. Mildenberger, J. Marlon, P. Howe, and A. Leiserowitz, "The Spatial Distribution of Republican and Democratic Climate Opinions at State and Local Scales," *Climatic Change* 145, nos. 3–4 (December 2017), https://link.springer.com/article/10.1007%2Fs10584-017-2103-0.

19. K. C. Seto, S. Dhakal, et al., "Human Settlements, Infrastructure and Spatial Planning," in *AR5 Climate Change 2014: Mitigation of Climate Change*, contribution of Working Group III to the Fifth Assessment Report of the Intergovernmental Panel on Climate Change, p. 927, https://www.ipcc.ch/pdf/assessment-report/ar5/wg3/ipcc_wg3_ar5_chapter12.pdf; Food and Agriculture Organization of the United Nations, "Livestock a Major Threat to Environment," November 29, 2006, FAONewsroom, http://www.fao.org/newsroom/en/news/2006/1000448/index.html.

20. M. Bloomberg and C. Pope, *Climate of Hope* (St. Martin's Press, 2017).

21. "A Digital Geneva Convention to Protect Cyberspace," Microsoft Policy Papers, https://query.prod.cms.rt.microsoft.com/cms/api/am/binary/RW67QH.

Chapter 10: The Hamilton Project

1. Hamilton was also in vogue in US policy circles in the early 1990s, when the Hamilton Project was created by Robert Rubin and others; see http://www.hamiltonproject.org/.

2. A. Hamilton, "The Continentalist, No. VI, [4 July 1782]," *Founders Online*, National Archives, https://founders.archives.gov/documents/Hamilton/01-03-02-0031.

3. M. K. Curtis, "In Pursuit of Liberty: The Levellers and the American Bill of Rights," 1991, *Constitutional Commentary*, 737, https://scholarship.law.umn.edu/concomm/737.

4. Credit Suisse Research Institute, *From Spring to Revival: Regime Changes and Economic Transformation*, November 2011, p. 15, https://publications

.credit-suisse.com/tasks/render/file/index.cfm?fileid=88E49EF1-83E8-EB92
-9D5152FC5FD1076F.

5. A European Minister of Economy and Finance, "Communication from the Commission to the European Parliament, the European Council, the Council and the European Central Bank," European Commission, December 6, 2017, https://ec.europa.eu/info/sites/info/files/economy-finance/com_823_0.pdf.

6. The proceedings from the Euro at 20 conference are also worth a look; see "The Euro at 20," IMF Conference, Dublin, Ireland, June 25–26, 2018, https://www.imf.org/en/News/Seminars/Conferences/2018/05/17/the-euro-at-20-dublin. Also see "The Five Presidents' Report: Completing Europe's Economic and Monetary Union," European Commission, June 22, 2015, https://ec.europa.eu/commission/publications/five-presidents-report-completing-europes-economic-and-monetary-union_en.

7. Maddison Historical Statistics, Groningen Growth and Development Centre, Historical National Accounts database, University of Groningen, https://www.rug.nl/ggdc/historicaldevelopment/na/.

8. "National Security Strategy of the United States of America," Office of the President of the United States, December 2017, https://www.whitehouse.gov/wp-content/uploads/2017/12/NSS-Final-12-18-2017-0905.pdf.

9. E. Osnos, "Making China Great Again," New Yorker, January 3, 2018; E. Wong, "A Chinese Empire Reborn," New York Times, January 5, 2018.

10. "Vice President Mike Pence's Remarks on the Administration's Policy towards China," Hudson Institute, October 4, 2018, https://www.hudson.org/events/1610-vice-president-mike-pence-s-remarks-on-the-administration-s-policy-towards-china102018.

11. Claessens and Kose, "Financial Crises."

12. P. Pan, "China Rules," part 1, "The Land That Failed to Fail," New York Times, November 18, 2018, https://www.nytimes.com/interactive/2018/11/18/world/asia/china-rules.html.

13. Analysis drawn from data at World Bank Open Data site, https://data.worldbank.org/; Investment Company Institute, "Research and Statistics," https://www.ici.org/research/stats.

14. "Foreign Observers Comment on Xi's Report to CPC Congress," China Daily, October 18, 2018, http://www.chinadaily.com.cn/china/19thcpcnationalcongress/2017-10/18/content_33419856.htm.

15. Perkins, The Roosevelt I Knew.

16. Analysis drawn from data at National Bureau of Statistics of China, http://www.stats.gov.cn/english/; Ministry of Civil Affairs of the People's Republic of China, http://english.gov.cn/state_council/2014/09/09/content_281474986284128.htm.

17. G. Knudsen, "Award Ceremony Speech," December 10, 1906, The Nobel Prize, https://www.nobelprize.org/prizes/peace/1906/ceremony-speech/.

18. J. S. Nye Jr., "The Kindleberger Trap," *Project Syndicate*, January 9, 2017, https://www.project-syndicate.org/commentary/trump-china-kindleberger-trap-by-joseph-s--nye-2017-01?barrier=accesspaylog.

19. M. Abi-Habib, "How China Got Sri Lanka to Cough Up a Port," *New York Times*, June 25, 2018, https://www.nytimes.com/2018/06/25/world/asia/china-sri-lanka-port.html.

20. Van Creveld, *More on War*; Grayling, *War*.

21. See General Gerasimov's essay: G. Valery, "The Value of Science in Foresight," *Military Industrial Courier*, February 26, 2013, https://www.vpk-news.ru/articles/14632; also H. Foy, "Valery Gerasimov, the General with a Doctrine for Russia," *Financial Times*, September 15, 2017, https://www.ft.com/content/7e14a438-989b-11e7-a652-cde3f882dd7b.

22. The US Army Futures Command in Austin, Texas, is one of the areas of thought leadership in new aspects of warfare such as urban-based war.

23. There are already several frameworks in existence to guide ethical work: UNESCO's Universal Declaration on the Human Genome and Human Rights (November 1997), UNESCO's International Declaration on Human Genetic Data (October 2003), UNESCO's Universal Declaration on Bioethics and Human Rights (October 2005), and the European Union's Additional Protocol to the Convention on Human Rights and Biomedicine Concerning Genetic Testing for Health Purposes (November 2008).

24. J. L. Yellen, "Labor Market Dynamics and Monetary Policy," speech at the Federal Reserve Bank of Kansas City Economic Symposium, Jackson Hole, Wyoming, August 22, 2014, https://www.federalreserve.gov/newsevents/speech/yellen20140822a.htm; D. Yagan, "Is the Great Recession Really Over? Longitudinal Evidence of Enduring Employment Impacts," UC Berkley Working Paper, November 2016, https://eml.berkeley.edu/~yagan/GreatRecessionScars.pdf; G. D. Rudebusch and J. C. Williams, "A Wedge in the Dual Mandate: Monetary Policy and Long-Term Unemployment," Federal Reserve Bank of San Francisco Working Paper 2014-14, May 2014, http://www.frbsf.org/economic-research/files/wp2014-14.pdf.

BIBLIOGRAPHY

Acemoglu, D., and P. Restrepo. "Secular Stagnation? The Effect of Aging on Economic Growth in the Age of Automation," National Bureau of Economics Research (NBER) Working Paper 23077, January 2017.

Acemoglu, D., and J. Robinson. *Why Nations Fail: The Origins of Power, Prosperity, and Poverty.* Crown Business, 2012.

Achen, C. H., and L. M. Bartels. *Democracy for Realists.* Princeton University Press, 2016.

Ahamed, L. *Lords of Finance.* Windmill Books, 2010.

Albright, M. *Fascism: A Warning.* HarperCollins, 2018.

Alesina, A., and E. Spolare. *The Size of Nations.* MIT Press, 2005.

Alletzhauser, A. *The House of Nomura.* Arcade, 1990.

Allison, G. *Destined for War: Can America and China Escape Thucydides's Trap?* Houghton Mifflin, 2017.

Amromin, G., M. De Nardi, and K. Schulze. "Inequality and Recessions." Chicago Fed Letter 392, 2018.

Angell, N. *The Great Illusion.* Cosimo Classics, 2007.

Ansar, A., B. Flyvbjerg, A. Budzier, and D. Lunn. "Does Infrastructure Lead to Economic Growth or Economic Fragility? Evidence from China." *Oxford Review of Economic Policy* 32, no. 3 (2016): 360–390.

Auer, R., C. Borio, and A. Filardo. "The Globalisation of Inflation: The Growing Importance of Global Value Chains." Bank for International Settlements (BIS) Working Papers, Monetary and Economic Department, Working Paper 602, 2017.

Autor, D., D. Dorn, and G. Hanson. "The China Syndrome: Local Labor Market Effects of Import Competition in the United States." *American Economic Review* 103, no. 6 (2012): 2121–2168.

Autor, D., D. Dorn, G. Hanson, and K. Majlesi. "Importing Political Polarization? The Electoral Consequences of Rising Trade Exposure." National Bureau of Economics Research (NBER) Working Paper 22637, 2017.

Bagehot, W. *Lombard Street: A Description of the Money Market*. Wiley, 1999.

Baker, P., and E. Vernon. *The Agreements of the People, the Levellers and the Constitutional Crisis of the English Revolution*. Palgrave Macmillan, 2012.

Barrone, G., and S. Mocetti. "What's Your (Sur)Name? Intergenerational Mobility over Six Centuries." VOX CEPR Policy Portal. May 17, 2016. https://voxeu.org /article/what-s-your-surname-intergenerational-mobility-over-six-centuries.

Baverez, N. *Chroniques du déni français*. Albin Michel, 2017.

Beeman, R. *The Varieties of Political Experience in Eighteenth-Century America*. University of Pennsylvania Press, 2006.

Berlin, I. *The Power of Ideas*. Pimlico Press, 2001.

Bernanke, B. *Essays on the Great Depression*. Princeton University Press, 2000.

———. "The Macroeconomics of the Great Depression." National Bureau of Economics Research (NBER) Working Paper 4814, 1994.

Bhagwat, J. *In Defence of Globalization*. Oxford University Press, 2004.

Bickerton, C. *The European Union: A Citizen's Guide*. Pelican, 2016.

Bingham, T. *The Rule of Law*. Allen Lane, 2011.

Bloom, N., C. Jones, J. van Reenen, and M. Webb. "Are Ideas Getting Harder to Find?" Stanford University Working Paper, version 0.62, February 2017.

Bocola, L., and A. Dovis. "Self-Fulfilling Debt Crises: A Quantitative Analysis." National Bureau of Economics Research (NBER) Working Paper 22694, 2016.

Bolleyer, N., and E. Bytzek. "Origins of Party Formation and New Party Success in Advanced Democracies." *European Journal of Political Research* 52, no. 6 (2013): 773–796.

Borio, C. "Secular Stagnation or Financial Cycle Drag." *Business Economics*, Palgrave Macmillan, National Association for Business Economics, 52, no. 2 (April 2017): 87–98.

Buchholz, T. *The Price of Prosperity*. HarperCollins, 2016.

Buckles, K., D. Hungermann, and S. Lugauer. "Is Fertility a Leading Economic Indicator?" National Bureau of Economics Research (NBER) Working Paper 24355, 2018.

Buera, F., and E. Oberfield. "The Global Diffusion of Ideas and Its Impact on Productivity and Growth." VOX CEPR Policy Portal. June 12, 2016. https://voxeu .org/article/global-diffusion-ideas.

Campbell, K. *The Pivot.* Twelve/Hachette Book Group, 2016.

Case, A., and A. Deaton. "Rising Morbidity and Mortality in Midlife among White Non-Hispanic Americans in the 21st Century." *Proceedings of the National Academy of Sciences* 112, no. 49 (December 8, 2015): 15078–15083.

Case, S. *The Third Wave.* Simon and Schuster, 2016.

Chambers, D., E. Dimson, and J. Foo. "Keynes the Stock Market Investor." *Journal of Financial and Quantitative Analysis (JFQA)* 50, no. 4 (2015): 431–449.

Che, Y., Y. Lu, J. Pierce, and P. Schott. "Does Trade Liberalization with China Affect US Elections?" Finance and Economics Discussion Series, Divisions of Research and Statistics and Monetary Affairs, 2016-039, Federal Reserve Board, Washington, DC, 2016.

Chen, S., and J. S. Kang. "Credit Booms: Is China Different?" IMF Working Paper 18/2, January 2018. https://www.imf.org/en/Publications/WP/Issues /2018/01/05/Credit-Booms-Is-China-Different-45537.

Chen, S., L. Ratnovski, and P. H. Tsai. "Credit and Fiscal Multipliers in China." IMF Working Paper, December 12, 2017.

Chernow, R. *Alexander Hamilton.* Penguin, 2004.

Conconi, P., G. Facchini, and M. Zanardi. "Policy Makers Horizon and Trade Votes." CEPR Discussion Paper DP 8561, September 2011.

Corsetti, G., L. Feld, R. Koijen, L. Reichlin, R. Reis, H. Rey, and B. Weder di Mauro. "Reinforcing the Euro-Zone and Protecting an Open Society." VOX CEPR Policy Portal. May 27, 2016. https://voxeu.org/article/reinforcing -eurozone-and-protecting-open-society.

Crabtree, J. *The Billionaire Raj: A Journey through India's New Gilded Age.* OneWorld, 2018.

Cragg, R. *The Demographic Investor.* Pearson Education, 1998.

Currie, J., H. Schwandt, and J. Thuilliez. "When Social Policy Saves Lives: Analysing Trends in Mortality Inequality in the US and France." VOX CEPR Policy Portal. August 10, 2018. https://voxeu.org/article/trends-mortality-inequality -us-and-france.

De Burca, G., and J. H. H. Weiler. *The Worlds of European Constitutionalism.* Cambridge University Press, 2012.

Deschouwer, K., ed. *New Parties in Government: In Power for the First Time.* Routledge, 2008.

Diamond, L. "Facing Up to the Democratic Recession." *Journal of Democracy* 26, no. 1 (January 2015): 141–155.

Dobbs, R., A. Madgavkar, J. Manyika, J. Woetzel, J. Bughin, E. Labaye, and P. Kashyap. "Poorer Than Their Parents? A New Perspective on Income Inequality." McKinsey Global Institute. July 2016. https://www.mckinsey.com/featured -insights/employment-and-growth/poorer-than-their-parents-a-new -perspective-on-income-inequality.

Downing, T. 1983: The World at the Brink. Little, Brown, 2018.

Drezner, D. The Ideas Industry. Oxford University Press, 2017.

Eagleton, T. The New Politics of Class: The Political Exclusion of the British Working Class. Oxford University Press, 2016.

Easterlin, R. "Explaining Happiness." Proceedings of the National Academy of Sciences 100, no. 19 (September 16, 2003): 11176–11183.

Eichengreen, B., A. J. Mehl, and L. Chitu. "Mars or Mercury? The Geopolitics of International Currency Choice." National Bureau of Economics Research (NBER) Working Paper 24145, 2017.

Eichengren, B., D. Park, and K. Shin. "The Global Productivity Slump." National Bureau of Economics Research (NBER) Working Paper 21556, 2015.

Eisinger, J. The Chickenshit Club: Why the Justice Department Fails to Prosecute Executives. Simon and Schuster, 2017.

Engen, E., T. Laubach, and D. Reifschneider. "The Macroeconomic Effects of the Federal Reserve's Unconventional Monetary Policies." Finance and Economic Discussion Series 2015-005, 2015.

Eubanks, V. Automating Inequality: How High-Tech Tools Profile, Police, and Punish the Poor. St. Martin's Press, 2017.

Ferrie, J., C. Massey, and J. Rothbaum. "Do Grandparents and Great-Grandparents Matter? Multigenerational Mobility in the US, 1910–2013." National Bureau of Economics Research (NBER) Working Paper 22635, 2016.

Findlay, R., and K. O'Rourke. Power and Plenty. Princeton University Press, 2007.

Foreign Affairs. The Clash of Ideas: The Ideological Battles That Made the Modern World—and Will Shape the Future. Edited by G. Rose and J. Tepperman. Foreign Affairs, 2012.

Foreign Affairs. "Out of Order: The Future of the International System." Foreign Affairs, January–February 2017.

Freedland, J. "US Politics: As Low as It Gets." New York Review of Books, September 9, 2016. https://www.nybooks.com/articles/2016/09/29/us-politics-as -low-as-it-gets/.

Freedman, L. The Future of War. Allen Lane, 2018.

Friedman, B. The Moral Consequences of Economic Growth. Vintage Books, 2015.

Fukuyama, F. Political Order and Political Decay. Profile Books, 2014.

Funke, M., M. Schularick, and C. Trebesch. "Going to Extremes: Politics after the Financial Crisis, 1870–2014." CESifo Working Paper 5553, 2015.

Gagnon, E., B. K. Johannsen, and D. Lopez-Salido. "Understanding the New Normal: The Role of Demographics." Finance and Economics Discussion Series 2016-080, 2016. Washington: Board of Governors of the Federal Reserve System. http://dx.doi.org/10.17016/FEDS.2016.080.

Galbraith, J. K. *The Affluent Society*. Penguin, 1998.

———. *The Great Crash 1929*. Mariner Books, 1997.

Gibbon, E. *The History of the Decline and Fall of the Roman Empire*. Delmarva, 2013.

Gillingham, J. R. *The EU: An Obituary*. Verso Books, 2016.

Goldin, I., and C. Kutarna. *Age of Discovery*. Bloomsbury, 2016.

Goodhart, D. *The Road to Somewhere: The Populist Revolt and the Future of Politics*. C. Hurst, 2017.

Gordon, R. "Is U.S. Economic Growth Over? Faltering Innovation Confronts the Six Headwinds." National Bureau of Economic Research (NBER) Working Paper 18315, August 2012. http://www.nber.org/papers/w18315.

———. *The Rise and Fall of American Growth: The US Standard of Living since the Civil War*. Princeton University Press, 2016.

Gorton, G., and G. Ordonez. "Fighting Crises." National Bureau of Economics Research (NBER) Working Paper 22787, 2016.

Graves, R. *Goodbye to All That*. Anchor Books, 1957.

Grayling, A. C. *War: An Enquiry*. Yale University Press, 2017.

Greenwood, R., A. Shleifer, and Y. Yang. "Bubbles for Fama." Harvard University Working Paper, February 2017.

Guilluy, C. *La France périphérique*. Champs/Flammarion, 2014.

Hamilton, A., J. Jay, and J. Madison. *The Federalist Papers*. Wider Publications, 2008.

Harmel, R., and J. D. Robertson. "Formation and Success of New Parties." *International Political Science Review* 6, no. 4 (1985): 501–523.

Harris, J. A. *Hume: An Intellectual Biography*. Cambridge University Press, 2016.

Heisbourg, F. *La fin du rêve européen*. Stock, 2013.

Hill, C. *The World Turned Upside Down: Radical Ideas during the English Revolution*. Temple Smith, 1972.

Hobbes, T. *Leviathan*. Penguin Classics, 2001.

Hopkirk, P. *The Great Game: On Secret Service in High Asia*. Oxford University Press, 2001.

Houellebecq, M. *Soumission*. Flammarion, 2015.

Howe, N., and W. Strauss. *The Fourth Turning*. Broadway Books, 1998.

Hu, G., J. Pan, and J. Wang. "The Chinese Capital Market: An Empirical Overview." National Bureau of Economics Research (NBER) Working Paper 24346, February 2018.

Inglehart, R., and P. Norris. "Trump, Brexit and the Rise of Populism." Kennedy School of Government, Harvard University, Working Paper Series, August 2016.

International Monetary Fund (IMF). "Neoliberalism: Oversold?" Finance and Development, June 2016.

Israel, J. *A Revolution of the Mind*. Princeton University Press, 2010.

Johnson, I. *The Souls of China: The Return of Religion after Mao*. Allen Lane, 2017.

Kagan, R. *The World America Made*. Vintage Books, 2013.

Kanter, R. M. *Move: How to Rebuild and Reinvent America's Infrastructure*. W. W. Norton, 2016.

———. *Move: Putting America's Infrastructure Back in the Lead*. W. W. Norton, 2015.

Keynes, J. M. *The Economic Consequences of the Peace*. Dover, 2004.

Kierzkowski, H., ed. *Europe and Globalization*. Palgrave Macmillan, 2002.

Kiley, M., and J. Roberts. "Monetary Policy in a Low Rate World." Brookings Papers on Economic Activity (BPEA), BPEA Conference Drafts, March 23–24, 2017.

Kim, J., and J. Millen. *Dying for Growth: Global Inequality and the Health of the Poor*. Common Courage, 2002.

Kindleberger, C., and R. Aliber. *Manias, Panics, and Crashes*. 7th ed. Palgrave Macmillan, 2015.

King, A., and I. Crewe. *The Blunders of Our Governments*. Oneworld, 2013.

King, M. *The End of Alchemy*. Little, Brown, 2016.

Kotlikoff, L., and S. Burns. *The Coming Generational Storm*. MIT Press, 2004.

Krishnamurthy, A., and A. Vissing-Jorgensen. "The Effects of Quantitative Easing on Interest Rates: Channels and Implications for Policy." National Bureau of Economics Research (NBER) Working Paper 17555, October 2011.

Krugman, P. *Geography and Trade*. MIT Press, 1991.

Kuhn, T. *The Structure of Scientific Revolutions*. University of Chicago Press, 1996.

Lang, V. F., and M. Mendes Tavares. "The Distribution of Gains from Globalization." IMF Working Paper 18/54, March 2018.

Loughlin, L. "Towards a Republican Revival?" *Oxford Journal of Legal Studies* 26, no. 2 (2006): 425–437.

Loughlin, M. "The Constitutional Thought of the Levellers." *Current Legal Problems 2007*, ed. C. O'Cinneide and J. Holder, 60 (2007): 1–39.

Maestas, N., K. Mulle, and D. Powell. "The Effect of Population Ageing on Economic Growth, the Labor Force and Productivity." National Bureau of Economics Research (NBER) Working Paper 22452, 2016.

Mahbubani, K. *The New Asian Hemisphere*. Public Affairs, 2008.

Mair, P. *Ruling the Void: The Hollowing of Western Democracy*. Verso Books, 2013.

Mallaby, S. *The Man Who Knew*. CFR Books, Penguin, 2016.

Marshall, T. *Prisoners of Geography*. Elliott and Thompson, 2015.

McCarthy, M. *The Moth Snowstorm: Nature and Joy*. John Murray, 2015.

Meiksins Wood, E. "Why It Matters." *London Review of Books,* September 2008, 3–6.

Mendle, M. *The Putney Debates of 1647.* Cambridge University Press, 2010.

Mian, A., and A. Sufi. *House of Debt.* University of Chicago Press, 2014.

Mian, A., A. Sufi, and E. Verner. "Household Debt and Business Cycles Worldwide." *Quarterly Journal of Economics* 132, no. 4 (November 2017): 1755–1817.

Milanovic, B. "Global Income Inequality by the Numbers: In History and Now." World Bank: Development Research Group, Policy Research Working Paper 6259, 2012.

———. *Global Inequality: A New Approach in the Age of Globalization.* Harvard University Press, 2016.

Miller, R., and M. O'Sullivan. *What Did We Do Right?* Blackhall, 2011.

Morris, I. *Why the West Rules—for Now: The Patterns of History, and What They Reveal about the Future.* Profile Books, 2010.

Mounk, Y. *The People vs. Democracy.* Harvard University Press, 2018.

Mudde, C. "The Populist Zeitgeist," *Government and Opposition* 39, no. 4 (2004): 542–563.

———. "The Study of Populist Radical Right Parties: Towards a Fourth Wave." C-REX Working Paper Series 1, 2016.

Mulford, D. *Packing for India.* University of Nebraska Press, 2014.

Müller, J. W. *What Is Populism?* University of Pennsylvania Press, 2016.

Nye, J. *Soft Power: The Means to Success in World Politics.* Public Affairs, 2004.

Orwell, G. *1984.* Penguin, 2003.

Osnos, E. *Age of Ambition: Chasing Fortune, Truth and Faith in the New China.* Farrar, Straus, Giroux, 2014.

O'Sullivan, M. *Ireland and the Global Question.* Cork University Press, 2006.

Otto, M. *Teeth: The Story of Beauty, Inequality, and the Struggle for Oral Health in America.* New Press, 2016.

Perkins, F. *The Roosevelt I Knew.* Penguin Classics, 2011.

Pettit, P. *Republicanism: A Theory of Freedom and Government.* Oxford University Press, 1997.

Pew Research Center, Global Attitudes and Trends Survey. 2017. http://www.pewglobal.org/database/.

Piketty, T. *Capital in the 21st Century.* Harvard University Press, 2014.

Piketty, T., L. Yang, and G. Zucman. "Capital Accumulation, Private Property, and Inequality in China, 1978–2015." VOX CEPR Policy Portal, July 20, 2017. https://voxeu.org/article/capital-accumulation-private-property-and-inequality-china-1978-2015.

Piris, J. C. *The Future of Europe.* Cambridge University Press, 2012.

Polyani, K. *The Great Transformation: The Economic and Political Origins of Our Time*. Beacon Press, 2001.

Popper, K. *The Open Society and Its Enemies*. Vol. 1, *Hegel and Marx*. Routledge, 1995.

Quah, D. "The Global Economy's Shifting Centre of Gravity." *Global Policy* 2, no. 1 (January 2011): 3–9.

Rachman, G. *Easternisation: War and Peace in the Chinese Century*. Bodley Head, 2016.

Rajan, R. *Faultlines*. Oxford University Press, 2010.

Rajan, R., and L. Zingales. "The Great Reversals: The Politics of Financial Development in the Twentieth Century." *Journal of Financial Economics* 69, no. 1 (2003): 5–50.

Rees, J. "Leveller Organization and the Dynamic of the English Revolution." PhD diss., Goldsmiths, University of London, 2014.

———. *The Leveller Revolution*. Verso Books, 2016.

Rodrik, D. "The Inescapable Trilemma of the World Economy." *Dani Rodrik's Weblog*, June 27, 2007. https://rodrik.typepad.com/dani_rodriks_weblog/2007/06/the-inescapable.html.

Rodrik, D., and M. Rosenzweig, eds. *Handbook of Development Economics*. Vol. 5. North Holland, 2009.

Rostow, W. *The Stages of Economic Growth*. Cambridge University Press, 1999.

Rovny, R. "Where Do Radical Right Parties Stand? Position Blurring in Multidimensional Competition." *Central European Political Science Review* 5, no. 1 (2013): 1–26.

Santolaria, N. *Comment j'ai sous-traité ma vie*. Allary Editions, 2017.

Sarrazin, T. *Deutschland schafft sich ab*. Deutsche Verlags-Anstalt, 2010.

Schell, O., and J. Delury. *Wealth and Power*. Little, Brown, 2013.

Schneider, W. *The Great Leveller: Violence and the History of Inequality from the Stone Age to the Twenty-First Century*. Princeton University Press, 2017.

Schwab, K. *The Fourth Industrial Revolution*. Crown Business, 2016.

Shorrocks, T., and J. Davies. *Personal Wealth from a Global Perspective*. Oxford University Press, 2008.

Simms, B. *Britain's Europe: A Thousand Years of Conflict and Cooperation*. Allen Lane, 2017.

———. *Europe: The Struggle for Supremacy*. Allen Lane, 2013.

Sinn, H.-W. *The Euro Trap: On Bursting Bubbles, Budgets, and Beliefs*. Oxford University Press, 2014.

Solow, R. M. "Growth Theory and After." *American Economic Review* 78, no. 3 (June 1988): 307–317.

———. "The Last 50 Years in Growth Theory and the Next 10." *Oxford Review of Economic Policy* 23, no. 1 (Spring 2007): 3–14.

Soros, G. *The Tragedy of the European Union.* Public Affairs, 2014.

Spengler, O. *The Decline of the West.* Oxford University Press, 1991.

Spiegel, M. "Did Quantitative Easing by the Bank of Japan Work?" Federal Reserve Bank San Francisco, economic letters, October 20, 2006.

Steil, B. *The Marshall Plan.* Simon and Schuster, 2018.

Stiglitz, J. *The Euro: How a Common Currency Threatens the Future of Europe.* W. W. Norton, 2016.

———. *Globalization and Its Discontents.* W. W. Norton, 2003.

Strauss, W., and N. Howe. *The Fourth Turning: An American Prophecy.* Broadway Books, 1997.

Subramanian, A., and M. Kessler. "The Hyperglobalization of Trade and Its Future." Peterson Institute for International Economics, Working Paper 13-6, 2013.

Sullivan, A. "Democracies End When They Are Too Democratic." *New York Magazine,* May 1, 2016. http://nymag.com/daily/intelligencer/2016/04/america-tyranny-donald-trump.html.

Taroor, S. *Inglorious Empire: What the British Did to India.* Hurst Books, 2016.

Taylor, J. "The Financial Crisis and the Policy Responses: An Empirical Analysis of What Went Wrong." National Bureau of Economics Research (NBER) Working Paper 14631, 2009.

Ther, P. *Europe since 1989: A History.* Princeton University Press, 2016.

Thornton, D. "Evidence on the Portfolio Balance Channel of Quantitative Easing." Federal Reserve Bank of St. Louis Working Paper Series 2012-015A, 2012.

Toffler, A. *The Third Wave: The Classic Study of Tomorrow.* Bantam Books, 1989.

Tucker, P. *Unelected Power: The Quest for Legitimacy in Central Banking and the Regulatory State.* Princeton University Press, 2018.

Vance, J. D. *Hillbilly Elegy: A Memoir of a Family and Culture in Crisis.* Harper-Collins, 2016.

Van Creveld, M. *More on War.* Oxford University Press, 2017.

Van Reybrouck, D. *Against Elections: The Case for Democracy.* Penguin, 2017.

Volo, J. *The Boston Tea Party: Foundations of Revolution.* Praeger, 2012.

Von Beyme, K. "Right-Wing Extremism in Post-War Europe." *West European Politics* 11, no. 2 (1988): 1–18.

Von Clausewitz, C. *On War.* Wordsworth Editions, 1997.

Wattenburg, B. *Fewer: How the New Demography of Depopulation Will Shape Our Future.* Ivan R. Dee, 2004.

West, G. *Scale: The Universal Laws of Growth, Innovation, Sustainability, and the Pace of Life in Organisms, Cities, Economies, and Companies.* Penguin, 2017.

Williamson, S. "Current Federal Reserve Policy under the Lens of Economic History: A Review Essay." Federal Reserve Bank of St. Louis Working Paper 2015-015A, 2015.

Woetzel, J., N. Garemo, J. Mischke, M. Hjerpe, and R. Palter. "Bridging Global Infrastructure Gaps." McKinsey Global Institute. June 2016. https://www.mckinsey.com/industries/capital-projects-and-infrastructure/our-insights/bridging-global-infrastructure-gaps.

Woodford, M. "Quantitative Easing and Financial Stability." National Bureau of Economics Research (NBER) Working Paper 22285, 2016.

Woodhouse, A. S. P. Puritanism and Liberty. Dent and Sons, 1974.

Wright, T. "Trump's 19th-Century Foreign Policy." Politico, January 20, 2016. https://www.politico.eu/article/donald-trump-19th-century-foreign-policy-presidential-campaign/.

Zemmour, E. Le suicide français. Albin Michel, 2014.

INDEX

MICHAEL O'SULLIVAN grew up in Ireland, where he studied economics and finance in Cork before earning MPhil and DPhil degrees in international finance as a Rhodes Scholar at Balliol College, Oxford. He then continued life teaching in the Department of Economics at Princeton University and later moved back to Europe as an investment strategist at UBS. He has worked as chief investment officer in the wealth management division of a major bank, where he uses the tough discipline of market forces to assess what is happening in the world in real time. (All views and opinions expressed in the book are his own and do not in any way reflect the views or position of any investment firm.)

Follow *The Levelling*
Instagram: @levellingbook
Twitter: @levellingbook
YouTube: The Levelling
(youtube.com/user/thelevelling)

PublicAffairs is a publishing house founded in 1997. It is a tribute to the standards, values, and flair of three persons who have served as mentors to countless reporters, writers, editors, and book people of all kinds, including me.

I. F. STONE, proprietor of *I. F. Stone's Weekly*, combined a commitment to the First Amendment with entrepreneurial zeal and reporting skill and became one of the great independent journalists in American history. At the age of eighty, Izzy published *The Trial of Socrates*, which was a national bestseller. He wrote the book after he taught himself ancient Greek.

BENJAMIN C. BRADLEE was for nearly thirty years the charismatic editorial leader of *The Washington Post*. It was Ben who gave the *Post* the range and courage to pursue such historic issues as Watergate. He supported his reporters with a tenacity that made them fearless and it is no accident that so many became authors of influential, best-selling books.

ROBERT L. BERNSTEIN, the chief executive of Random House for more than a quarter century, guided one of the nation's premier publishing houses. Bob was personally responsible for many books of political dissent and argument that challenged tyranny around the globe. He is also the founder and longtime chair of Human Rights Watch, one of the most respected human rights organizations in the world.

•　　•　　•

For fifty years, the banner of Public Affairs Press was carried by its owner Morris B. Schnapper, who published Gandhi, Nasser, Toynbee, Truman, and about 1,500 other authors. In 1983, Schnapper was described by *The Washington Post* as "a redoubtable gadfly." His legacy will endure in the books to come.

Peter Osnos, *Founder*